Major Conflict

Major

One Gay Man's Life in the Don't-Ask-Don't-Tell Military

Conflict

Jeffrey McGowan, MAJ, USA (Ret.)

BROADWAY BOOKS

NEW YORK

PRINTED IN THE UNITED STATES OF AMERICA

BROADWAY BOOKS and its logo, a letter B bisected on the diagonal, are
trademarks of Random House, Inc.

Visit our Web site at www.broadwaybooks.com

First edition published 2005

Book design by Donna Sinisgalli

Library of Congress Cataloging-in-Publication Data
McGowan, Jeffrey.
Major conflict : one man's life in the Don't-Ask-Don't-Tell military /
Jeffrey McGowan.—1st ed.
p. cm.
1. United States—Armed Forces—Gays—Government policy.
2. United States—Armed Forces—Biography. I. Title.
UB418.G38M35 2005
355'.0086'6420973—dc22
[B]
2004057017

ISBN 0-7679-1899-1

10   9   8   7   6   5   4   3   2   1

To my grandparents, who loved me unconditionally and who will always be my heroes, and to the men and women who serve in silence, your sacrifice and perseverance will be recognized soon.

ACKNOWLEDGMENTS

★

Whenever I used to pick up a book, I would thumb past the acknowledgments so I could dive right into the first chapter. Now, of course, I realize that no book is written truly alone and I will always stop to find out about the people who made a difference for the author. I could probably write a book recognizing the many contributions of the people that I cite below. However, even though space is limited, I wish to dwell a moment on several very important people without whom my efforts would never have come to fruition.

I want to begin with my agent, Ian Kleinert, who is a consummate professional and a genuinely good person, whom I respect greatly. Ian has been there for me every step of the way, looking out for my best interests. He is probably the most patient person I know, having taken countless phone calls from me, as he guided me through the entire process. His agency has the feel of a large family that really cares about the people they represent. I am truly lucky to be associated with such a wonderful group. A special note of thanks to Kathy Barboza who was always helpful and kind over the phone, a company couldn't have a better person to greet its clients when they call.

I wish to thank my editor, Stacy Creamer, for believing in me and giving me the opportunity to tell my story. She is a great listener and a warm person who was easy to work with. Her insight taught me many things about writing and I admire her greatly for her keen intellect and sophistication. I also wish to recognize her assistant, Tracy Zupancis, whose diligence and thoroughness will make her an editor in chief one day. Her kind, gentle manner always brightened my day whenever we spoke.

Of course, how could I not take a moment to recognize the men in my life, Greg, Paul, and Billy. To Greg Torso, thank you for being there for me. Your recollections and insight, not to mention your journals, gave me the added perspective that allowed me to look at my life more deeply, resulting in a more nuanced book. Thank you for helping me with your opinions and revisions. Special thanks to Chelsea and Dave for letting me use your home and for your insightful feedback. To Paul, thank you for understanding. To Billy, I love you, I want to spend the rest of my life with you. To my mother, I love you.

To my friends, Willy, Jeffrey, Charles and Maurice, Andrea and Claudio, Carla and Michael, Michael Littler, Sari, Julia, Jason West, John Shields, Erna Berger, Dr. Duggan, Christine Karam, Emily Kerr, Steven and Denise, Tara, Larry Cavazza, Cindy Delgado, and Judy Mayle, you guys are simply the best.

To my beloved and much missed friend Vincent, you inspired me to be more than I could be on my own, I miss you deeply and will love you always. To Jed, his partner, your loyalty, love, generosity and kindness make you a true hero and I am honored to call you my friend.

To my boss, Jim Stephens, thanks for being a great leader and busting my balls relentlessly to be the best salesman I could be. To my district, Amy, James, Tom, Paul, Pete, Ted, Tom, and Chris, There isn't a better bunch to work with anywhere.

To my comrades in arms, in particular Duncan Barry and his lovely wife, Tonianne, Paul Mapp, Brian Hathaway, and Mike Poling, thank you for being heroes and patriots, I love and respect you guys because you made me a better person.

Finally, if I missed anyone, thank you for being there for me.

INTRODUCTION

★

The ancient yellow school bus was obviously not built for comfort. And it certainly wasn't built to travel over the sun-baked roads of Jubail, Saudi Arabia. The road was lined with crevices and holes, and as the old bus rolled into one and then the other, it felt as if my kidneys were being dislodged and my lunch would soon be out the window. Add the heat—a relentless, blinding, 110 degrees—and it's not a great leap to say that we were living and working in a place not unlike hell. The view through the dust-caked windows often confirmed our suspicion that we'd been dropped to that lower place. Toothless men wearing torn and shabby robes stood by squat, sun-bleached buildings made of concrete block, eyeing us with suspicion and hate. It wasn't hard to imagine one of these men, rushing toward the old yellow bus, a bandolier of C-1 or dynamite strapped around his waist, in order to take out the Western infidels. I knew I wouldn't feel safe until we were wheels-up in the transport plane.

This tour of duty had been an especially hard one. Six long months of MREs (meals ready to eat, also called Mires) and sleepless nights spent on uncomfortable cots. But it was all good now. Now that we were leaving the kingdom, it was all just sandy water under the bridge. We were on our way back to civilization, back to Europe—to Germany, to be precise.

Sitting on the plane, I couldn't help but think how much the axis of the world had changed in just one short year. Prior to this mission into Saddam's hell, we were still in full Soviet mode, covertly moving along the East German borders, working up battle plans in the event of a thermonuclear war. We were busying ourselves with the day-to-day tasks of war without actually firing a shot. Staring out the window on my way back to Germany, I couldn't help thinking, God love the gentlemanly tones of the cold war! But all that had come to a thunderous halt when one egomaniacal tyrant decided to tinker with the geography of the Arabian Peninsula. Saddam Hussein embarked on a gamble that he'd eventually lose, and lose big, leaving his elite Republican Guard with fifty thousand fewer men.

Before the war actually began we all thought it was going to be a toe-to-toe heavy-metal battle. We had acquired much recon and been briefed on the fighting capabilities of the Republican Guard, which, with over more than five hundred thousand troops, was the fourth-largest army in the world. We knew our mission, and we were going to have to hit them with the force of a jackhammer. Plain and simple: that was our job. Our task was clear, and there was no room for error.

Of course we had great confidence in our own capabilities. We were the best-trained army on the planet, and we were able to maintain a high level of readiness on every terrain imaginable. What we didn't realize, though, was just how easy it would be, how one-sided the victory would end up being.

Technically it was a three-day war, supremely executed by all the armed forces of the United States. When it was over, we pretty much owned Kuwait and had to remain there to keep the peace until the oil-rich country was back to normal and reestablished as a free and sovereign nation.

I served as a lieutenant in Operation Desert Storm and Desert Shield. For six months I served proudly and without question in these campaigns and as a result was awarded a bronze star and various campaign medals. The unit I was in received a valorous unit citation. I think I was most proud of this since, as their leader, it felt as if my own sons were being honored. After the war I felt as if I was on top of the world. Finally, I was truly where I wanted to be: a leader, an officer, a gentleman, a soldier. Still, something was missing. Sitting on that plane heading back to Germany, I knew that in order to achieve my goals I'd made a great sacrifice, namely a big chunk of myself, and I was beginning to wonder how long I could continue being just half a person.

★ ★

I'd always believed that everything was possible, that any problem put in front of me could be solved with hard work, strong will, and unwavering determination. So I thought that this problem, this feeling of incompleteness and need for companionship, wouldn't be any different. I'd figure out a plan, execute it, and *presto!* I'd be whole, problem solved. I was wrong. In the end the problem was, in fact, unsolvable, at least unsolvable as long I stayed in the military. At some point I'd have to make a choice.

As we landed at Rhein-Main Airport I pushed all these thoughts from my mind and did what I usually did: focus on my next assignment, focused on work at the expense of my feelings. I knew I'd be promoted to the rank of captain soon, and with that commission the possibilities would be endless.

In the end, I just couldn't continue with the charade. Initially, I worked harder than ever, taking on the toughest assignments in the hope that I might beat the odds, redefine the game, and find my way. But at the same time, I was finally realizing that it was time to move on.

Once I'd made the decision it felt as if a great fog had lifted. Everything in my life started to ring as clear as a bell. I knew that it would be hard, that I'd have to start all over, but I knew any difficulties would now be cushioned by the fact that I'd never have to lie about myself again.

* *

We all make sacrifices. We all make compromises. I wanted to be a soldier. So I compromised for a while. I sacrificed a part of myself in order to achieve my goals. But had I continued on any longer, my accomplishments would have amounted to a Pyrrhic victory. I wasn't prepared to keep compromising. I left the military in order to save myself. This book is that story, a unique inside look at the U.S. military, where I served as a gay soldier in the Gulf War.

A R 635-100
S-12 Moral or professional dereliction in interests of national
    security.
(7) Commission or attempted commission of a homosexual
    act.
    Upon substantiation of allegation this gives rise to serious doubt as to the advisability of permitting the officer in question to retain a commission or warrant and requires a review of his overall record. The commanding officer will refer the individual for medical evaluation, immediately revoke his security clearance and deny any access to classified defense information.
    Punishment under Uniform Code of Military Justice, Article 15: Elimination action may be originated via court-martial.

The above are charges and specifications from the Uniform Code of Military Justice (UCMJ). What it states in layman's terms is simple: once it is deemed that the accused is a homosexual or has engaged in a homosexual act, he will immediately be dismissed from the U.S. armed forces regardless of tenure or past military record.

Imagine, if you will, having to live with this statute's consequences hanging over your head for most of your adult life. Imagine having to worry every single step of the way, on assignment as a commander on the battlefield during the Gulf War, during peacetime in Kuwait and Germany, as a special weapons officer in the nuclear reliability and security program, that somehow, someone has found out, and that someone is now revealing your secret to someone else, effectively ending your career, a career you've devoted yourself to heart and soul, a career you've truly believed in from day one, a career that was a childhood dream, a calling. Forget becoming a colonel. Don't even think about becoming a general. That's all over now. Everything you've done in your life up to this point has now become null and void. All because of your sexual orientation. All because you're a man who loves men. All because that orientation was deemed, a very long time ago, somehow suspect and a threat to the interests of our national security, not to mention simply unbecoming of an officer and a gentleman.

* *

I am Major Jeffrey McGowan. I lived under just these conditions for twelve years while proudly serving this great country of ours. I now respectfully add my voice to the ever-growing chorus of gay former soldiers who've served well and served proudly under the cloud of a policy that makes the challenge of the military an even greater one than it needs to be.

I have no ax to grind. I knew what I was getting into. And I'm proud of my accomplishments in the military. This book is merely my attempt to shed some light on the issue and perhaps give hope to the many patriotic gay men and women who even now, even today, are serving honorably in the U.S. armed forces, men and women in Iraq, in Afghanistan, and all over the world, working hard (and sometimes dying) to defend the interests of our country and to preserve our unique way of life.

More than anything, however, this book is a personal journey, one man simply coming clean with himself, telling the truth about being a gay man in the military, as an officer and as, I hope, a gentleman.

CHAPTER ONE

Toy Soldiers and Saris

I've always wanted to be a soldier. In fact, I can't remember a time when I could imagine being anything else. It was, I think, my destiny; my path was preordained. I guess I was lucky since this tunnel vision made life easier for me. While friends flailed around in their late teens and twenties, changing majors, jobs, cities, I stayed the course. There was never any question in my mind. And I knew this at a very young age. It just always felt like some fundamental part of my being. Becoming a soldier seemed as necessary to me as fulfilling the most basic of needs. There was hunger, thirst, sleep, and then there was soldiering. Later on there would also be sex and love, but I don't want to get ahead of myself.

I don't come from a military family. In fact, though the men in my family served in the armed forces, they served only when drafted, and when their term of enlistment was up, they hurried back to civilian life. A man had a duty to his country, I was told, but once that duty was fulfilled there were far better things to do with your time than playing with guns and bombs, especially if you lived in the greatest city in the world.

That city was New York, of course, where my family had lived since the turn of the last century. I've traveled all over the world as a soldier, and I still believe that New York City is hands down the most amazing place on the planet. To grow up in New York is like being born with a special talent, like being given something extra. Rich, poor, white, black, Asian, Latin, Arab, Jew, gay, straight, and all points in between, nowhere on earth does such diversity exist side by side in such relative harmony.

And nowhere is the mix more pronounced than in Queens, particularly in Jackson Heights, where I grew up. Ironically, the area was originally developed in 1908 as a white, middle-class "restricted residential community" by a group of real estate men in anticipation of the opening of the Queensboro Bridge in 1909. It was meant to be a suburban escape from the increasing ethnic mix of Manhattan. The only diversity in this early Jackson Heights, before restrictions against Jews were lifted after World War II, was, oddly enough, a thriving community of gay vaudevillians who began moving in after the number 7 train was built in 1917, connecting the neighborhood directly to Times Square. Since the forties the neighborhood has morphed into one of the most ethnically diverse areas in the country. When you walk down Thirty-seventh Avenue, it's like being in Shanghai, Moscow, Calcutta, and Bogotá all at once. Walk a block down any main drag in the neighborhood and you'll likely hear a half-dozen languages being spoken and pass a half-dozen restaurants, each serving totally different ethnic cuisines. Though the whole world is represented, the newer residents are now primarily South Asian and Latino, and you'll have a better chance of seeing a woman in a bright sari passing an Ecuadoran restaurant serving roast guinea pig than coming across, say, a Carrie Bradshaw wannabe in her favorite Manolo Blahniks on her way to cocktails. I feel lucky to have grown up in this colorful, vibrant neighborhood. Like many neighborhoods in New York, especially those in the outer boroughs, Jackson Heights feels like a small town, a little village tucked in the great metropolis, a place where people know one another and take the time to say hello.

I grew up on Eighty-second Street, right across the street from St. Joan of Arc, the Catholic church where I went to grade school every day and to Mass every Sunday. My family was Protestant, but since the Catholic school was the best in the neighborhood, I was duly baptized and then spent the next sixteen years of my life as a student in the Catholic educational system. I have fond memories of getting up every day and putting on my uniform: the gray polyester trousers, the green jacket, the white shirt with the green clip-on tie, and then walking out the front door of my apartment building and simply crossing the street to school. The nuns still wore habits in those days and didn't think twice about smacking you one good if you got out of line.

It was in the school yard of St. Joan of Arc when it first became clear just how much I wanted to be a soldier. Like most young boys I got pretty rambunctious in the school yard, wrestling, fighting, chasing this boy or that girl, but what I loved most of all was playing war games—staging epic battles, killing spies, chasing down the enemy. On one occasion I got so involved in being a dive-bomber that I ripped my jacket straight up the back and was sent home by one of the nuns with a note reading, "Please take a moment to explain to young Jeffrey that he is not, in fact, a Stuka dive-bomber, but rather a student who needs to learn how to behave like the fine young gentleman we at St. Joan of Arc know him to be."

Once a week I was allowed to go out for lunch with my friends. I was given $1.25, which bought me a slice of pizza, a Coke, and some penny candy. My friends and I were pretty much free to explore the neighborhood after school and on weekends as long as we returned home in time for dinner. The neighborhood was tight-knit, everyone knew everyone else, so nobody really worried. How things have changed! When I think of the paranoia today, of the stress parents seem to be under, worrying about the safety of their children even when they're just down the block, I can't help thinking that I grew up in a kind of golden age. It sounds funny, since the truth is that my childhood coincided precisely with the city's fiscal crisis of the 1970s, when the crime rate skyrocketed, the city's reputation plummeted, and everyone else in the United States became convinced that New

York City was one of the most dangerous places on the planet. But believe it or not, growing up in Jackson Heights in the 1970s, long before things turned around under Rudy Giuliani, I never once was threatened or felt unsafe. Who knows, maybe I was just plain lucky. Then again, I think Jackson Heights was, and is, a pretty special place.

My parents were quite young when they had me, so it was decided that I would be raised by my maternal grandparents. They raised me as if I were their own son. My grandmother was from Ohio, the daughter of Scottish immigrants. My grandfather was English, first generation. For forty years he took the subway to Twenty-third Street to go to work at the Metropolitan Life Insurance Company. One of my most vivid memories is of him walking down Eighty-second Street, on his way home from work. My grandmother and I made a habit of waiting for him every day on the stoop of our building. Around five-thirty he'd come into view, striding toward us, always wearing a hat and puffing on a big cigar, looking very much the gentleman, circa 1950. He had a great sense of style and a kind of old-world outlook that allowed for a healthy joie de vivre and professional success at the same time.

As a little boy I was in awe of him. He was the most generous, kindest, smartest man in the world as far as I was concerned. Two or three times a week, sitting on the stoop with Grandmother, I'd notice a brown paper bag at his side as he approached, and I'd stand up and rush to meet him, knowing that the bag held a gift for me, usually a toy soldier or tank, a toy gun or knife, or later, a Matchbox car or one of the Hardy Boys books. It didn't take long for me to amass a huge collection of soldiers and tanks and artillery with which to stage epic battles alone in my room.

My grandfather read voraciously, four or five books a week. I owe my love of books to him. He made time every week to sit down and read with me. He'd bring me books from the Hardy Boys series but also books about history and war, books about monarchies, flags, baseball, dinosaurs. I loved adventure stories the best and truly believed that one day I would have adventures of my own, that one day I'd be just like one of the brave, heroic figures I was always reading about.

My grandparents came of age during the Depression and, like many of their contemporaries, they remained cautious about money for the rest of their lives. But they were never too frugal to help out a man down on his luck, to do the Christian thing when called upon, and in one particular case, literally to give a man the coat off their backs.

One day in January the three of us were on our way home when we passed a homeless man lying on top of a small stack of cardboard in front of the delivery entrance to the neighborhood Genovese drugstore. It was bitter cold, and he was poorly clothed for the weather. His legs were exposed, and the skin on them looked thick and dried and cracked, like the hide of an elephant. What's more, his legs were covered with sores and scabs. He'd fashioned himself a pair of shoes out of old newspapers, cardboard, and rags. He just lay there, unmoving, but awake, I think, lost in his own despair, I assumed. It was the middle of a weekend afternoon, and the street was busy with shoppers. People rushed by without even looking at the man, not an uncommon reaction even now in New York, but more so then since the fiscal crisis and the resulting cutbacks in social services had exacerbated the homeless problem to the point where regular New Yorkers had little choice but to become immune to such a ubiquitous sight.

On this particular day we, too, simply walked on by. No one spoke about it, and soon we were back in the warmth of our apartment. While pulling off my coat, I rushed to the kitchen to find something to eat. "Where you going?" my grandfather asked. "I'm hungry," I said. "Hold on," he said. "What do you say we go back out and get a slice of pizza?" As much as I knew I'd prefer a slice of pizza to almost anything my grandmother had in the kitchen, I hesitated because it was almost time for the latest episode of *Lost in Space*, and I really didn't want to miss it. "Come on," my grandfather said, as my grandmother handed him the winter coat he hardly ever wore anymore. He was still wearing his regular coat, so I was a little confused. Maybe he was getting it dry-cleaned, I thought. I guess the end of the story is obvious. On our way to the pizza parlor we passed the homeless man again, and my grandfather stopped and said, "Here you go, pal," then set the coat down next to him. "God bless you," the man said, quickly laying the old overcoat across his body like a blanket. My grandfather didn't say a word, just kept walking, but he must've seen me looking at him because after a few minutes he turned to me and said, matter-of-factly, "If you can do something good for someone, Jeff, do it. Chances are it will come back to you."

Not long after this incident my grandfather died, leaving a big hole in the lives of my grandmother and me. He suffered a stroke while he and Grandma were in the Catskills. He lingered in the hospital for several weeks. When I went to see him, he appeared thin and drawn, the light in his eyes dimmed, though he seemed to make an effort to be cheerful and upbeat for my benefit.

I was twelve years old when he died, and even at that age I sensed, in the vague way that children know things, that our family was different, though nothing was ever explained to me. His absence made this difference suddenly seem more pronounced. My grandmother took impeccable care of me, but I felt deeply lonely with my grandfather gone. To this day, even though I had him so briefly, my grandfather's warmth and personal philosophy has been the most profound influence on my life.

★ ★

Twenty families lived in the six-story apartment building in which I grew up. Everyone knew everyone else. I was often enlisted to help an older resident move a bureau or a sofa or to help someone bring laundry up from the basement. The other residents in turn kept tabs on me, gave me advice, asked about my grades, encouraged me in every way. In the evenings the hallways were always filled with smells of cooking: pot roast, curry, pasta sauce—a mélange of ethnic cuisines prepared in an effort to keep the bond alive with the home country. In the winters the radiators would hiss and knock, and the aroma of food at dinnertime would be even stronger. Coming out of the cold into the overheated hallway filled with the smell of home cooking was the best welcome in the world.

After St. Joan of Arc I went on to Archbishop Molloy High School, which I hated. I don't think it was the school itself, it was just the idea of school, period. An indifferent student, uninterested in extracurricular activities, I cruised along in neutral, unsure what I wanted, unsure of myself. I hung around the neighborhood a lot, and went to an occasional school dance to meet girls from our sister school. But I felt awkward and clumsy at these and began to feel different from other people for the first time in my life. A chasm was beginning to open up, though I didn't know it at the time, separating me from the rest of the world. So much has happened in the last thirty-five years, and in the last ten years alone, that it's easy to forget just how difficult things were back in the seventies for young gay men and for gay boys. That's not to say, of course, that life is a cakewalk for young gay people today, but I'm not sure I even knew the word *gay* in 1979, when I was fifteen.

Like most teenage boys I did, however, know the words *queer* and *faggot.* When I was about thirteen, I got into the habit of hanging out in front of the building with a group of neighborhood boys, most of them older than me. I wanted to be cool. One summer afternoon we were out in the street playing stickball when a guy from the neighborhood went by on roller skates. He was in his early twenties, I guess, and seemed to go everywhere on his skates, usually in tight cutoffs and often shirtless. He had a perfect body. Looking back now, I feel pretty sure he was gay, though who knows? What mattered was that he was perceived that way by the super's kid from my building, who felt compelled to spit on the ground as he rolled by and yell, "Queer!" with so much disgust in his voice that I jumped a little.

The guy turned his head back to us, looking a bit startled, and then raised his middle finger as high as he could and shouted, "Fuck you!"

The super's kid rushed forward with the ball in hand. "What didya say, faggot?" he yelled, then threw the ball directly at the guy, just narrowly missing his head. The guy said nothing. He simply skated away and didn't look back.

"Fucking faggots," the super's kid said, spitting again, and running up the street to get the ball. There was so much venom in his voice that I almost found myself wanting to defend the skater. But I kept quiet, knowing that defending a *faggot* was the fastest way to be banished from the land of cool. And besides, a large part of me actually agreed with the super's kid.

So despite the changes that were taking place in the seventies, in San Francisco mostly, and in the West Village in Manhattan, for those of us still in high school then, it might as well have been the fifties or the sixties. The one gay character on prime-time television—on the series *Soap*—was a pre-op transsexual. The message was clear: male homosexuality was incompatible with masculinity, incompatible, even, with owning a penis.

And so I was clumsy and awkward at the high school dances, and I goofed around a lot. But I was absolutely convinced that I would one day marry a woman. I didn't feel particularly feminine, so I couldn't be gay. And I certainly didn't want to lose my penis. I wanted to be a soldier so I couldn't be gay because soldiers aren't gay. Soldiers are masculine. That's what I was learning, that's what I internalized, and that's what I've spent the last twenty years of my life attempting to exorcise.

CHAPTER TWO

Starbursts and Cigarettes

After graduating from Archbishop Molloy High School in 1982 I seriously considered joining the service. The idea of college was anathema to me. I wanted to have some adventure and see the world and get on with my life as a soldier. I went into a recruiting station one day just to look around, and one of the cadre talked me up and basically conned me into giving him my phone number. For the next few months I was inundated with calls encouraging me to sign up. I was torn. While I knew I wanted to be a soldier, I realized I wanted to be an officer and I'd need college for that. Unable to make a decision, unwilling to commit at the time, I decided the best thing to do would be to work for a little while. I figured that if I was going to continue living at home with my grandmother, the least I could do was to help her out financially.

I found a full-time job at the flagship Doubleday Bookshop on Fifth Avenue between Fifty-sixth and Fifty-seventh Streets, directly across the street from Trump Tower. The store's been gone for years. Today the space is occupied by Prada, and if you watch *The Apprentice*, you can actually see it at the end of every episode, when the person who's been fired comes down at the end and rides away in a cab.

It was a very special store in its time. A book superstore before superstores had been invented, with four floors of books and an exposed elevator in the center with a window that allowed passengers to look out onto the sales floor. In its own way it was considered a kind of literary landmark, the place where the rich and famous would come for their book needs when in the Big Apple. As a nineteen-year-old kid from Queens the experience was thrilling at first; I was easily starstruck. During my time there I met and waited on the likes of Mick Jagger, Keith Richards, Sylvester Stallone, Shimon Peres, Cher, Ed Koch, and many others. It was the place Imelda Marcos came for books. Her husband owned the adjoining building directly to the north. And it was the place where I met the first man with whom I had a relationship, though maybe "relationship" is stretching it a little, maybe "relationship" is stretching it a lot, but it was the closest I would come to one for a long, long time.

He didn't start working at the store until the winter of 1985, when I was in between semesters in my freshman year at Fordham University. I'd applied to a handful of schools in the New York area in 1983 and was surprised when I received an acceptance letter from the well-known school. I hadn't even taken the time to visit the campus up in the Bronx, thinking that my acceptance was such a long shot. Having spent so much time in Catholic schools I was attracted to the Jesuit tradition at Fordham, the phrase *"homines pro aliis,"* Latin for "men and women for others" jumping out at me from the school's brochure.

Financing school was tough, though. Through federal grants and savings I was able to come up with the first semester's tuition, but I'd have to commute. Fortunately one of the first things I did when I enrolled was to stop by the ROTC office on the campus. I learned about their scholarship program and decided to go for it. I'd have to prove myself first, though, maintaining at least a 3.0 GPA my first semester. That first semester was really when my life began to change. The two years off from school had apparently done me a world of good; I wanted to be there, and I wanted to learn. As a result, I ended up getting a 3.8 GPA, and I got the scholarship.

In many ways January 1985 was a watershed month for me, a

month in which both my professional and my personal life would change dramatically and move in directions I'd never imagined. When I wasn't working at the bookstore, I spent much of my time waiting anxiously for my grades to arrive from Fordham. My grandmother had spread the word throughout the building, so everyone was rooting for me, waiting with me, and, when the news finally arrived, everyone celebrated. My grandmother was so proud and happy that, knowing how hard the long commute was for me every day and how much I wanted to live on campus, she went ahead and paid for my room and board without telling me. I was stunned. I have no idea how she figured out how much it was and where to send the money order and all that. She was seventy-eight years old, after all. We had a rotary phone. She believed most of what was written in the *National Enquirer*, especially anything to do with aliens. I suppose I underestimated her. What I never underestimated, though, was her enormous heart, which I'll be grateful for until the day I die.

The other event that shook up my life in January 1985 was meeting a guy whom I'd become involved with off and on until we finally lost touch in the early nineties. The first time I saw him he was working a cash register in what we affectionately called "the pit." It was the busiest cash-wrap area in the store, and most of the new clerks were thrown in there at first as a kind of initiation. His name was Greg, and he was a tall, skinny guy, good-looking, with short, straight brown hair. I was drawn to him right away, though I can't say I understood why. I didn't think of myself as gay then, and I don't think I was even capable of translating my attraction to Greg into a language that made any kind of emotional or sexual sense. It was as if a light switch had been flipped on and I had no idea how the switch worked, what it was connected to, or where the source of energy was located. All I knew was that something that hadn't been lit before suddenly now was, and I was drawn to it like the proverbial moth to the flame. That switch has been turned on for me twice since Greg, and each time I've gotten better at recognizing all the qualities of the light, and at understanding the source, and at making sure not to hurt the person inside the light. But with Greg I was a novice, I was totally lost, and he ended up being the first great casualty in my journey toward self-acceptance.

Greg and I became fast friends, taking lunch together, spending our break time together. It got to the point where if you saw one of us you were bound to see the other. He said he wanted to learn Spanish, so I started giving him lessons. We walked to the train together at night, down Fifth Avenue and over to Grand Central, where sometimes we'd sit on a closed OTB (Off Track Betting) counter and talk. He'd smoke three or four cigarettes and I'd eat a pack of Starbursts, and we'd talk about religion (he was an atheist, was reading too much Sartre, I thought) and politics (he was a big liberal, I was a small one). We'd talk about everything, and in the evenings we'd talk more on the phone. Sometimes we'd talk for two or three hours. One night we went out with a bunch of people after work and had too many beers and on the way to the train Greg just came out and said how much he liked me, that he was attracted to me. I said I was flattered but I wasn't into men, and he said sorry, sorry, but after that moment I found myself even more drawn to him.

The truth was I'd never been so close to a gay man before. And being so close, and seeing how perfectly at ease he seemed to be with his sexuality, all my preconceptions about gay men—that they were effeminate, that they were weak, that they were only hairdressers and dog groomers and interior decorators—began to fall away in the face of the evidence now before me. Greg wasn't a theoretical gay person, some perfect stranger who rolls by on his roller skates whom I know nothing about, but a real person, standing in front of me, talking to me, at ease in his body, not so strange or unfamiliar or that much different from me at all.

While this was happening at the bookstore my first semester on campus at Fordham was in full swing. The two parts of my life seemed oceans away, irreconcilable, as different as the idyllic Rose Hill campus of Fordham—with its bucolic setting and nineteenth-century buildings—was from the crime-ridden streets of the Bronx just be-yond the campus walls. At Fordham I was the hard-drinking ROTC guy. I thought of myself as a leader, all-American, a man's man. I overcompensated at school, throwing myself more dramatically into typical college-boy activities, as if by doing this I'd cancel out all the uncomfortable feelings Greg was bringing up in me. And in a way it worked. Basically, he stopped existing when I was on campus.

Though I studied hard, ROTC was my primary focus. The weekly training convinced me more than ever that I was meant to be a career officer. The ROTC staff at Fordham was fantastic. One per-son stood out, however, and he would become my close mentor and friend for years. His name was Sergeant Major Robert Carpenter. He was a Green Beret who had served three tours of duty in Viet-nam. He started his career in the 82nd Airborne in 1961 and was se-lected to become a Green Beret not long after being made sergeant. Originally from Virginia, he'd gone into the army out of a great love for soldiering and to make a better life for himself. He was everything I wanted to be. All of us in the ROTC idolized him. Not only was he a great soldier, he was a great man, someone who just totally kicked ass. From him we learned not only our basic soldiering skills, but the culture and ethos of army life as well. His stories, especially his Viet-nam stories, which he told like a pro, taught us that becoming a sol-dier is far more than just learning how to fire weapons and how to employ tactics and strategy; it involves becoming part of a special community, learning a new language, a new spirit, embracing ideals unique to army life.

We couldn't have been more different. He was from the South and had only a high school education. I was a city kid from Queens going to college. But he had a way of making all of that irrelevant; he's what I refer to as "true blue." He served selflessly, enduring great hardship on numerous deployments to protect our interests and our country. Guys like him are why we're free, why the United States re-mains the greatest power on earth. He was a father figure not only to me, but to almost everyone who had the privilege of being trained by him. He was my hero, and I always wanted him to be proud of me. I hope that if he reads this book, he'll understand.

The problem was that as I tried making Robert Carpenter my role model, I kept running into a kind of disconnect on those occasions when I failed to keep my two lives separate, when I wasn't able to keep Greg out of my mind. What would Sergeant Major Carpenter think about that? I didn't even have to ask myself the question. I felt certain that he'd disapprove and disapprove mightily. And so I'd try even harder to convince myself that what I was feeling for Greg was nothing at all, really, that I was completely straight after all. There was simply no room in the self-image I was creating for the feelings Greg was stirring up in me.

But I was learning fast that it wasn't something I could control entirely. I found myself spending more and more time with Greg, going into work on my days off just to see him, going out with him after work for drinks, spending even more time with him on the phone at night. At work, when we were alone, I'd massage his shoulders and back playfully; one day, as we were sitting on the OTB counter at Grand Central, I lifted up his hand without thinking and looked at it, then took hold of it and tucked our locked hands between us. From that day on, though it made me nearly sick with fear, this was something we always did there, on the closed OTB counter at Grand Central; we secretly held hands while he smoked his cigarettes and I chewed my Starbursts.

It began to feel almost like an addiction, something I was forever trying to stop. Just when I would get to a place where I'd feel certain that what I was feeling for Greg was simply the bond of male friendship, I'd say something or do something that went past the boundaries of simple friendship. After hanging out upstairs at Grand Central, we'd usually go down to the number 7 train below, where he'd wait for the westbound train to Times Square, and I'd wait for the eastbound train to Queens. One night as my train pulled in I jumped up from the bench Greg and I were sharing on the subway platform, planted a kiss firmly on his left cheek, and then rushed into the train just as the doors were beginning to close. As the train pulled away I looked through the graffiti-scrawled window to see Greg still sitting on the bench, looking somewhat stunned, one hand pressed up against the kissed cheek. A few nights later, standing in Rockefeller Center, the RCA Building lit grandly in front of us, I suddenly found myself grabbing Greg's shoulder and turning him toward me and saying, "I like you. I want you to be my pal." Later on that night, as we passed under the marquee of the Guild Theater on Fiftieth Street, Greg turned to me and said with a smile, "I like you, too, Jeff. I want you to be my pal." And I said, "Ah, c'mon, you like me more than that," and Greg's face fell, he seemed embarrassed, then a little angry, and without thinking I pulled my ROTC pin from the front pocket of my jeans and handed it to him. "I want you to have this," I said, and all the anger and embarrassment rushed from his face and he smiled again and hugged me.

I didn't realize it at the time, but this act of giving my ROTC pin to Greg, of connecting the two seemingly irreconcilable aspects of my life in one simple action, was the closest I would come to uncompart-mentalizing my life, or bringing together the soldier and the man, for several years.

But the ROTC pin wasn't enough, of course, for Greg. Having come out at seventeen, leaving Pittsburgh to come to New York, Greg was light-years ahead of me on the gay curve. He was ready to have a relationship, and he became increasingly less tolerant when I'd suddenly close up and continue to insist that I was straight. I sensed that he'd fallen in love with me and that this love gave him an almost Herculean patience when it came to my being totally honest about my sexuality. But even that had its limit, and one night near the end of April everything snapped and he reached that limit.

There'd been some talk at work about us, and I'd gotten paranoid. I was working the twelve-to-eight shift, he was working the nine-to-five, and when I came in at noon I ran into him taking a smoke break in the back staircase that led up to the sales floor. I told him we had to cool it, we couldn't hang around each other so much, and then I told him that should the subject of his own sexuality ever come up with anyone at work, he should act as if he was straight, he should deny being gay. Looking back now, I honestly can't believe how naïve I was, and how selfish. Did I really believe Greg would do such a thing? Did I really believe I had a right to ask him to lie about himself? Amazingly, I think I did. But I underestimated him.

A confused look came over his face. He took a quick, long drag on his cigarette, staring at me the whole time, incredulous, as if he were seeing me for the very first time. Then, stabbing out the cigarette hard in the big plastic ashtray that was kept on the ledge there, he said, shaking his head, "I love you, Jeff, but I can't do that. I just can't. . . ." I thought he was going to start crying, but he pulled himself together and flung open the door to the sales floor and rushed out. "Wait, Greg," I said, and I raced out after him, grabbing his arm just as he reached the large display table covered with travel books in the center of the store. It would have been hard to find a more conspicuous place, but I wasn't thinking. "Ouch, damn it, Jeff," Greg yelled, rubbing his arm. I'd grabbed too hard. "Why don't you just rip my arm out of the socket, you idiot," and he turned and continued walking toward the information desk in the front of the store. "Wait, Greg, I'm sorry—I . . ." and then I looked around and saw that, with the exception of the cashiers in the pit ringing up sales, everything else in the store had slowed down or stopped completely. I felt as if I'd been dropped into a film that had suddenly been switched to slow motion. Customers on the open staircase above the travel section paused between steps and looked down. Clerks shelving books in the back slowly turned their heads toward me. People browsing the green Michelin guides stopped browsing and looked up. Jane Light, the older woman who ordered the travel books and anchored the information desk, stopped talking and dipped her head down and looked out over her glasses at me.

I froze. It felt as if the ground had just disappeared from under my feet. I got hot and dizzy, and I imagine I turned beet red. I looked down at the table of travel books, then squatted down, as if I were looking for something in the overstock section below. I tried to breathe while listening to the store return to normal. I heard Jane Light's voice resume, and footsteps on the stairs again. And then I grabbed a travel guide, hurried back to the door to the back staircase, rushed inside, and took the steps down two at a time.

We avoided each other the rest of the afternoon, and when he left at five, I was relieved. This was it, I promised myself. No more hanging around with that faggot. I wasn't going to do it. But then around seven-thirty he called the store, slightly drunk, from J's downtown.

"We have to talk, Jeff," he said, sounding frantic, as if he'd been crying.

"No, nothing to talk about," I said curtly, ready to hang up on him.

"Meet me, Jeff, please, meet me in front of the church at Fifty-fifth when you get off."

There was a pleading in his voice. I hesitated, but then hung up. Thirty seconds later the phone rang again. I picked it up.

"What," I said. "What do you want from me?"

"Please, Jeff, you owe me this much, just meet me in front of Fifth Avenue Presbyterian when you're done with your shift. We can talk on the way to the train."

"What will it take for you to understand?"

"Oh, I understand, Jeff, I understand you better than you understand yourself!"

"Fuck you," I said under my breath. I was standing at the information desk. "And don't come up here. Don't come up here! Stay down there at your faggot bar!" And I slammed the phone down. I was so angry I felt sure that if Greg had been standing in front of me I would've beat the shit out of him.

After finishing my shift I hurried through the revolving doors and started walking briskly down Fifth Avenue. It was the last week in April, an unusually warm night, humid, windy, strange. It felt like rain. They'd been calling for rain all day, and I'd brought my big golf umbrella with me to work. At Fifty-sixth Street, while waiting for the light to change, I took off my suit jacket and flung it over my shoulder and loosened my tie.

I'd calmed down since the phone call from Greg and managed to get him out of my head. I had homework to do when I got home and ROTC matters on my mind. The light changed and I crossed Fifty-sixth Street. I passed Harry Winston, the famous jeweler, and was just approaching the Rizzoli Bookstore in the middle of the block when I noticed a figure standing up on the steps of the church. I realized that it was Greg, always so solemn, with his books and his worn-out shoes, his school-boy sweaters and his old blue corduroys that shone from too much wear. I froze, then made a beeline to the street, started walking across Fifth, trying to act as if I hadn't seen him. But he'd seen me, and he started coming after me. "Jeff! Jeff! Wait!" he shouted, and I started to run then, down Fifth Avenue. But he was faster than me, and by the time I reached Fifty-third Street he'd caught up with me. The light was red and there was traffic and I felt trapped.

"You fucking hypocrite!" he shouted. It was obvious he'd had a few more beers since the phone call.

"Do you know how ugly hypocrisy is? Do you know how ugly that is? It's the ugliest thing in the world, Jeff; it's the ugliest thing you can be. And it's like a disease, it's like a cancer, it's insidious, it's going to eat you up until you're empty, until you're dead!"

I didn't look at him. I didn't speak. I tried to act as if he were a crazy homeless person. I couldn't wait for the light to change. I had to get away from him, so I turned down Fifty-third and starting jogging away. He jogged after me. It started to rain hard—one of those tremendous spring storms. I opened up my umbrella and, realizing I wasn't going to outrun him, just walked briskly across Fifty-third Street, trying my best to ignore him. But he didn't have an umbrella of his own, and as he yelled at me he kept trying to get under mine, and I kept hurrying up and pulling away, leaving him stranded in the downpour.

"Christ, Jeff, do you think I'm blind? Do you think I'm an idiot? I see. I know. You keep saying, 'I'm straight, I'm straight, I'm straight,' but I see what's in your eyes when you look at me! Look at me! Look at me! Look at me now, Jeff! You fucking asshole, I can't believe I ever got involved with you. What am I doing? What am I doing? I can't be-lieve . . . it wasn't supposed to be like this. Do you think I moved from Pittsburgh to New York so I could sneak around with some fucked-up closet case? You're straight? Straight! Do straight boys hold hands? Do you hold hands with your straight friends on the OTB counter at Grand Central? Do you talk on the phone with your ROTC buddies for hours every night? Go ahead, walk away, I'm soaked, fine, it's just water, Jeff, it's only rain, natural, a natural substance, I won't melt, un-like you. I know you can hear me. You'll be hearing this voice for the rest of your sad sorry life unless you get your shit together and face up to what's happening inside you. God, Jeff, you want everything to make so much sense! You want the whole world to make sense! You want *structure*. Your religion, the military. You need those nice, neat lit-tle hiearchies where everyone knows exactly what everything is and precisely where everyone stands. Everything wrapped up in these nice, tight little boxes. Fuck you! Go ahead, just keep walking, just keep walking, dry, stay dry, Jeff, make sure you always stay perfectly dry!"

He reached over and pulled the umbrella away from over my head, and I pulled it back, but even that short amount of exposure left me half drenched, it was raining that hard. "See, Jeff, it's just water, it's just rainwater, it won't hurt you. It's the most natural thing in the world!" We'd reached the Citicorp Building, and I ran down the steps to the plaza and the entrance to the subway station. When I got out of the rain, I stopped and closed my umbrella and turned around. Greg had stopped midway down the stairs. He stretched open his arms and raised his face directly into the rain, then looked down at me. "You're not going to stay dry forever, Jeff," he yelled. I wasn't sure, there was too much rain, but it looked as if he was starting to cry, the way his head fell and started to shake a little. I turned and quickly fished a token from my pocket, rushed through the turnstile, and, without looking back, hurried down the steep escalator to the trains below.

*   *

We didn't speak to each other for the next month. I managed to focus on school and ROTC and avoid him as much as possible at work. But when the semester was finished, I started full-time at the bookstore for the summer. And slowly, we drifted back together. This time it became more serious. We played on the store softball team together, and after the second game a bunch of us went to a BBQ on the Upper West Side. Halfway through the meal, Greg got up and went to the bathroom. A few minutes later, I followed him, and we kissed for the first time, his back to the bathroom door in case anyone walked in on us. We went to the movies. We saw Arnold Schwarzenegger in *Red Sonia* in a crowded, smoky Times Square movie theater, the two of us hunched down low in our seats, knees touching the whole time, our fingers occasionally locking together as we passed the Coke and popcorn back and forth between us. Periodically Greg would light up a cigarette and then rest a hand on my knee. Afterward we had dinner at the Beefsteak Charlie's nearby on Forty-fourth Street and Broadway, where Greg had waited tables for a few years (the space is now used by ABC's *Good Morning America*). The following week we spent a day together up at the Cloisters (Greg lived close by, in Inwood), listening to Gregorian chants in the courtyard, walking through Fort

Tryon Park, the Hudson and the Palisades spread out so grandly below us.

For his birthday in July I invited him out to my apartment, and we walked over to Flushing Meadow Park and made out on the ground in front of the Unisphere, the big silver globe left over from the 1964 World's Fair. I don't know what came over me. I mean, it was broad daylight, in the middle of the afternoon, in a city park. There was a group of Mexicans playing soccer on the dustbowl of a field in front of us. I bought us two Cokes and two hot dogs at a cart, and we sat down on the grass nearby and watched them play. Occasionally the number 7 train, up on its elevated track, would rumble by behind us. A Mets game was in progress, so every now and then we could hear the crowd cheering and the organ playing over at Shea Stadium. It was Greg's twenty-third birthday, so after finishing our hot dogs we started horsing around, kind of wrestling, and I said I had to give him his birthday punches. I started out softly, just tapping him, really— Greg was thin and somewhat delicate—punching him lightly on the arm. And he was laughing at first and pretending to struggle, but as the numbers grew higher, I don't know why, the punches grew progressively harder. I began to feel something well up in me, not anger, really, but something else, I've never known what to call it, and as I got closer to twenty the punches got even harder and Greg started saying, "Stop, Jeff, stop," though still laughing, still taking it all good-naturedly—but then at twenty-one I just let loose and really smacked him hard on the arm, and I saw the look on his face, a little water welled up in his eyes, and then twenty-two, harder, and his laughing stopped, then twenty-three, and I was holding him down now. "And one to grow on," I said, and hauled off and popped him as hard as I could. "Ow—fuck, Jeff, damn," he said, crawling away from me on the grass and rubbing his arm. He was trying his best to hold back the tears now, and I looked at his face and suddenly was filled with such regret and longing at having hurt him, and such overwhelming desire, that I crawled over and took him in my arms and kissed him deep on the mouth. We collapsed onto the grass, rolled around, our mouths locked together, our tongues twisting around each other. We both got hard instantly and the rolling around turned into a kind of wrestling, and I feel certain that had we not been interrupted, we would have soon been tearing off our clothes. But *"Maricón!"* came flying at us from a dozen different sources, like a swarm of flies. The Mexicans were shocked. *"Maricón!"* again, and laughter, and then the soccer ball came flying toward us, just barely missing Greg in the head, and we stood up and hurried off toward the train and Queens Boulevard.

My grandmother was out when we arrived back at the apartment. I think we both knew what this meant. We went directly to my room. I closed the door, snapped the fan on high, and we fell into the bed together, resuming the kiss that the Mexicans had interrupted, hardly missing a beat. We were sweaty now, and the cool air felt good on our skin. The noise from the fan sealed the room shut, in a way, so that it seemed at that moment that nothing in the whole world existed except Greg and me. We kissed until our lips ached, and then I found myself pushing Greg's head down to my crotch, and before I knew it he had me in his mouth and I was exploding.

In those few moments during the orgasm the world seemed to switch from color to black-and-white, and now, suddenly, though a part of me wanted just to enjoy the easy languor of lulling about in the afternoon heat with Greg, a larger part of me had me jumping up and pulling on my white briefs and jeans and rushing off to the bathroom. When I returned to my room, I was hoping Greg would be dressed and ready to go, but he was still lying there in the breeze from the fan, a peaceful half-smile on his face.

"You should get dressed," I said. "My grandmother might come home."

"Oh, okay," Greg said, and he lazily pulled himself up and started putting his clothes back on.

After he was dressed he said, "So, what should we do now?"

"I really need to do some stuff around here. How about if I just see you tomorrow at work? You know how to get to the train from here, right?"

Greg looked a little crestfallen, but he said okay and stood up and drew near to kiss me good-bye. I grabbed him and kissed him hard in the middle of the forehead. "Happy birthday," I said. He looked a little startled but just smiled and turned around. I walked him to the front door, and he was gone.

After he left I straightened my bed and sprayed the room with Lysol, convinced that the smell of sex was everywhere, and then I tried to put the whole thing out of my mind. But a few hours later it was all I could think of again, and I decided to try to write a note to let him know how I felt. I wanted it to be clear that I liked him a lot as a friend but that the sex wasn't going to happen again. I wasn't gay; we were just friends. After a half-dozen false starts I finally came up with this draft, which I ended up copying onto a yellow notepad and giving to him the next day at work.

I thought of you the other day
I was sad because I did not
Adequately express all I had to say
I am not a writer or poet
But I was moved to say these words

I thought of you yesterday
They were good thoughts and sustained me.
It was your birthday and I was happy for you.
I want you to know that I care!
My caring is different, I know
But I feel that in the long run
Your dignity is most important
And your greatest gift to me.
I believe in you, I hope in you and for you
I trust you!

I could ask to know no better and yet
I know you can and will be better.
Your birthday makes me think of
The journey you will make
All your triumphs and struggles, your
Happiness and hurt.
I am awed and wish to be a part of it.
Mushy sounding, but from the heart.

I suppose it was a function of my confusion and emotional immaturity that allowed me to believe that this note said what I wanted it to say. I handed it to Greg in an envelope the next day at work and told him to wait until he got home to read it.

For the next month or so I felt like a crazy man half the time, crazy thinking about Greg, and then crazy with guilt after having sex with him. Greg complained that we spent less time just hanging out, but I always felt so guilty afterward that I couldn't bring myself to hang out with him the way we used to. I was learning to compartmentalize my sex, to keep it in a nice box that had nothing to do with the rest of my life. Greg didn't want to be kept in a box.

Finally, the summer ended, and I threw myself back into school and ROTC, deciding once and for all that I wasn't gay, and that the thing with Greg was just a phase. I went back to part-time at the store and managed to avoid Greg as much as possible. There was one last fight, and that was it. Deep down, I think I knew Greg was right, but I wasn't anywhere even close to dealing with it. And being a soldier meant too much to me. So I deliberately switched off the light, leaving him in the dark, and he gave up, I suppose, and I suppose I broke his heart again, for the second time in a single year.

CHAPTER THREE

The Boy on the Rock

That fall I kept myself busy with school and ROTC and a part-time schedule at Doubleday. Greg got a new job, at a small, academic publisher downtown, but he continued to work part-time at the bookstore at night. This made things easier. Though we still ran into each other occasionally when our shifts overlapped, we didn't see each other much and were able to abide by a relatively civil truce when we did. And this is how it went for the next few years. I had classes all week, Wednesdays were ROTC, and I worked at Doubleday Thursday through Saturday. Unlike high school, at Fordham I tried to get involved as much as possible, socially and otherwise. I studied hard and partied a good deal. And that year, my sophomore year, I even got involved in student government, getting elected president of my class.

Like most of my friends, I dated girls casually in these years and had a few of the standard late-night drunken fumblings that characterize college life. Commitment was never much of an issue. The most memorable of these casual dates was a girl named Eileen, whom I met at Clarke's, one of the local watering holes that catered to Fordham students. It was the spring of my junior year, and my roommates and I were hanging out at the bar at around one in the morning. Eileen walked up to me and introduced herself. She looked familiar and I said so, and she said she was in my Soviet foreign-policy class.

We hit it off right away. She was sweet and smart and had a great sense of humor. There was a softness to her that seemed to blunt my own oversize clumsiness. We talked for a few hours at the front end of the bar. Periodically, one of my roommates, none of whom was getting lucky that night, would interrupt us to monitor my progress, jealous that I was one step closer than he was to getting laid. One of them would appear to make some lame remark and then disappear. I figured since Eileen was willing to put up with them she was pretty interested in me. After the bartender had made last call around three-thirty, she asked me to walk her home. I said sure and then yelled over to my roommates that I was leaving.

Eileen and I talked nonstop all the way up Fordham Road, laughing at our own bad jokes, and at the thought of my roommates hovering over us at the bar, watching my every move. When we finally got to her room in the mini-skyscraper on campus, known as the "Fives," she turned around and looked at me keenly. Without really thinking I gave her a long lingering good-night kiss that lasted for about twenty minutes, and then we exchanged numbers and kissed again, briefly.

We arranged to meet again the following weekend at Clarke's. We closed the place again and I walked her home, but this time, when we got to her door in the "Fives," she invited me in. Truth was, I'd enjoyed her company and her conversation so much that I'd kind of forgotten about sex. And as we started making out and then actually having sex, I found myself disappointed because I thought it would be more exciting than it was. This wasn't the first time I'd had sex with a woman, but it was the first time I'd had sex with one to whom I felt so connected, whom I liked so much. Everything worked perfectly, physically speaking, but the whole thing felt perfunctory, it lacked real passion, it lacked the vitality and sheer animal quality I'd felt with Greg and would later feel with other men. Eileen was beautiful and I liked her, but having sex with her felt like an intellectual exercise. It seemed entirely quantifiable, easily explained, unlike sex with a man. For me, the experience of sex with another man, I'd already learned, was unquantifiable; you just knew it was great. And it was this very fact that made it so special; it was the fireworks I'd been watching in the movies for years finally translated into the language of my own heart. Andrew Sullivan once said that having sex with a woman was like watching black-and-white TV, whereas having sex with a man was like watching the same TV in full Technicolor. I couldn't agree with him more.

This little dalliance with Eileen went on until I went off to ROTC Advanced Camp in July. The night we said good-bye I think it was clear to both of us that when I returned in August and when we got back to school in the fall, we'd probably not be an item. We'd had a good run, but I think she sensed the limits of my affection early on and, sensing them, had limited her own. Still, I firmly believed that it was just a matter of finding the right girl, and that someday I'd find her and marry her and we'd have kids and the whole bit. I didn't know it at the time, but this little spring-into-summer affair with Eileen would actually be my last shot at that, since it would be my last relationship with a woman.

Having said good-bye to Eileen, I went off to Advanced Camp. One of the most exciting things for me during college was experiencing what it was like to be in the field as a soldier. Every year up to this point we'd been sent to West Point for a weekend training exercise. These training exercises and our weekly classes were basically preparation for what is now called National Advanced Leaders Camp. When I went, though, it was called simply Advanced Camp.

Scheduled during the summer between the ROTC cadet's junior and senior years of college, it is the culmination of everything the cadet has learned up to that point and, more important, serves as an evaluating tool for the military. Cadets are rated on a scale of one to five, a one meaning you're simply not cut out to be a soldier, a five meaning you're the cadet equivalent of an Eisenhower. This score plus your GPA determines whether or not you're placed on active duty. The camp also gives the cadet the chance to experience a little bit of every branch of the army so that he or she can decide where they most want to serve.

Today the camp is held only at Fort Lewis, Washington, but when I went they had Advanced Camp at Fort Bragg, North Carolina, as well. I was sent to Fort Bragg. The whole experience was a nonstop adrenaline rush: constant activity played to a loud hard-rock sound track that included songs like "Rock You Like a Hurricane" and "Hell's Bells." Typical components were: Basic Rifle Marksmanship, Fire Support, Machine Gun Training, Hand Grenade Assault Course, and Confidence Training (Rappel, Obstacle Course, etc.).

It was at Advanced Camp that I first developed my lifelong obsession with being a paratrooper. The Eighty-second Airborne assigned a brigade to Advanced Camp every year. It was with the Airborne that I formed my first real impression of the army away from cadet land and a better appreciation of what I was in for if I wanted to go on active duty.

The most powerful experience I had while at Advanced Camp occurred about halfway through the course. It was a hot and clear Carolina day. As we made our way through an obstacle course on one of the western ranges, it felt as if the sun were getting closer to us with each step, beating down on us without mercy. In addition to the heat, this particular obstacle course made the afternoon feel like a crucible in which we were being tested mightily. The course included a timed portion that took us through a deep, muddy trench lined on both sides by sergeants barking at us like mad dogs. Coming out of the trench, I found myself covered head to toe in filth and smelling pretty bad, but feeling, somehow, exhilarated, as if I'd reached a new level of endurance. After the trench, there was a five-story tower. As we'd been instructed, I climbed to the top and slid down the long wire on the other side, letting go at just the moment we'd been trained to, and dropping down into the cool stream below. It was great to be in the water, feeling all the dirt slide off my tired, sweaty body. I relaxed for a moment and tried to actually enjoy it until one of the cadre above started yelling at me to get out of the way so that the guys behind me didn't fall on top of me. As I swam downstream to the rendezvous point I suddenly heard behind me at the drop point a loud crack followed by a dull kind of thud. I turned back to the hanging wire and saw, on the jagged outcrop of rock that stuck out just below the tower, the crumpled body of a cadet who must've been just behind me. I waited for him to stand up, to roll over, anything, but he just lay there motionless, and I started getting an awful sinking feeling in my gut. I tried to see if I recognized him, but the way his body was twisted away from me I couldn't make out a face. I was frozen there in the cool stream, treading water, transfixed by the scene transpiring in front of me. "Get up, get up, fuckhead, get up," I heard myself saying, under my breath, pushing the water out around me harder and harder. But he still wasn't moving, and I began to realize it was probably very, very serious. I can't remember how long I stayed there, treading that black water. I remember thinking, I can't move; I can't look away, until he moves, until he gets up. But he didn't move, no matter how much I willed him to, and the water seemed to grow colder and colder until I started losing feeling in my feet. Just as they reached him and began to survey his injuries and take his vitals, making sure not to move his body, I was yanked out of my state by the brusque voice of one of the cadre yelling at me to come out of the water and get with the group.

I swam downstream. The sight of the kid's body so impossibly arrayed across the rocks was terrifying. The image of his young, twisted body was immediately seared into my mind. I had never seen anything like it before, nothing even close, and I found myself getting a little queasy and a little short of breath as I pulled my body out of the water and joined the rest of the group. We sat silent, shivering, crestfallen, all the young, male energy that had filled the air just a few moments ago having instantly vanished. Deflated, barely able to look at one another, we waited quietly as they retrieved the boy's body from the rocks. At one point I turned my head away from the recovery scene and looked at my fellow cadets sitting around me. Just a few moments earlier their faces had been the faces of young, vibrant men, invincible, eager to take on the world. Now all I saw were boys, little boys, some fighting tears, faced for the first time with evidence of their own mortality, evidence of their own limits, and most of all, the hard cold evidence of one of the most sobering realities of army life.

After about a half hour, without any sort of explanation, they moved us downstream to the next site. It was hard, of course, to recapture the energy we'd had before the accident, to reinflate ourselves, so to speak, but that seemed to be what they expected, so we all did our best. As the afternoon progressed, the heavy-metal music they played through the loudspeakers to pump us up seemed callow and crass, a kind of mockery of the boy whose fate was still entirely unknown to us. I was distracted and sluggish the rest of the afternoon, unable to shake the image of the boy on the rock from my mind, and increasingly angered by the total silence coming from on high regarding the incident. By the end of the day I was so worked up that for the first time I found myself questioning whether or not I actually wanted to be an officer, whether or not the army life was actually the life for me.

That evening the sergeant in charge of our platoon called a meeting to discuss the day and to assign the next day's leadership positions. Before he could even start he was bombarded with questions about the accident. He tried to update us on the injured cadet's condition and what had apparently caused the mishap, but we were all too worked up to absorb his rather clinical explanation. We started talking among ourselves, recounting our own reactions and thoughts. We were all feeling a little bit raw that night, some of us almost teary-eyed, and more clumsy with our feelings than usual. We needed more than the normal cut-and-dried response. The sergeant seemed to get it and listened to us patiently, murmuring reassurances, and when the geyser of emotion seemed to have run its course, he got straight to the point about the boy on the rock.

"He's alive, but, unfortunately, the word is the boy's pretty fucked up," he said. "They say he'll probably never walk again. Spinal cord. Not much they can do."

Walking back to my bunk that night, I tried to process what he'd said and what I'd seen that afternoon and how I felt. Nothing seemed to want to come together. It just seemed so ludicrous, so enormously random and unfair. Now this boy of no more than twenty-two was doomed to spend his entire life in a wheelchair, his strong limbs left to shrivel away pathetically, all the freedom and vitality of his youth snatched away in an instant, without even as much as a peep of explanation from the universe.

Accidents and death happen in every profession, I reminded myself; but I hadn't chosen just any profession, I'd chosen the only one in which a pledge of your life, your very breath and blood, is a prerequisite. Is this what I really wanted? Advanced Camp was merely a training exercise. You're not supposed to get killed or maimed or paralyzed in training. This was a fluke, this boy on the rock. I tried to comfort myself, lying in bed that night, but it wouldn't work. The reality of my choice had been made clear. I'd have to be prepared for this sort of thing. If we ever went to war, it would no doubt be a lot worse. I was fast learning that there was a big difference between rhetoric and reality, and that life, and life in the army especially, is serious business indeed.

CHAPTER FOUR

Coins and Butter Bars

The accident notwithstanding, my experience at Advanced Camp was overall a good one. I'd gone down to North Carolina thinking it would be a piece of cake and discovered it was pretty challenging. I ended up being evaluated as a three out of that possible five. Not bad, but no Eisenhower. I was disappointed, felt I could've gotten a four had I gone in a little more focused, and I caught hell from the cadre when I returned to school. But after a few ass-chewings they let the matter go. And for senior year, I was promoted to commander of the entire corps of cadets.

By the time I officially started my senior year at Fordham, I'd already made up my mind that I wanted to serve in the infantry and go into the Eighty-second Airborne. I let the detachment commander know and asked him to do what he could for me. I even wrote a letter to the battalion saying that I wanted to serve with Second Battalion, 505th Parachute Infantry Regiment (PIR). It turned out that I would actually serve with them a few years later, though in a different capacity. Of course I didn't know that at the time. I felt pretty confident I was going to get what I wanted. But the army was short artillery men in the late eighties, so I ended up being assigned there. I was disappointed at first but then less so once I'd learned a bit more about the artillery. I was to report to Fort Sill, Oklahoma, two weeks after graduation.

I was the first in my family to graduate from college, and my grandmother was thrilled. For years afterward she bragged to everyone just how proud she was on my commencement day at Fordham and how much it would've meant to my grandfather had he been alive to see it. I was glad to make her proud.

I was commissioned a few days after commencement in a ceremony that was subdued compared to the large graduation ceremony at Fordham. The detachment commander put us in formation and called each one of us up to pin the "butter bar," the bar for second lieutenant, on our shoulders. After a few perfunctory remarks the formation was dismissed. Then, as the time-honored tradition dictates, each newly minted second lieutenant took his first salute, bearing a coin that tradition also dictates he give to the officer from whom he's chosen to receive this first salute.

The tradition of giving coins in the military is a fairly old one. It's a form of reward and recognition that commanders at all levels use in place of medals. The coins are larger than regular currency, more like medallions, usually one and a half to two inches in diameter. Every unit has one that is unique to it, bearing the insignia or arms of the unit or some other symbol, like airborne wings or unit patches on either side. They're used to encourage esprit de corps. For example, every member of a unit will be given one on the condition that they bear it all times as a symbol of pride and belonging. Sometimes they hold more practical value; for instance, a general will award one that, when presented to a commander, guarantees a three-day pass or some other incentive. Soldiers tend to collect them over the lifetime of their career.

For those of us who trained under SMG Robert Carpenter, it was a no-brainer which officer we'd take our first salute from and present our coin to. And so we all lined up and stood patiently as, one by one, we filed by our mentor and hero, and he saluted and graciously received our coins of gratitude.

CHAPTER FIVE

Steel on Target

I was a soldier at last! And off to strange and distant lands! Well, Oklahoma, at least. Some people say New Yorkers are the most provincial people on earth, after Parisians, and I guess I was no exception. Like most New Yorkers, I tended to believe that the city of my birth was the center of the universe. Anything west of the Hudson River (with the exception, maybe, of Hoboken and Jersey City) was, in my mind, inspiration for TV shows like *Little House on the Prairie*. I knew that where I was going was different from where I'd been; what I didn't realize was just *how* different. I remember getting off the plane and finding myself discombobulated by the people in the airport. For some reason, and to this day I don't know why, there seemed to be a disproportionate number of disabled people: people missing hands, legs, hunchbacked people. Looking back on it now I don't think Lawton, Oklahoma, had a higher number of people with birth defects or disabilities at that time, I think I was so freaked out by being in a new place that all I could see was difference. By the time I walked out of the airport things seemed to normalize, and I didn't spot one person missing a limb. But still, what a different world I had entered. Oklahoma! Where the wind comes sweeping down the plain! Isn't that how the song from the musical goes? I'd been to North Carolina, but that was still the East Coast, not that much different from New York, really.

I think it's a matter of scale. Everything seemed so much bigger, wider, more open, so much space that seemed to be unclaimed, unlike New York, where people buy even the rights to the sky. My concept of Oklahoma had come mostly from the movie version of the musical: pastures of velvet green gently swaying in the wind and carefree young girls in pigtails running around beneath a big clear blue sky, breathing in the freshest of air, delirious with joy. Sitting in the back of the cab on my way to Fort Sill, I was amazed at how perfectly the actual place seemed to match my romantic preconception of it. Looking out the window, I marveled at the fields as we drove along the highway. They seemed endless and so green, a shade of green I swear I'd never seen before, rolling out beneath a sky so big and so deeply blue that it almost seemed as if I'd arrived on a different planet. Large bales of hay dotted the flat landscape along with cows mindlessly chewing their cuds. I tried to joke with the driver by asking him what breed of large dogs they were, but he wasn't amused. He simply grunted kind of grudgingly just like a New York cabbie, and I realized things weren't completely different here in the Midwest; I was still on planet Earth.

Still, I was quickly learning that New York is not, in fact, the center of the universe. And years of traveling around the country has made me realize that Lawton, Oklahoma, is far more like the rest of America than New York City is. Living well and simply and knowing how to enjoy the real things in life, that's what people in the heartland seem to know best how to do, and I've come to appreciate that a great deal. Every romance has its moment of clarity, however, the moment when real life comes clamoring back in. As we entered the town I realized I wasn't in the Rodgers and Hammerstein musical after all. Every army town has a group of businesses that thrive with the proximity of the troops. These businesses reflect the makeup of those troops—most soldiers are young men. In many ways a federal installation is a kind of great piñata of cash waiting to be broken open. Lawton was no exception. It had a dreary strip of topless bars, pawnshops, army-navy stores, Korean and Vietnamese restaurants, German bakeries, paintball suppliers, hunting shops, and, of course, a good many used-car dealerships.

A young soldier doesn't make much money. There is an impression around the country that if you join the service you'll get great pay, excellent benefits, and a good pension. This is a half truth, at best. First, the pay isn't outstanding. On average it's roughly 6.5 percent lower than civilian salaries. Second, the benefits are pretty good and there is a pension, but they lag far behind what can be had in the private sector. As a single guy on his own I never had a problem, but raising a family on army pay is no easy task. It's troubling to me, especially now, when we're asking so much of the members of our armed services, to see young servicemen and -women struggling to support their families, even sometimes having to go on welfare. Though the pay gap between military and civilian workers has decreased slightly over the past few years, and the imminent-danger pay for soldiers in combat has increased, there's still a long way to go. I think it's shameful that the men and women we ask to defend our country sometimes have to struggle to meet the basic needs of their families.

None of this was on my mind, however, when I arrived at Fort Sill on that hot afternoon at the end of June 1988. No, at that point everything was up. All the buckets were full. Fort Sill, Oklahoma, may not have looked like the setting for a Broadway musical, at least not one by Rodgers and Hammerstein, but I sure as hell felt as if I were in one. Everything was about possibility and hope. I'd yet to earn even an ounce of cynicism. Though the question of my sexuality had caused me some pain in college (and much more pain for Greg, though I was far too callow to be aware of the pain I'd caused him), I'd somehow managed to stuff the genie that Greg had nearly succeeded in freeing forcefully back into the proverbial bottle of my own denial. Not only did I get the genie bottled, it seemed as if the original seal had never been broken. I was a free man now, young, bursting with excitement, having realized a dream born so many years before in Jackson Heights. I was a soldier now. I was a lieutenant in the United States Army.

Like any young person who has had a dream come true, I saw only good things ahead of me. I couldn't wait to get up in the morning so I could put on my uniform and go off to work. Everything was new and interesting and worth learning more about. To top it off, I was now getting a decent paycheck every two weeks, something I'd never experienced, even when I worked full time in the summers as a bookseller for Doubleday. Being on my own and supporting myself for the first time was a great feeling. I'd never before felt so independent, that it was only me calling the shots. It wasn't just the paycheck that was fueling this, of course. Along with the tremendous pride I took in being a lieutenant there was also a certain amount of validation that came with it, the respectability that is automatically granted to soldiers. Everywhere I went, people acknowledged me because I wore the uniform, and this acknowledgment gave me a great sense of pride and power and responsibility. Though I had wanted to serve in the Airborne, I soon discovered that the Artillery has an illustrious history of its own and is, in fact, an excellent branch in which to serve. I'd done some research, but it wasn't until we passed by Key Gate on the afternoon of my arrival in late June that I began truly to appreciate the unique role the Artillery has played and continues to play in the U.S. military. What remains of Key Gate are two sides of a large stone wall with an iron gate in the center. On the left side two large cannons are affixed to the wall, crisscrossing each other. To the left of the cannons are the words "Fort Sill, Oklahoma," and to the right "Home of the Field Artillery." A large, old cannon sits in front of the other side, beneath the words "Key Gate." Within the fort itself the sides of the road are dotted with vintage artillery pieces, statues commemorating this war and that battle, and many generals and famous commanders, including Major General Philip H. Sheridan, who first staked the site of Fort Sill out of the Indian Territory in 1869, and the fort's namesake, Brigadier General Joshua W. Sill, who was killed in the Civil War. Everything was neatly manicured. It had the feel of a very old, very prestigious and historic country club. Passing by all of this history, as if I were touring a kind of outdoor military museum, it occurred to me at one point that I didn't recognize quite a few of the cannons, rockets, and missiles on display. I wanted to get a closer look, so when the driver left me off in front of Snow Hall, where I was to sign in and get settled, I decided to take a walk around. Examining the artillery pieces more closely, I realized just how much the branch has changed over the centuries.

The Artillery is considered the senior branch of the army since the first unit constituted by the colonies was an Artillery battery. What Artillery is, basically, is an amazingly lethal weapons system. Its mission is this: "To destroy, neutralize, or suppress the enemy by cannon, rocket, and missile fire, and to help integrate all fire support assets into combined arms operations." The cannons are assigned to the divisions and provide the critical, all-weather capability to engage the enemy with a wide range of munition types. They can be dropped from planes, lifted by helicopter, or simply rumble along with the tanks. The missiles can engage targets up to one hundred kilometers away. And the MLRS (Multiple Launch Rocket System) can blanket a one-square-kilometer piece of terrain with a thick cloud of white-hot shrapnel. These three systems in combination provide the generals in charge with the unmatched ability to reach out and target the enemy long before the tanks and infantry even arrive. Artillery has been responsible for roughly a quarter of all casualties in the last several conflicts in which the United States has been involved. What role does the soldier play within this massive system of lethal weaponry? It is his role to make sure these machines work properly, of course. The artilleryman is trained to, above all, "put steel on target." Artillery is in many ways a thinking man's branch of the army. Gunnery, the science of computing ballistic firing data, is more involved than, say, shooting an M16A2 rifle. It also requires a much broader view of the battlefield. It often falls to Artillery to help integrate all the supporting pieces on the battlefield. For instance, the artilleryman assigned to a battalion of infantry will coordinate all tactical air support, the engineers, and naval gunfire.

After walking around and checking out all the vintage artillery I finally entered Snow Hall to sign in and get myself settled. Fort Sill is a national historic landmark. It is also the only remaining active army installation of all the South Plains forts built during the Indian Wars. Any doubts I had as to why the place was considered worthy of historic landmark status were immediately put to rest when I walked into Snow Hall. The place has the feel and smell of a very old high school and isn't very well lit. Newly minted lieutenants take classes here on everything from tactics to cannon gunnery. It was in these classrooms where I would learn everything I needed to know about being an artilleryman. It is also the place where new doctrine is developed and serves not only as the artillery training center for the United States but for the entire free world. Foreign militaries send their best officers to train alongside us, where they learn the staff-planning process at all levels and how to use equipment their own governments have, in many cases, purchased from ours. It exposes them to our values and helps to maintain friends and allies throughout the world. It works, though not everyone remains friendly. Libyan leader Muammar Qaddafi took the signal officer course here, but he's far more the exception than the rule.

Most of the classes I took in Snow Hall weren't that difficult. The most glaring exception to this was gunnery. It got so tough I began to question whether or not I was cut out to be in the "thinking man's branch" of the army after all. Gunnery is a catch-all term that describes the procedures used to calculate the trajectory of a round of flight to ensure that it lands where it's supposed to. In order to do this one has to use algorithms that account for things like wind speed, muzzle-velocity variations, and precise target locations. It's the kind of stuff that sends the old geek meter into the red zone for people who are really into that sort of thing. My background was in liberal arts—political science, history. I could talk for days about, say, the nature of the Soviet nomenklatura system or the impact of foreign aid on developing nations, but I was no math whiz. As we moved through the curriculum I found myself becoming increasingly frustrated and lost. I always seemed to be the last one getting the material, if I got it at all. Finally, as the possibility of my failing the class became ever more likely, I ended up getting a tutor. I worked my ass off, and when the final came, I managed to pass, but just barely. My instructor, who happened to be a Marine, congratulated me but then joked that the hammer in his toolbox probably understood the material better. I didn't think that was quite fair, but marines aren't often known for their tact, so I just smiled and tried to laugh at his lame joke.

As it turned out, the instructor who had the greatest effect on me at Fort Sill was a woman. Her name was Captain Bridgeport, though she was often referred to behind her back as Captain Bridgebitch. I'm sure had she known she wouldn't have cared, having developed a tough hide in her years in the service. I admired her. She was one of the first women to graduate from West Point and one of the few women to join the field artillery. I was drawn to her instantly, maybe because I, too, felt like something of a trailblazer, an outsider, though I didn't consciously see myself this way at the time.

Being something of a ballbuster, she wasn't a particularly popular instructor. She was especially hard on the West Pointers. Unlike some of the other instructors, who saw teaching as a kind of vacation from the real army, she took her job seriously. And it was obvious from the very beginning that she really knew her stuff. You could tell that she had high standards for herself, and because of this she expected, and often got, the very best out of everyone. On top of this it was clear to me from the start that she had a big heart.

Most of all, Captain Bridgeport had courage. When we listened to her talk about herself sometimes after class we learned just how difficult it had been for her breaking in as a woman. She was spit on, was verbally abused, and was, in a very real sense, forced to pay a far higher price than even the most average of men, simply for the privilege of serving her country. I often wondered where the kind of courage that Captain Bridgeport seemed to possess came from, and why, I sometimes asked myself, I didn't have some of it.

CHAPTER SIX

Skunks and Golden Dragons

 M y first roommate at Fort Sill was Tony Alvarez, another lieutenant. Originally from Fort Lauderdale, he was a great guy, laid-back
but quick as a whip. We hit if off instantly, and I learned a lot from
him. Since I graduated in June and went on active duty right after
graduation, I had to attend the officer basic course with the West
Point class. I found this a little intimidating because there's always
been an intense rivalry between West Pointers and ROTC graduates.
Luckily, Tony wasn't your average academy graduate, so we got along
fine. He'd been on active duty for four years at the academy, so he was
familiar with the day-to-day routine of a post, and he basically took
me under his wing.

In many ways my first six months at Fort Sill felt a lot like college.
We went to class and studied hard, and spent far too much time at
night sitting in bars with sawdust floors, listening to country music,
chasing whiskey shots with beer. Years later, when I saw the movie
Road House, with Patrick Swayze, I was reminded of those days with
Alvarez and the guys. The only difference between the bars in the
movie and the ones we hung out in was that the bars we went to didn't
have chicken wire strung up to protect the band.

We'd stay out until midnight, sometimes later if we went to the
strip club afterward, and then get up promptly at six-thirty the next

morning for PT (physical training). It was always about pushing your-self to the limit in the army, even when it came to having fun. And we were all so young and fit, our bodies seemed to be able to take just about anything. Later on, there were road trips to Oklahoma City and Dallas and Wichita Falls. It was usually Alvarez and I and a few guys from my unit—Dave Bartlett, Jay Squire, and Ron Citro, three West Pointers who really knew how to have fun but were serious about being soldiers as well. We had a great time together and we all got pretty close. We'd sit in the bar drinking and talking about school and women, mostly, and I really felt like a part of the group. I had dated girls in college after all. There'd been Eileen and a few others, so I never really felt like a total outsider. I was one of the guys, though there was always, in the back of my mind, some distant whisper, a phrase from Greg's outburst in the rain, the memory of some freshly squashed desire (a glimpse of a soldier's hairy legs; the clean-cut back of a neck; a strong, wide wrist banded with a watch that kept me just slightly apart. Still, it was usually just a whisper, and it became clear to me early on that the truth was I was far more like these guys than I was different from them. Despite coming from completely different backgrounds, we all shared similar hopes and dreams about the fu-ture; we liked a lot of the same music, movies, and TV shows; and we all shared a sense of humor that kept things light and helped us get through courses like gunnery.

I remember the night I first began really to appreciate Alvarez and the guys. It was one of those nights when you become convinced you'll be friends for life, when it becomes inconceivable that you'll drift apart and go on with your separate lives. That's exactly what happened, of course, but on this night I just couldn't imagine it.

It was the night before our first gunnery exam. I should've been home studying, but they'd convinced me to come out with them to the bar. The energy was high that night, and we drank quick and fast and soon found ourselves laughing hysterically at the story Dave was telling to a couple guys from another unit who'd joined us at our table.

We all knew the story already, but Dave told it in a way that made us laugh as if we were hearing it for the first time.

We'd been bivouacking on one of the ranges to learn how to call for fire. One night Dave and Ron, always the practical jokers, decided to put some food in front of the tent of a couple West Pointers they didn't like. They hoped to attract a skunk or a raccoon to scare the crap out of them since one of them couldn't be convinced that there weren't bears in the area. But they were disappointed in the morning when they saw that the food was untouched. That night Jay decided to get in on the action, so he placed some food in front of Dave and Ron's tent. During the night they heard some scratching at the entrance to their tent, and when they looked out were confronted with the largest skunk either of them had ever seen. Dave looked at Ron and said, in the gravest of tones, as if they'd just come under enemy fire, "Remain calm." But then he panicked. He leaped up and rushed out, tearing the tent stakes straight from the ground, leaving it half collapsed on top of Ron, and terrifying the skunk so that both of them got sprayed head to toe.

We were all laughing at the story we'd heard before, our laughter renewed and fortified each time Dave or Ron or one of us would repeat the phrase "Remain calm" in a deeply concerned voice, or when the image of Dave rushing out would flash back through our minds. I remember looking around in a boozy haze of hilarity and thinking how cool it was to have friends like this. These guys are rock solid, I thought, and I know they'll make excellent comrades in arms. I felt compelled to make an impromptu toast, so I called for another round of shots, stood up somewhat unsteadily, and raised my glass.

"To my best buds," I said. "You guys are the best. I'd like to take this opportunity to apologize for all the horrible things I'm going to do to you over the years, but then again you'll probably have it coming, whatever it is."

They all laughed and drank along with me. Alvarez flipped me the finger and Dave punched me hard in the arm while Ron yelled, "And fuck you, too, McGowan!"

"I smell a golden dragon!" Ron said then, and we all soon agreed to leave the bar and head to the Golden Dragon Strip Club.

This wasn't exactly how I'd imagined the army. I'd been part of one of the last groups to be commissioned formally as both an "officer and a gentleman," and I'd thought that meant we had to live by higher standards than, say, the privates in the army and the average Joe civilians. But this was pre-Tailhook, and there was a kind of renewed swagger in the military now that billions of dollars had been pumped in since Ronald Reagan had taken office seven years before. The Berlin Wall would soon collapse, and the Soviet Union would dissolve shortly thereafter, and we'd emerge as the world's sole superpower. There was a renewed sense of entitlement and pride, and in a way I think we were expected to live a little bit on the edge, to live wildly, like winners, now that the cold war had finally ended and it seemed as if the long national trauma of Vietnam had finally run its full course and, in a sense, been atoned for.

And so it was that we often went to the Golden Dragon Strip Club after spending a few hours at the bar. On this particular night I was pretty much six sheets to the wind, and that made it easier for me. I remember feeling strangely disconnected as the lap dancer, a petite redhead with enormous breasts, swiveled over my thighs. I remember thinking that she was Russian from her accent and how strange that was. The girls at the Golden Dragon were all local girls and were all clearly American. Later on I'd learn that it was something she put on, the accent, and that she wanted to be an actress, "like Meryl Streep," she'd say. She smiled when I got erect, but at that point in my life you could have rubbed me up against sandpaper and I'd have gotten hard, so I knew it really didn't mean anything. I heard Alvarez laughing somewhere behind me, and then another beer was suddenly put down on the table in front of me. I played along. I went through the motions. It was actually kind of fun. I really didn't mind coming to the Golden Dragon with the guys. What I minded was that I had to pretend that a woman's body meant the same thing to me as it did to them. In the strange illogic of denial, though, I still had every intention of getting married and having a family. This moment—me, a young soldier, drunk at the Golden Dragon Strip Club in Lawton, Oklahoma—was, I believed, just another chapter in the normal narrative of a regular guy. This is what you did. In a few years I'd be married with children and look back on these days with a kind of fondness. The fact that I wasn't really feeling much for the redheaded "Russian," the Meryl Streep wannabe, on my lap, or for the laughing blonde on Dave's lap, or for any of the women in the club for that matter, only meant, I insisted, that none of them were really my type. All I needed was to meet the right girl and everything would be okay.

But the genie was slowly slipping back out of the bottle (the seal had been broken, after all) and unlike other nights—when I'd been able to convince myself that I just hadn't met the right girl, and that Greg had been a phase, and that I was seeing in these scantily clad lap dancers the exact same thing that Alvarez and Dave and Ron and Jay were seeing—tonight the whole thing just kept collapsing in my mind. And I experienced a kind of vertigo. The mental fortress I'd built to protect me from the truth was under siege, and all that I felt was a kind of disconnection from everyone around me, and, more important, from myself. But then the redhead laughed loudly at something and leaned over to whisper something in the blond girl's ear, bringing me back to the room and back to myself, and I heard the old voice saying, "Yes, you will get married. These women are just not your type. Someone, the right one, will come along one day and everything will fall into place."

And so I rationalized the conflict away. And the mental fortress was no longer under siege. By laying half-truth over half-truth again and again and sealing it all with the most dogged self-righteousness, I managed to blur the issue sufficiently so as to avoid letting the real me take shape. It was more important for me to fulfill my dream of being a soldier than to face this fundamental part of myself, since I instinctively knew that embracing my desire for men meant ending my career. Looking back now, I'm amazed at the amount of energy I spent avoiding my own authenticity in an effort to fulfill some ideal dream of being a soldier.

⋆   ⋆

When I learned that my first assignment would be in Germany, I was disappointed. I still dreamed of going to Fort Bragg and becoming a paratrooper with the Eighty-second Airborne, but that was just not going to happen, at least not on the first go-round. Instead, I would be part of the Third Armored Division, also known as Spearhead for having played the leading role in the advance on Germany in World War II. I was assigned to the Second Battalion, Third Field Artillery, which was part of the First Brigade. The brigade was located north of Frankfurt in a small town called Kirch-Göns. Nicknamed "The Rock," the town had the reputation among those who'd served in Europe as being a kind of shit hole. Turns out my time in Kirch-Göns, and in Germany in general, was one of the greatest experiences of my life.

Despite not getting the assignment I wanted, I was on top of the world when I returned home to Jackson Heights after finishing the basic course at Fort Sill. I had finished my first big test in the army and now was on my way to Germany, where I would begin my career in earnest. That FNG (fucking new guy) feeling was fading fast, and my confidence in my ability was growing by the day. A few days home and I received a set of orders in the mail informing me that I'd be a fire support officer, which meant I'd be assigned to either an armor or infantry unit to call for artillery during combat. This was a typical assignment for somebody coming out of the basic course. As I reviewed the orders, my grandmother, clad in one of the flowery housedresses she invariably wore, walked in, looking glum.

"What's up, Gramma?" I asked.

"I can't believe you're going to Germany! I mean, can't you change this? It's so far away. I don't want you to go. I thought you were going to Fort Bragg."

"Well, not exactly, I wanted to go to Fort Bragg, but they said no. Lieutenants don't get a choice. We're just assigned randomly. The next assignment I get to choose."

"Well, I don't like it," she said, folding her arms. "I mean, how will we talk? It's so far away."

And then she began to cry. I took two steps to where she stood and gave her a big hug.

"Look, I promise that I'll call every week and I'll send you some beer."

"I don't drink beer!" She laughed a little and slapped my arm tenderly.

She was right, though, I thought, it was pretty far away; it was halfway around the world, in fact. But I was beginning to warm to the idea of living in Europe. I'm a big history buff and have a gift for languages, so I knew the experience would probably be a good one for me.

Knowing that I'd probably never live there again, I took one last long walk through Jackson Heights a few days before I left for Germany. Across Eighty-second Street and up Thirty-seventh Avenue, while the number 7 train, the Redbird, roared by on the elevated tracks every few minutes, making its way out to Flushing Meadow and to Shea Stadium. The loud, colorful neighborhood out in northern Queens, in New York City, had prepared me well. I was a soldier now and ready to see the world.

CHAPTER SEVEN

Old Castles and Licensed Whores

By the time my plane landed in Germany and I was actually on European soil, all my disappointment at not having been assigned to the Eighty-second Airborne had vanished in light of the opportunity to live and work in Europe. Few twenty-three-year-old American kids get that chance, and it had finally dawned on me just how lucky I was. I'd been reading books about history, mostly European history, my whole life, and now I had the chance actually to experience the places and the people, the food and the culture, that previously had existed only in the books I read and in my own imagination.

First thing, though, was sex. I had a vague understanding that the Europeans viewed the matter with a little more sophistication than we Americans, but I had no idea just how different it was. There in the shopping promenade of the airport, in full view, merchandise spilling over onto the clean white floor, was a sex shop. Large pink dildos, cheap satin lingerie, candy-colored vinyl bustiers, and a blur of contorted faces and knotted bodies on assorted magazines and video jackets greeted the weary traveler with an unapologetic brashness. I had to laugh and found myself feeling a little embarrassed at the same time. Need gum for the flight out? Why not buy a cat-o'-nine-tails duty-free since it's right next door? Want a newspaper or the latest issue of the *Economist?* Gee, before I do that, let me pick up some of that lube on sale two for one. It was like having a branch of the Pink Pussycat, the well-known sex shop in New York, located in the middle of JFK or La Guardia. I couldn't believe it. It was downright hilarious. I realized that I was gawking and smiling to myself, while everyone around me passed by as if it were nothing more interesting than a luggage store or one of those sunglass huts. People just hurried on by. Apparently, it was no big deal to accidentally crash your carry-on into a bin of edible underwear in the airport in Germany.

As I rubbernecked by, trying my best to look blasé, I imagined what would happen if a branch of the Pink Pussycat actually opened up in one of the New York airports. I knew it would never get past the initial planning stages, but if it did, and they managed to open the store, it would be headline news for days on end. The Catholic groups in Queens would be up in arms, the Queens Borough president would stage big press conferences, Evangelicals would be bussed and flown in from every far-flung corner of the nation to stage demonstrations. It would be clear to all that this was just one more sign that the republic was falling deeper and deeper into irreversible moral decline. Airport sex shops in America? Wasn't going to happen. But I wasn't in America anymore, and though it may seem a little silly, seeing this sex shop planted in the middle of a busy airport, seeing the whole subject of sex being treated with such an easygoing matter-of-factness, was my first lesson in the advanced education I would receive over the next several years, an education that would allow me eventually to view my own sexuality with the kind of matter-of-factness it takes to finally relax a little and live at peace with yourself.

As I reached the baggage claim area I began to realize how exhausted and hungry I was. All I wanted was a hot shower, something to eat, and a clean bed to collapse into. But doing all that wasn't going to be so easy. I was in a foreign country, and it was fast becoming clear that doing even the most mundane tasks—making a phone call, asking for directions, buying a hot dog—would take some time getting used to. Luckily I'd studied German at school and could recall enough to get me through the initial stages of my arrival. There'd be some time before our luggage would start circling around the carousel, so I ambled over to a kiosk to get a quick bite to eat. I was confronted with an array of wursts, gyros, and schnitzels. The person next to me said, *"Pommes frites, bitte,"* and was promptly handed a large bag of French fries slathered in mayonnaise. The smell of sausage and French fries mixed with the cigarette smoke coming from weary passengers waiting in line behind me put me at ease, and sparked memories of home and the people I'd spent most of my life with. Everyone was eating poorly and smoking heavily, and life was just grand! With a very greasy gyro in one hand and a small *orangensaft* in the other, I walked over to wait for my baggage.

Pleased with myself at having navigated the purchase of food, I relaxed a little and for the first time took a close look at the people around me. Large Arab families, the women and girls in head scarves and floral dresses, mixed with people from Germany, Russia, Italy, Spain, France, the Netherlands, all speaking their native tongues. The occasional sound of British English soothed me a little, but for the most part I was surrounded by a great babble of foreign language. And everyone seemed dressed up or, at least, dressed neatly, with some sense of style. With the exception of the Arabs, everyone was dressed in what today might be called business casual. I, on the other hand, had opted to travel in jeans and a T-shirt. As I looked closer, I was able to pick out the few Americans in the crowd who, like me, had chosen to travel halfway around the world in the closest thing they could find to pajamas. Baseball caps, sports jerseys, sneakers, ill-fitting sweats and oversized T-shirts—the Americans were a motley crew indeed among the more stylish Europeans. This is something I'd notice more and more as I traveled across Europe. And I rarely traveled in jeans and a T-shirt after that day.

Every new officer arriving in Europe for the first time is assigned a sponsor to help him get adjusted. Mine was a lieutenant named Ron Tama, who'd sent me a letter a few weeks before, telling me about the unit and what I could expect. Having gotten my bags, I made my way through the crowd until I saw a short, muscular guy holding up a sign with my name printed on it. It was Ron. His sharp features and strong jawline lent him the appearance of rugged intelligence. He extended his hand and introduced himself quickly.

"Ron Tama . . . Jeff?"

"Yep, how's it going?" We shook hands. He had a grip like a vise.

"Good, man, how was your flight?"

"Pretty long, almost seven hours."

"Well, don't worry, you'll get a chance to rest up at the BOQ."

"Cool."

"All right, grab your shit and let's get out of here."

He seemed like a nice enough guy, if somewhat intense. As we made our way to his VW Golf, he filled me in on the battalion's officers, the post, and the training. It sounded like a good deal, a pretty tight-knit group. Out on the autobahn Tama sped up to about a hundred miles per hour. The first thing I noticed, aside from just how fast everything was flashing by me, was the sheer number of military vehicles on the road. These days if you see a Hummer on the road in the United States, it's probably a private car. But back then, before the heyday of the SUV and its obscene, logical conclusion—the private Hummer—you'd almost never see one on the road in the States. Here in Germany in 1989, however, they were all over the place. And it made sense when you considered the fact that we had roughly three hundred thousand troops in the country at that time. Long convoys of armored vehicles up on heavy-equipment-transport trucks, fuelers, Hummers, and two-and-a-half-ton trucks seemed to be everywhere. Porsches, BMWs, and Mercedes Benzes darted nimbly in and out of the slow-moving formations. It was eerie, in a way, but the Germans were apparently used to it, having living with it since the end of World War II.

Pulling off the autobahn at our *ausfahrt* (exit), we came upon a charming little town called Butzbach. Butzbach is picturesque and

has a wonderfully warm feel to it. Off-white stucco buildings with exposed timber beams rise along cobblestone streets, housing quaint little shops and restaurants. In the center of town is the Marktplatz,
where a large circular fountain serves as a kind of rendezvous point.
It's a great place to spend a warm summer afternoon. Butzbach has
the simple and wholesome feel of a place that's been doing things precisely the same way for a very long time, which is no surprise since the
history of Butzbach goes back as far as the Roman Empire.

When I was there Schloss Kaserne housed administrative and
support units. If you had pay problems, housing questions, promotion
points to add to your records, you went to the *kaserne* (barracks) in
Butzbach. If you were new in country, as I was, you'd spend a week
or so there attending an orientation course. You learned how to con-
verse, how to convert money, what the driving laws were—all the basics. If you were an officer, you checked into your BOQ (bachelor
officer quarters) at your home post and went during the day for the
courses. This was changed later on so that everyone, regardless of
rank, had to stay at the Twenty-first Replacement Battalion. Apparently, too many officers were blowing off the courses, setting a bad example for the troops.

After checking into the replacement battalion at Butzbach, we
drove to the Ayers Kaserne at Kirch-Göns, where our unit was located. It was a postage stamp compared to the massive installations
you find in the United States. And it was completely fenced in and
heavily guarded. Armed guards manned the gate on a rotating basis
twenty-four/seven. At that time, most posts in America were completely open. Here it was different because the troops had been the
target of terrorist attacks in the 1970s by radical Marxist groups like
the Red Brigades in Italy and the Baader-Meinhof Gang in Germany.
Security was also a major focus because the Soviet Union had a ro-
bust espionage operation in the West that was designed to monitor our
deployments and equipment.

The entire post was maybe three miles in circumference, and the

BOQs were located on the backside of the *kaserne* next to the officers' club. Ron made sure I got settled into my BOQ and left me for the evening.

My BOQ was dingy and small and dirty, like some lonely furnished room straight out of a T. S. Eliot poem. You couldn't help but wonder if they deliberately neglected the BOQs as an inducement to marriage—this is what awaits you in the land of bachelorhood! And surely the rooms for "confirmed bachelorhood" would be much, much worse. Spartan would be an overstatement. There was a single bed with a lumpy mattress. There was one chair, a sofa, a TV set. The furniture was covered in some kind of thick brown industrial fabric that reminded me of the protective liner of a flak jacket. Despite being dotted with cigarette burns and covered in stains, some of which looked as if they'd been created before the Berlin Wall even went up, the stuff seemed absolutely indestructible, as if it would outlast the heartiest of cockroaches after a nuclear war. Putting my bags down on top of the old mattress, I reminded myself that I wouldn't have to stay here for long. After the orientation I'd be able to get an apartment of my own off post. In the meantime I was too tired to care all that much. Even the lumpy mattress didn't bother me that first night.

The orientation was pretty uneventful. By the end of the week I was beginning to understand why some officers skipped the classes. The kicker came unexpectedly at the end of the week. As a means of putting the skills we'd learned into practice, we would take a day trip in order to interact in German society.

"Tomorrow," our instructor began, picking up a piece of chalk and turning toward the blackboard. "You all are going to make sure you can get your sorry asses around this lovely host country of ours. But you have a choice." He started making a crude sketch of a castle. "First, you got history," he went on, pointing to his childlike drawing of two turrets. "Marienburg Castle. Leine River Valley. Nineteenth century. George V. Scenic. Educational. Postcard material for Mom.

Or . . . ," he continued, a slight smile edging up on the sides of his mouth, "you got big city," and he started drawing the outline of a woman's body, a very big woman, with enormous breasts and huge hips. "Frankfurt. Red-light district. Pussy," he said, circling the area around the crotch several times. "So what'll it be? Castle?" circling the castle. "Or pussy?" circling the crotch area of the sketch again. "Castle or pussy? Castle or pussy?" he kept going back and forth while he repeated this, circling the castle and the crotch area over and over again.

The whole class, myself included, erupted into laughter and whistles and cheers. I was one of only two officers in the class. The other, a second lieutenant by the name of Zach Forbes, an infantry officer who'd been assigned to Fifth Battalion, Fifth Cavalry Regiment, was sitting next to me. I was smiling and laughing as I turned my head toward Zach, but the truth was I felt a little uneasy. I think even if I'd been 100 percent straight, I'd have felt uneasy. Personally, I really wanted to see the castle. It functioned as a museum of the Hannover Royals, and I'd read a lot about them. And besides, I'd grown up in a big city, so big city was no big deal for me. In addition, I couldn't imagine that spending the day with a bunch of enlisted guys could lead to anything good, especially in the red-light district. I looked at Zach, but he said nothing and simply rolled his eyes.

"So what's it gonna be, fellas, old castle or red-light pussy?" the instructor shouted over the commotion.

"Do we have to go as part of a tour?" a sergeant in the back yelled, "or can we do our own shit?"

"Once you're off the bus you're on your own. It's just you and your cock."

The sergeant in the back then shouted, "Pussy!" setting off the whole class. Shouts of "Pussy!" came from every part of the room, along with more whistles and clapping and cheers.

"Well, there you have it. Can't say I'm surprised," the instructor said, turning to the blackboard and slashing a big X across the castle and then circling the crotch of the freakishly large woman he'd sketched one last time. "Pussy, it is! I'll let the driver know."

The next morning was bright and sunny. The fountain in the Marktplatz seemed cleaner and brighter than usual. The sun weaved its way through the narrow cobblestone streets of old Butzbach, past the old shoe store and the Italian restaurant where we often ate. Though I'd wanted to see Marienburg, I was excited about going to Frankfurt. I knew it wasn't quite Paris or Rome, but it was still an important financial center full of history and culture, and I was still pretty much the wide-eyed American, eager to soak everything in.

I knew that Frankfurt had been virtually leveled by the Allied bombing raids in the war, but that fact didn't really register until we pulled into the city center. Coming from Butzbach to Frankfurt was like traveling quickly a thousand years through time. Considered the skyscraper capital of Europe, parts of Frankfurt seemed more like New York to me than old Germany. Frankfurt was not the only German city left so devastated by the war, of course. As I traveled around the country over the next four years, I recognized scars from the war nearly everywhere. I'd be looking at some significant church or palace and suddenly notice a seam and realize that only half the building was authentic and that the rest had had to be rebuilt after the war. Seeing these healing scars so prevalent throughout Germany, I soon began to appreciate why the German people were now so ardently devoted to peace, often much to the chagrin of the Reagan administration. I remember the struggle to deploy the Pershing II missiles and the visceral reaction that decision sparked. Literally hundreds of thousands of Germans took to the streets to oppose the decision. At the time, being a casual observer who had yet to travel to Europe, I didn't really understand their outrage. I thought they were being ungrateful since, after all, we were putting the missiles there at our own expense in order to protect them and the rest of Europe. Once I was there, though, and able to see the scars from the devastation of World War II up close, I understood that it was much more complicated, that there's an enormous difference between the way readers experience history through books and the way the citizens of a particular nation experience history they lived through and remember.

They dropped us off at the Hauptbahnhof, the main terminus of the railways in the city, which was located on the south side of the Stadtmitte, the city center. On the bus ride down, Zach and I had agreed that it was probably bad form for officers to mix with troops in the red-light district, so we split up from the group and for the next three hours walked around the city together, checking out museums and historical sites and the shopping district. It was a nice morning, and we had no trouble navigating "our sorry asses" through the "lovely host country." Around noon we had lunch in a small café.

During lunch Zach asked me if I wanted to check out the red-light district. I hesitated but then, seeing his smiling, expectant face beaming at me, said, "Why the hell not?" I figured he'd probably think it was weird if I said no. And besides, I was genuinely curious, though a little fearful.

I tried to act casual and relaxed as Zach and I made our way to Kaiserstrasse (also known as Kstrasse), talking about old girlfriends and bad dates and parties we'd been to. I was still a bit uncomfortable, but all my reluctance seemed to vanish as we entered Kstrasse, my worries overridden by sheer curiosity and the vague stirrings of desire. With block after block of apartment buildings devoted exclusively to the sex trade, Kstrasse is a wild, wild place, like nothing I'd ever seen, and certainly like nothing that exists in the States. It seemed as if every single window had a red light in it and the windows seemed to go on forever, like a stage set that suggests a kind of infinity. Could there actually be this many women working as prostitutes squeezed into such a relatively small area of town? It was like walking into a fantastic dream.

Self-conscious and anxious to get off the street and out of view, we picked the nearest building and entered through the Gothic stone arch. The passageway was poorly lit and, ever the native New Yorker,

I worried that we were going to get mugged. A short distance ahead of us was a doorway covered with a set of thick, clear plastic curtains that you might see on the back-alley entrance to a restaurant kitchen. Through the curtains we could make out a dim light that seemed to be illuminating the fuzzy outline of several doorways at a greater distance. Classical music and then some jazz, I thought, too distant to identify, drifted softly from the doorway. We pushed through the plastic. As I listened to the curtains clap against each other and against the sides of the doorway, my grandmother's voice suddenly popped into my head telling me to wash my hands. I smiled to myself and walked forward.

We'd entered a large lobby with a smooth marble floor. Though still quite dark, it was clear we'd come into a pretty fine old building. The air was filled with the sickly-sweet detergent smell of a freshly mopped floor. I was a little surprised by this since I'd expected something far worse—a lobby crowded with whores and derelicts and drug addicts sprawling in the filth that comes from years of indifference and neglect and dissipation, kind of like the waiting room (now Vanderbilt Hall) in Grand Central Station in the mid-1980s. Instead, this fine old building looked as if it was as meticulously maintained as I imagined the Marienburg Castle was—very clean and ordered, in typically Teutonic fashion.

At the far end of the lobby I noticed a woman standing in the doorway of what looked like a single room. She wore red satin panties and a feathery red bra. She had shoulder-length, blond hair and perfect skin and not an ounce of fat on her perfectly shaped body. I was kind of stunned by just how beautiful she was and how healthy and normal she looked. Far from the strung-out, crazed hooker I'd imagined, she stood there calmly and entirely self-possessed, patiently observing us as we looked around. As we moved closer, she shifted slightly on her stilettos. I noticed a small sign with a picture of a woman on it hung up rather conspicuously just to the right of her door. Later, I would find out that this was her government license, certifying her status as disease-free, as determined by her last round of STD (sexually transmitted disease) tests, the date of which was stamped on the license. It reminded me of a cabbie's license in New York. Or the USDA stamp on a package of ground meat. Zach and I nodded to her and she nodded back with a slight, knowing smile. She smelled of what I think was Chanel No. 5. I tried not to stare but was curious about her room. I walked slowly past and looked inside. It was painted a garish color of pink, and the sheets on the bed were deep purple and lavender. There was a decent-looking chair and what looked like a suit holder in the corner. An array of sex toys were hung across one of the walls. A small radio sitting on the night table next to the bed played Mozart softly.

Despite the apparent civility and cleanliness of the place, I couldn't help feeling anxious, thinking that at any moment some armed German guy was going to jump out from the shadows and mug us. As Zach moved on and I followed him, I kept looking back over my shoulder to make sure no one was behind us. The last time I looked back, the red-pantied hooker had lit a cigarette and was turning and moving, high atop her red stilettos, into the room with a good-looking middle-aged man, a wisp of cigarette smoke trailing behind her. I'd not even seen the guy coming. The door clicked shut quietly and the Mozart vanished, leaving just the faint sound of a saxophone coming from somewhere and then just silence, which felt like an accusation, like Grandmother's wagging finger.

We walked on and came to a short staircase, three small steps down, that took us to a long, dark hallway that led to a larger staircase up to the second floor. It was a little brighter here, on the stairs, and I could just make out the color of the walls, a kind of light brown, lined at the top with a burgundy border covered with flowers, the whole thing so faded it looked as if it had been dipped in bleach. We took a right at the top of the stairs and walked into a long corridor, lit dimly by simple globe light fixtures installed into the ceiling about every five feet. The corridor was lined on both sides with rooms, most with the door open, and a girl standing in the doorway or sitting on a chair or lying on the bed inside the room. I wondered what distinguished the girl down below from all these other girls and, when I couldn't figure it out, decided that in our anxious haste we'd missed an entire wing of the whorehouse. That first girl was just the first in the first-floor line of girls. And maybe it was a matter of seniority, I thought, the girls down below having worked longer.

Some of the second-floor girls wore relatively modest silk bathrobes; others had on skimpy lingerie; while the boldest, having dispensed with modesty almost completely, opted for only half an outfit, exposing either their breasts or bottoms, but never both. They appeared to be mostly European, and mostly German, and every single one of them was drop-dead gorgeous. All conversation stopped when we started moving down the corridor. They observed us intently as we walked by, the smokers stopping mid-drag, raising an eyebrow. And we looked them up and down, though each time one of them engaged her eyes with my own, I had to look away, move my eyes forward to the next girl, or down to Zach's ass just a few feet in front of me, which was, I'd happened to notice, as we'd climbed the stairs, not bad at all. Toward the end of the line of girls Zach stopped and started chatting quietly with one of the girls. I passed him by and moved to the end of the hallway. I wondered what could possibly motivate such beautiful women, or even not-so-beautiful women, to do this kind of work.

"How did you get into this line of work," I would ask.

And the girl would say, matter-of-factly, that it was just her thing. "Some people like to jump out of airplanes," she would tell me, "or climb mountains or whatever and this just happens to be my adrenaline hit—taking on all you hot American soldiers and tourists and the dirty old German bankers from Deutsche Bank."

"And who does your outfits," I would say.

"Why, Patricia Field, of course, who else?"

I laughed at myself, as Zach started walking toward me, having apparently failed to reach a deal with the girl he'd been talking to. It really was a different world, I thought. All my life I'd been taught that prostitution was degrading and violent and something to be hidden away from the public eye. But walking through these halls, I got the distinct impression that that just wasn't the case anymore, at least not here in Germany. About a year later I was talking to a stripper we'd hired for a bachelor party, and she told me that prostitution in Germany is just another job, like being a secretary or a paralegal or a waitress. Women go to work to pay for college, save up for vacations, or simply for the adventure of it. The government monitors everything, so it all runs pretty smoothly and safely. Looking back, I now realize that that particular stripper was an exception, and that she either wasn't telling me the whole story, or she wasn't seeing it clearly herself. Truth be told, although the government monitored and controlled prostitution, it was technically still illegal, dangerous, and certainly not "just another job." Two years ago, in 2002, thirteen years after my experience in the Frankfurt brothel, the German government actually legalized prostitution, and the life is still difficult and dangerous. Many of the prostitutes, some say at least half, are actually illegal immigrants, so the protections designed to protect them as sex workers don't even apply.

When Zach reached me, I pushed through the fire door to the stairwell and started climbing the steps to the next floor. Opening the door to the third floor, we found ourselves walking into a totally different world from the one down below. This was apparently the African floor. Occupied entirely by black women, the energy here was far less subdued, more celebratory, freer. The women danced with one another in the middle of the hallway to a Milli Vanilli song that blared from a boom box in one of the rooms. They barely noticed us as we negotiated our way through the crowd of bodies. Slowly, as it became clear they'd received visitors, they collected themselves and moved back to their respective rooms and stood waiting or sat down on the chairs just outside the rooms. Unlike the reserved German girls downstairs, these girls had no problem talking to us, even yelling at us.

"Hey, pretty white boy, whatchuwant?" one toward the far end yelled. "You come to make love with an African goddess?" she went on, and then laughter scattered through the hallway.

"Why you so quiet?" another one said, then, "Girls—they look so nervous!"

"We have to calm 'em down," the girl next to her said, laughing with her friend.

Nervous was an understatement. Maybe the first two floors were a ploy, I thought, set up to lure in unsuspecting idiot white boys like me for the entertainment of the wild she-devils up on the third floor. As I tried to look cool, though sweat was now dripping from my forehead, and make my way down the hallway, one of the women reached out, grabbed my crotch, and held on, firmly. I turned my head abruptly and looked at her. She was smiling big, a Madonna-like gap between her two front teeth.

"Hey GI, wanna fock?" she said, still smiling, and still holding on to my crotch.

I was momentarily stunned. My mind raced, what the hell did "fock" mean? *Fock, fuck,* I thought, *right,* I got it. I tried to regain my composure and answer her as politely as possible.

"No, thank you," I said, sounding, I'm sure, like the whitest GI on the face of the planet. "I have a girlfriend, but thanks, thank you very much."

This was completely untrue, of course, and the girl didn't care one way or the other. She tightened her grip on my crotch and started massaging me, and I felt myself starting to get hard. I pushed her hand away and walked on, feeling humiliated, and the laughter and yelling grew louder.

"He got one a dem skinny white tings?" one of the shorter girls yelled. She was kind of plump and had had her hair straightened. She was laughing so hard it looked as if tears were streaming down her face, and when someone else yelled, "Not so skinny on a big guy like dat!" She collapsed into the arms of another girl, whose shoulders were shaking from laughter.

"You gonna tell your girl you made love to a goddess?" said another, with arms akimbo and a look of truly venomous sarcasm across her face that made me think of what battery acid does to a car hood.

"Go home and tell her to come back wit you and we teach her a couple a tricks."

Zach bumped into me then, as if he'd tripped, and kind of pushed us both through the door onto the stairwell. We stood for a moment, laughing at ourselves, Zach with his back up against the door as if to keep the women from chasing us.

"Geez-o-peets," Zach said, "what the fuck was that?"

"Yeah, I know, they kicked our ass, didn't they?"

"Geez-o-peets, Christ, I feel like a log on a table saw," he said. "You want to check out the fourth floor or just give it up?"

I looked at him steadily. A part of me just wanted to get the hell out of there but curiosity got the better of me.

"Let's do one more floor," I said finally. "But if it's as fucked up as this one, last man out buys beers."

So up we went to the fourth floor. A sense of deep relief washed over me as we entered the floor. It was quiet here. There was a kind of dismal tranquillity to everything. All the women were Asian. A few were quietly chatting among themselves, but most were simply standing or sitting, waiting. The scent of coriander and ginger hung heavily in the air. Despite their reserved manner it looked as though these Asian girls specialized in the more exotic sexual activities. Every room was outfitted with a swing and a lot of bizarre leather equipment. Halfway down the hall Zach suddenly stopped in front of a particularly beautiful Chinese girl. She was maybe five feet two inches, with long shiny black hair and a petite, nicely proportioned body. She had a squarish face with high cheekbones that gave her a kind of serene dignity. Her eyes were soft and a little bit sad.

I listened to Zach negotiate with her. Her voice was soft when she spoke to Zach in just barely passable English, though harsher and much louder when she was interrupted by two of the other girls and forced to reply, first in German, and then in Chinese. I heard her tell Zach she was from Hong Kong. Behind us, one of the other girls said something in Chinese, and everyone starting giggling. I began to sweat again, thinking of the floor down below, but the giggling soon ran its polite course and petered out.

"So how much will it be?" Zach said

"Pipty mahk for bof."

"Both? Both what?"

"Suck n fock."

"Okay, and . . . okay," Zach stumbled over the words a little.

"Anything you want, you ask an ah give you plice."

"No, what you said first, that'll be okay," Zach said, and he walked into the room past her. She quickly turned around and closed the door behind her.

Meanwhile, I suddenly found myself standing alone in the hallway, blinking like an owl. The other girls seemed to be eyeballing me now with renewed intensity.

"Hey, GI, you wanna have fun? Whassa matter? You no look so good."

I looked hard at them, unsure what to do, and I guess I must've looked pretty intense.

"Oooh," one of the girls said. "He bery mad, I think. Wha happen . . . you wanna go in room wif friend. Jus knock is all right."

"Hey, you come here I make better," another one said.

"Smile, it not so bad," said a third. "We give special for the soldier, bery special for the American soldier. You soldier boy?"

At that moment I knew I had to get out of there. It would be too humiliating to just stand there and wait for Zach. I fixed my gaze on the light above the door at the end of the hall and walked resolutely toward it. I felt like shit. My emotions were all mixed together, and I couldn't make sense of anything. I guess I hadn't really expected Zach to actually *do* anything. Part of me thought he was just plain stupid for doing it, but another part of me gave him credit for being so fearless. He was a good-looking guy, and for a fleeting moment I saw his ass again on the stairs and wondered what he would look like doing it with the girl from Hong Kong. But then I felt guilty about having this thought and pushed it from my mind. Being here in the whorehouse was hard for me because I couldn't be in the moment. I found myself getting angry that I felt pressured to take a girl myself. Deep down I knew that what I wanted simply wasn't here. And I resented the fact that it seemed so easy for Zach.

Suddenly, standing there in the midst of all these beautiful Asian prostitutes, an American soldier they said they'd treat special, I felt like an enormous fraud. It was the same feeling of fraudulence and inauthenticity I'd experience a few years later while I was waiting for a plane in full uniform at La Guardia Airport in New York. A woman approached me holding the hands of her two young sons. The boys, both of whom looked to be about five or six—they may have been twins—trailed a half step behind their mother, as if they were afraid of where she was dragging them. By the time she reached me she had a big smile on her face, and she quickly introduced herself and then pulled her sons forward to shake my hand. The boys came to me shyly but then beamed when I shook their tiny hands. The woman said her sons had never met a real soldier before. I knelt down when one of the boys asked a question and stayed there while the other boy asked another; when they both seemed satisfied, I stood up and shook the mother's hand. The mother thanked me and took her sons back to their seats in the waiting area, and I was left standing there feeling like a million bucks. But it was a hollow feeling; something wasn't quite right. I knew that her wanting her sons to meet me had nothing to do with me personally. It was the uniform, which, in many people's minds, still stands for all the ideals of a great democracy, and it is for little boys, and now, increasingly, little girls as well, a clear representation of something they can aspire to *be*.

On career day in the fifth grade, say, there is the *policeman*, the *fireman*, the *soldier*, the *teacher*, and on and on. Becoming one of those things is presented almost as if it's an existential choice, as if that is what you'll actually *be*, as opposed to what you will, in fact, simply *do*. As they began to announce preboarding for my flight, the hollow feeling seemed to deepen. It occurred to me that when I was in my uniform, I felt as if I were onstage, as if I were an actor performing a role. This in itself is not such a bad thing, really. It's the one of the things that assure the smooth functioning of the military, in fact—clear-cut roles, duties, privileges, places within a strictly defined hierarchy of titles and responsibilities. But maybe I'd taken it too far. I'd come to believe that I was, above all, a soldier, rather than simply a man who happened to have made a career out of soldiering. I'd become the role, and because I perceived the role of soldier and homosexuality as mutually exclusive, I'd manage to forfeit one of the most important aspects of myself.

Rushing out of the whorehouse into the Frankfurt street that day back in 1989, I tried to shake all the unease from my mind. I sprinted down the street, trying to physically outrun my feelings, to sweat out the desires, to run back to myself. I don't know how far I ran, but it seemed like miles. When I finally stopped, exhausted, sweaty, I felt calm again. I reminded myself firmly that I would have a family one day. I reminded myself that if I kept thinking about men, that wouldn't happen, at least not in the way I'd imagined it.

Back on the bus that day I was talking to one of the sergeants when Zach came running up. He bounded up the stairs, came down the aisle, and sat down next to us, smiling and breathing hard. His hair was disheveled and his face was red.

"Missed you, buddy," he said. "Where'd you get off to?"

"I got bored," I said, "so I thought I'd just come back to the bus."

"And just where, pray tell," asked the sergeant, "did you two fine gentlemen spend the day?"

He was looking directly at me. My face went blank. Zach took a deep breath and said, quickly, "We just walked around, basically."

The sergeant looked at us curiously. His looked seemed to indicate that he, too, had seen the inside of one of the apartment buildings in the red-light district that day.

"Yeah," I said firmly, "we just . . . walked around."

Riding back on the bus that Friday afternoon, it occurred to me that my formal education as a soldier had finally come to an end. No longer a cadet in training, Monday morning I would report to the Headquarters and Service Battery with the title fire support officer (FSO).

CHAPTER EIGHT

Meeting the Troops

The day after the Frankfurt trip with Zach and the orientation class, I reported to headquarters to meet my new boss and fire support sergeant. I'd been assigned to a Fire Support Team (FIST), the group responsible for calling for artillery fire for a particular infantry company. We were attached to A Company, Third Battalion of the Fifth Cavalry, which was a mechanized infantry company consisting of fourteen Bradley fighting vehicles.

My unit was to be deployed in three days as part of Exercise Centurion Shield, the latest iteration of the REFORGER exercise (more about this later). It was mind-boggling to me the way the unit shifted into action, making all the last-minute preparations to load the track vehicles onto the flatbed trains so they could be transported to the "maneuver box," the name given to the area of the country in which the exercise would take place.

And it wasn't just my unit, of course. As I walked across the post on that cool October morning I saw that the whole place was frantic with preparations, the *kaserne* having been transformed into a virtual hive of activity. Every unit was out in front of its barracks, conducting thorough inspections of every single piece of equipment in its possession. The normally placid motor pools, row after row of huge tanks, silent behemoths parked snugly one right up against the next in order to save space, were all out of place, jutting out at odd angles, surrounded by equipment and the soldiers who were making adjustments and repairs. Troops laughed and joked as they prepared for the maneuver, packing up equipment, changing tires, checking oil—a flurry of dipsticks going up and down like the pistons of an engine, the whole thing working so smoothly and with such precision it really did seem like a well-oiled machine.

For a moment, walking past the railhead, I suddenly felt as if I were in an old Hollywood war movie. Everything seemed to be working so well it almost felt choreographed, as railcars slowly and ponderously backed up to the platform under the careful supervision of a sergeant wearing a fluorescent safety vest. As each car gently made contact with the thick rubber blocks placed there to protect the cement structure, a soldier walked onto the flatbed and began the process of guiding his vehicle onto the car, using a carefully defined set of hand signals. Once in place, enormous chains were applied to the front and back of the vehicle and then ratcheted down. Though the whole process was done slowly and with a kind of steady precision, it wasn't quite what I'd imagined. Everything seemed to lack the pomp and formality all my training had taught me to expect. Looking back now, I realize I was still very much the cadet at this point, still very much wrapped up in the romance of army formalities and too invested in the rhetoric of soldiering to appreciate fully the reality of army life. These people preparing for Exercise Centurion Shield weren't playing at soldiering, they were actually doing a job, they were working. Their uniforms weren't perfectly pressed and starched; some were actually a little ratty and covered in oil and grease. There was little, *none* in fact, of the self-consciousness that so often accompanies the activities of cadets in training. No, I wasn't in a movie, after all.

★ ★

My life as a cadet was finally over. This was the real world at last. I spent the next six months unlearning a lot of what I'd been taught during my four years of training and learning how to translate the rest into a language I could actually use and apply to my real job as a second lieutenant.

When I reached headquarters the duty NCO (noncommissioned office) directed me to the FIST office down the hall. It was a large, spacious office that would be my home for the next year or so. I took a seat self-consciously and waited for about ten minutes when suddenly I heard voices in the hall. They were talking loudly and laughing, and they seemed to be coming my way. I got anxious for the first time, thinking about the fact that whomever I was going to meet would probably be reporting to me.

In walked a tall blond staff sergeant with a full mustache, followed by an even taller NCO with light brown hair and a huge dip of tobacco stuck in his lower lip. Behind them was a major. He was shorter then the two NCOs. He was also one of the fittest men I'd ever seen in my life.

"Ah, fresh meat!" the major said with a broad smile. "Top o' the mornin' to ya, Mac," he said, a little ironically, extending his hand to me, "John Taglia here."

"Jeff McGowan," I said, a little hesitantly, caught off guard by his casualness. Since I was the lower-ranked officer it would have been customary for me to report to him. None of that seemed to matter to him, though. He waved his hand through the air as if pushing away a cloud of formality and quickly got down to business, jabbing a finger at the two smiling sergeants standing on either side of him.

"This is Staff Sergeant Reid," he said, pointing to the big blond, "your team chief, and this is Staff Sergeant McNeil," he went on, pointing to the tobacco chewer. "Same battalion but with Bravo Company. Both of them are total and complete scoundrels, and you'll learn a lot from them. All right," he said, smacking me on the shoulder and winking, "go get your cherry popped. I've got a meeting," and he turned quickly on his heel and walked out, leaving me standing there, smiling like an idiot, not sure what to do.

Staff Sergeant McNeil cleared his throat and extended his hand.

"Hey, sir, welcome aboard," he said. I shook his hand. I liked Mc-Neil right away. He struck me as being competent and smart, and he had a genuine warmth that put me at ease.

"Welcome, sir," Staff Sergeant Reid joined in, putting out his hand. "How was the trip? And inprocessing?"

"Everything went really well," I said, "no problems at all. So what's next?"

"Come with us to the motor pool and you can meet the team. Tomorrow I'll take you to A Company, where I'll introduce you to the commander."

McNeil broke off from us as we approached the line of vehicles, letting us know that he had some business with the maintenance technician. When Reid and I arrived at our team vehicle, the engine cover was open and a rag was lying on the lip of the hood. The laser was in its upright configuration. Two of the team were on top doing something with the compartment that held the laser while another guy was packing large, heavily padded boxes into the back.

"All right, guys," Reid said, "gather round and meet the new lieutenant."

For a moment everyone simply stopped what they were doing and looked up, first at Reid, then at me. Then slowly they began to walk to the front of the vehicle and form a line. In a way, I'd been waiting all my life for this moment, being presented as an officer to the group of men I'd lead. For the guys on the team, though, it was just another distraction in an otherwise long day. I found myself feeling awkward and clumsy and unsure how to hold my body in place. A part of me wanted to smile and laugh and treat them like new friends, put them at ease, but I reminded myself that I was in charge now, and that that wouldn't be appropriate. So I opted instead for a kind of professional aloofness that I thought made me look authoritative, but actually made me look, I'm almost certain, like a bit of a pompous, insincere asshole.

I went down the line and shook hands—too hard, I realized afterward—with every guy on the team, and listened to them tell me their names. Privates all, and most of them relatively new to the unit and not used to being around an officer; they seemed a little cautious, eyeing me as if I were a strange curiosity. The appearance of an officer was so rare in the daily lives of these guys that it usually served only to raise the tension level and get in the way of the work at hand.

As I made my way down the line, listening to each man introduce himself to me, I was struck by how diverse a group it was. There was, for example, Private First Class Fair, a black soldier from rural Georgia; there was Specialist Rodriguez, a Latino from Los Angeles with tattoos all up and down his arms; there was the white kid from Delaware, Private Johnson, who'd joined the army, I'd later learn, solely for the college money; and there was Sergeant Grajaba from San Antonio, who, I'd soon discover, had a wicked sense of humor and a knack for irreverence that often got him in hot water with his bosses, though never with me. Looking at the whole motley crew of them, I couldn't help but wonder just how a group of young men like this, with seemingly so little in common, would be able to function as a unit in close quarters for a long period of time.

After the last man had introduced himself and I'd shaken his hand, I stepped back and tried to think of something to say. The introductions had put me somewhat at ease, but I was still struggling to find the right tone, to strike a balance between friendly approachability and authoritative distance. I tried to imagine what a great general would say upon meeting his troops for the first time. What would Patton have said, I asked myself, and then immediately, in an effort to regain some sense of modesty, pushed the thought from my mind: *You, sir,* I thought, *after all, are no George S. Patton,* echoing Senator Bentsen's memorable slam against Dan Quayle during the vice presidential debates of the election the year before. Still, I was inspired. So I decided to give an impromptu pep talk that was brief, powerful, and, judging by the expressions on the faces of Fair and Rodriguez and the others, totally inappropriate. I'm sure they all had a good laugh over the new lieutenant later on that day.

"Men," I started. "let me begin by saying just how honored I am to have the opportunity to serve with you. And I want you know from the get-go that I am fully—I mean fully—committed to helping you realize your true potential as the most devastating, rock-solid FIST the U.S. Artillery has ever known. Your skill and lethal power will make you stand head and shoulders above your peers in the greater Artillery community."

Fair and Rodriguez exchanged glances at this point but I went on, convinced that any new leader has to fight for the loyalty of his troops.

"Let me just say this. My goal is simple. I want us to be feared on any battlefield we might find ourselves. And we can only do it together. Men, let's be clear. Make no mistake about it—I am committed to you one hundred fifty percent and I expect nothing less than one hundred fifty percent from each and every one of you in return. You will engage training, maintenance, everything—like you would the enemy! And above all, above all, men, fight hard to be all that you can be!"

The speech by itself was not actually so inappropriate, it was just ill-timed and kind of out of place. I mean they were doing maintenance, for God's sake not fighting their way up the beaches of Normandy! For my own part, I walked away feeling elated at how my first meeting had gone, completely oblivious to the cool, though respectful, reception it had gotten. I wasn't going to let anything ruin my first day on the job!

CHAPTER NINE

Reforger

My experience in Germany was, in most respects, wonderful. We worked hard, and I learned a great deal, and I bonded with a group of men who, sexual orientation aside, seemed very much like me. We spent a lot of our time in the field doing maneuvers and exercises, and whenever we had a couple free days we'd take a day trip, most of Europe being virtually a day trip away.

When I arrived in Germany at the end of the Reagan era, the military was like a college football player, pumped up and ripped on steroids. A decade's worth of lavish military spending had created a psychology of invincibility and swagger. Everyone had a certain look, an air of untapped power, as if we were spoiling for something, anything at all, to happen. Nobody seriously believed that a war was imminent, but the attitude was that active duty no longer meant just sitting around and drawing a paycheck; it meant working hard in preparation for something, though no one knew exactly what.

At that time an average unit spent roughly 250 days a year in the field, training. There was an open-minded attitude about it. Mistakes weren't viewed so much as failures as opportunities for soldiers and units to see what they'd done wrong and to learn from the experience. Those with big egos were quickly disabused of their own brilliance by objective assessments based on the facts as captured by impartial third parties.

In addition to this, once a year we participated in what was called REFORGER, a shorthand term for Return of Forces to Germany. This annual exercise, started in 1969 in an effort to demonstrate continued U.S. commitment to NATO (North Atlantic Treaty Organization) after withdrawing roughly twenty-eight thousand troops from Europe in 1968, tested the ability of the army to deploy forces from the States in the event of a Soviet invasion or some other outbreak of aggression or war. It was an immense and powerful display of force designed not only to give our commanders and generals an opportunity to test our readiness but also, and perhaps more significant, to remind the Soviets of the very real threat we posed to any form of aggression they might be considering against Europe or our other Allies around the world. The Soviets denounced the first REFORGER in 1969 as a "major military provocation." The end of the cold war, coupled with huge advances in computer technology, brought REFORGER to a close, in 1993, when the last one occurred as mostly a computer-driven logistical exercise in which only one part of one unit was deployed from the United States.

During REFORGER, troops from as many as six divisions would come from the States and draw prepositioned equipment in Belgium and the Netherlands and in a matter of weeks deploy to Germany alongside those of us already stationed in the country. Then the maneuvers would begin, right through the cobblestone streets of quaint German towns and over the fields of the German countryside. I realize that this is hard to imagine. I mean, picture a convoy of M1 tanks rolling down the main street of your own hometown! Once a year we went to a different part of the country, deployed thousands of troops, then tore up fields and streets and damaged property and infrastructure, in the process of our "show of strength."

What did the Germans think of all this? The impression I got over the four years I spent there was that the population was pretty much divided on the issue. Divided not only in terms of the annual exercise, but in terms of our mere presence in their country as well. It was mostly a generational thing, which makes sense if you think about it. Older Germans tended to support our presence, while people my own age tended to despise us with a ferocity that often took me totally by surprise. Many of those who hadn't lived through the devastation of the war viewed us as unwelcome occupiers bent on prolonging the cold war instead of working toward a definitive and lasting peace. To them, the REFORGER exercise was simply visible proof of the arrogance of both superpowers. Anyone who lived through the war, however, understood that though the Americans weren't perfect, they were a far better alternative to the overlords in the East. With a massive force—millions strong and armed to the teeth—just a stone's throw away, our presence was a pragmatic and comforting counterweight to the Soviet threat.

*   *

The exercise we were about to deploy was to take place in the south of Germany near Munich. Our equipment would be sent ahead by freight, and we would then drive down separately. Once there, we would conduct final checks and then begin tactical operations.

It was still a little unclear to me just what was meant by "tactical operations." Everyone I asked simply said we'd do a lot of driving through the countryside and through a few small towns. I couldn't imagine how the actual fighting exercise would fit into the whole scheme of things. I'd learn soon enough.

Having driven down and spent a day in final preparations, we were ready to begin Exercise Centurion Shield the following morning. It was bitter cold on that first morning. I'd positioned myself in the turret of my vehicle, and as we moved into the operational area and then into the first town the wind was so cold it felt as if my face were burning. Trying to ignore the cold, I let my mind wander a little as we pushed through the town in a neat row, like baby ducks crossing a lake behind their mother, toward our first objective. Suddenly, my radio flared to life, spitting out voices giving reports and orders. I jerked myself upright and began to focus on what was going on. An ambush had been set up about a mile and a quarter ahead of us, just outside of town, and we were the first company to receive contact. The enemy was positioned on a small ridge next to a group of farm buildings. A Hummer marked with blue tape had moved quickly to our column and informed the lead vehicle that it had been hit; it was out. This caused the flurry of communications as the column swung into action to defend itself, pulling off the road and into the open field to engage the enemy.

The column of Bradleys parted like the Red Sea and began a mad dash across the field, destroying a whole crop of what looked like beets. The vehicles quickly deployed into a formation that maximized firepower and speed, aggressively moving against the farm buildings, turrets swiveling wildly in order to engage multiple targets. It was determined that the enemy was located in the farm buildings, so my boss called for fire on them, and I quickly responded by getting the ball rolling with the tubes waiting for use.

In my naïveté I found myself overly concerned about the state of the beet field, convinced that a mistake had been made, that we'd inadvertently moved across the wrong field, that a field left fallow for just this purpose was right ahead of us and we'd engaged too soon. Wouldn't we get in trouble for destroying this poor farmer's field? Why weren't they stopping the exercise? Was it my fault? Had I missed something, a signal, an order? Had I overlooked something during the preparations? For a moment, looking down at the ruined crop of beets, I became convinced that I would end up being the most quickly relieved lieutenant in the history of the U.S. Army. As the line of vehicles continued to rumble across the field, it began to look like a very large pig pen, the crops smashed into a thick slurry of mud, with huge ruts forming that were beginning to bog down the Bradleys.

But apparently no mistake had been made. The referee stood by, serenely watching the carnage of the beet field, until the battle had actually run its course. Signaling with a small flag, he drove first to Captain Kreuz's Bradley and conferred with him and then moved on to the enemy position. The boss's voice came over the radio and explained that the company had taken casualties and that the two Bradleys at the front of the column had been destroyed and would have to report to a holding area. The idea was that if you got "killed," you left the game for however long it would normally take to either repair or replace your vehicle. The logisticians got a great workout by implementing the repair procedures and ordering.

Once the adjudication process was complete we got on our way again, re-forming on the road and moving off smartly. There was another small town about two miles ahead of us. At a little over a mile out we stopped and pulled into a defensive formation—half the turrets were pointed to the right, half were pointed to the left and one was pointed to the rear. Three of the Bradleys lowered their ramps, and about eighteen troops slowly disgorged themselves, looking like troglodytes who had been awakened from a deep sleep. Quite frankly, they were taking a long time to get their bearings and put all their gear on. I could sympathize with them because I knew that spending hours being tossed around inside a Bradley was not the most pleasant experience in the world. It fell to these troops to carefully reconnoiter to determine if there was an ambush waiting for us. As they checked out the town, it was up to my team and me to submit possible targets to the gun batteries in the event we had to fight at this location.

About a half hour later, the grunts returned, looking refreshed and alert. Amazing, I thought, what a little fresh oxygen and light can do for a man! The commander signaled that all was clear, and we pulled back onto the road to continue our convoy. We pulled out in the same order and proceeded on through the town. As we moved through, I watched as curious onlookers began to congregate on their front lawns and in their front windows to get a good look at the Americans. Slowly, we negotiated our way through the narrow streets of the old town, occasionally tearing up a cobblestone or two or crushing a piece of the curb, or flattening a hedge that had gotten in our way. At one point, the Bradley just ahead of us got too close to a metal divider and caught the edge of it. The divider crumpled almost instantly, snapping free from its supporting columns, and ending up a twisted and jagged reminder that the Americans had passed through yet again. Just as I'd been in the beet field, I was amazed that this seemed to be accepted as business as usual. Later on, I would learn that during every one of these exercises an MDCO (maneuver damage control officer) was positioned behind every unit. It was his job to identify all damage done and to provide the owner with the proper paperwork for reimbursement. The total for repairs on an exercise like this could run as high as a hundred million dollars. What's more, the exercises had been going on for so long that some Germans would actually *try* to get commanders to cross their property so that they could be reimbursed for damages. In some cases, if a field was torn up, we were billed not only for the loss of any current crop, but for every crop it was estimated that plant would have yielded over the course of its natural life span. We did these exercises at least twice annually, so over the years quite a lot of money was paid out to the Germans for damaged crops and torn-up cobblestones.

As we pulled out of town I couldn't help but admire the beauty of the small piece of German countryside we hadn't managed to turn to mush, and as I looked back to face the vehicle in front of us I was confronted with a horrible sight. The road banked gently to the right. Captain Kreuz had placed one of the M1s from the platoon of tanks at the head of the column, and dragging along behind that tank was a mangled Mercedes Benz with what appeared to be a driver still behind the wheel. At first I didn't believe my eyes. I actually shook my head, thinking I wasn't seeing things right, since what I was looking at didn't seem possible. And it got worse when it became clear to me that the tank driver and the tank commander apparently hadn't even noticed and were driving blithely along, enjoying the same scenery I'd been looking at just a moment ago. It made me think of those stories you hear about dog owners tying their beloved dogs to the back of their cars at a campsite or something, then forgetting about them and driving two hundred miles until some shocked stranger at a red light points out to the clueless owner the dead and mangled dog still attached to the rear bumper.

But Captain Kreuz noticed. He was the shocked stranger, in this case. His Bradley suddenly jerked out of the formation as he simultaneously ordered the whole column to stop. For a twenty-six-ton vehicle, the Bradley can move pretty fast in a pinch, and it was doing just that now. Kreuz was halfway out of the turret, waving his arms frantically, trying to get the attention of the tank commander. But the commander just continued on, oblivious, until Kreuz grabbed a full bottle of water and hurled it at the guy, who, catching sight of the small missile flying past his face, finally realized something was wrong. As the massive tank slowed and finally came to a halt, Captain Kreuz ripped off his helmet and scrambled off the Bradley to the rear of the tank. The tank commander was next to him a moment later, and then he jumped back onto the vehicle; I could see him reaching for his map. They were calling for help. Then the executive officer spoke over the radio. There'd been an accident, we were told. We would be here for a while. We were to move into a larger formation and begin maintenance on our vehicles.

Once we took our position in the perimeter, I decided to get a closer look at the accident. As I approached the scene I noticed the tank crew standing off to the side of the road in a drainage ditch. They all looked pretty shaken up. The section leader seemed especially upset; he looked to be on the verge of tears. Captain Kreuz tried to calm everyone down. His crew was in the field holding bright orange pieces of vinyl. He had obviously called for a medevac. Just then the blaring horns of an ambulance and fire truck could be heard on the road behind us.

As I approached the mangled Mercedes lodged up under the M1 tank on that cold October morning in the south of Germany, I found myself experiencing a horrific sense of complicity. My heart was racing as I got close to the vehicle. Each step closer seemed to come with increasing difficulty, as if I were slowly falling into one of those dreams in which you find yourself walking and walking and walking but unable to move, unable to get anywhere at all. Suddenly, I was in the cool stream again at camp, treading that black water, frozen, looking up at the boy on the rock, waiting for him to stand, to scream, to laugh, to lift up his hand and flip the finger at us all.

Reaching the accident I saw that the hunter green Mercedes was worse than it had looked from a distance—it had been reduced to a mere crumpled hulk, a mangled jumble of steel and shattered glass. It seemed impossible that anyone could be pulled out of there alive. Reaching the driver's side of the car, I found myself getting a little queasy and short of breath. What I saw was imprinted on my memory as indelibly as the image of the twisted body of the boy on the rock.

The body of a young man was slumped over the bent steering wheel. Blood was splattered everywhere in semicongealed rivulets, some actually dripped from the frame of the car as I stood there and watched. It looked as though the bottom half of the man's body had been crushed by the tank as the Mercedes had crashed into the back of the armored behemoth. The windshield was completely shattered, and its frame had actually been loosened and was now jutting out from the body of the car. The car was pinned under the back end of the tank, and the frame was bent so that one of the rear wheels was slightly up in the air. I just couldn't understand how this happened, and once again a great curtain of sadness descended on me as I was forced back to the memory of the cadet at camp, the boy on the rock. It was another training exercise and another casualty, with no good reason to answer the simple question, Why? I thought that maybe the second time around I might have a different reaction, but here it was again, and once again I was simply flailing against questions I couldn't possibly answer.

Staring at his lifeless, ruined body, I couldn't help thinking about war and death and my place as a soldier within the context of these two words. There was so much silence here, so much absence rising up off the dead German's body, it almost seemed substantive, as if the absence and the silence were positive conditions rather than the result of the mere lack of sound and being. I sensed that there would probably always be a disconnect between all the reasoned arguments for war and war itself, war as it presents itself finally to you as a game you score by keeping track of deaths and injuries. My Catholic training had morphed slowly over the years into a kind of secular spirituality, but it was still informing my outlook on things in a very real way. Although I'd dedicated myself to the army, made a career out of soldiering, I still had questions—not about the reasoned arguments for war, I had no question about those—but about the thing itself, which you can see only in a moment like this, when it's presented to you in all its bald vulgarity, in the form of the dead, mangled body of an innocent civilian.

I had not yet seen war, but I was beginning to understand why it is that the most reluctant warriors are those who've actually seen battle and that this reluctance, this caution, increases in direct proportion to the amount and intensity of the soldier's experience on the battlefield.

A part of me believed that all this hand-wringing was a good thing since it meant my humanity would always remain in tact. What makes a soldier most effective is the power he's given within the context of combat to actually kill fellow human beings. A soldier is by definition one who is given this ultimate power within the strictly defined rules of war. In order to counterbalance the awesome responsibility of wielding this power, a soldier must discover within himself even deeper reserves of compassion and empathy than the average citizen. These deep reserves are what keep the soldier's moral compass in place, especially in moments of great duress during wartime, when the line between fair combat and calculated brutality can become so easily blurred.

I was told to step back as the emergency personnel from the local town and the medevac people swarmed the vehicle. The sergeant in charge of the tank crew started speaking quickly.

"Sir," he said, addressing Captain Kreuz, "I just didn't see him or anything. The first I knew anything was wrong was when you flagged us down, when you threw the water bottle." His voice was raspy, and it quavered as he tried to hold himself together.

"How come your radio was off?" Kreuz asked him.

"Sir, we've been having commo problems for a while, and I thought we had got it fixed. I hadn't noticed that it was out again. You said you wanted radio silence on the road marches, and I thought everything was cool."

Kreuz looked at him steadily and then turned to the other sergeant standing on his left.

"You see anything?"

"Well, sir, the rad was at the intersection and fell in with the convoy and was trying to dart in and out of the formation. It looked as though he mistimed passing in front of Staff Sergeant Barnes's vehicle and ran into the back and got caught underneath." *Rad* is a term the troops used to refer to a German.

"All right, the battalion commander called and told me that CID (Criminal Investigation Division) will be here to investigate and take statements. I want you to be honest and forthright. Staff Sergeant Barnes, I want you to report to the ALOC, where you and your section will meet with the chaplain and get the vehicle checked for damage." ALOC stands for Administrative Logistics Operations Center, and this was where vehicles were repaired and casualties treated.

I was feeling numb at this point. All I could think was, What a stupid, stupid way to go! How did your brother, son, lover, die? they'd ask. Oh, he drove underneath the back of an M1 tank and got stuck. Why hadn't he waited until we passed or taken a different route to get where he was going? How would his family take this? Did he have a wife and kids? Did he have a boyfriend? What would the family and friends think of us? I knew I'd never get the answers to these questions. We would all simply drive off and continue the exercise, leaving the tank and its crew behind to deal with the ramifications of being inside the vehicle that had dragged a German to his death, and experiencing, as we all would that day to some degree, the vague horror of the kind of shapeless complicity that never quite attaches itself to anything and never quite goes away, and always seems to end up as the mere complicity of survival.

This would become even clearer to me years later, after the war, when I was at Fort Bragg with the Eighty-second Airborne. This was during peacetime, mind you. One of the special incentives they devised was this: if we made it through eighty-two days without a death among us, we'd be issued a three-day pass. In the four years I was there we were given that three-day pass only once. Granted, if you take any large group of people and monitor them over time, odds are some are going to die, whether they're doing nothing or taking huge physical risks. But still, at Fort Bragg, we'd reach, say, day seventy-five, and all the troops would begin to get excited, talking about where they planned to go, what they planned to do with their three-day pass. And then it would come down that so-and-so had been injured and then died at such and such a place, and as the news spread around the post that strange unease would pass from soldier to soldier, unit to unit, and we'd all experience the odd sensation of guilt about being, still, on this side of survival.

★ ★

After a few hours of waiting and watching the local German and army emergency personnel do their thing, there seemed to be a collective sigh of relief when the word finally came down to mount up and move out. We all were eager to get back into the exercise and forget about the accident. The battalion commander decided to make us lead company, which was a subtle nod to Captain Kreuz that the commander had not lost confidence in him or the company.

We drove for hours, encountering no resistance, meeting our various objectives and continuing on to the next. Armored warfare is very fluid and can cover huge distances rather quickly. Whereas a light force of infantry on foot might attack an objective three miles away from its staging area, an armored force can move upwards of sixty miles without batting an eye. But riding in these vehicles is no day in the park. The whole thing is often extremely uncomfortable and gets exhausting pretty quickly. If you had to ride in a turret the way I did, you were completely exposed to the elements, rain or shine. Of course this was great in the warm weather, but in the cold, surrounded on all sides by metal that made it seem even colder, it could be hell. For those on the inside of the vehicle it wasn't much better; being tossed around, they often suffered from aching backs and exhausted muscles.

This was our basic routine for the next two weeks—long days of driving through small German towns, with the occasional run-in with the enemy. The exercises were done not so much to benefit the individual troops but for those higher up who were responsible for planning and movement. The exercises allowed generals and others to observe large forces being moved around and to cope with the logistics that came with that.

This first exercise gave me the opportunity to begin to bond with my team and for them to bond with one another. Over the two weeks I learned quite a bit about who they were and what they wanted out of life. For some of them, the army was a way out: out of poverty, a troubled home life, or both. These guys were often turned into immediate heroes in the small, depressed towns from which they usually came. Others saw it as a means to pursue the American dream, serving in the army to get educated and eventually to move up into the middle class. Some found comfort in the regularity and predictability of army life, thriving in the culture of discipline and loyalty.

Spending two weeks with these men, in such close quarters, I managed to earn their respect and to learn how to lead them at the same time. I often thought of the dead German beneath the M1 tank and, as I grew closer to my men, found myself feeling ever more protective of them. I became increasingly convinced that I'd do almost anything I could to cover their backs, and to save their very lives.

★ ★

Three things that will always lift a trooper's spirits: mail, a long hot shower, and a clean uniform. We were granted our showers and clean uniforms on day nine of the exercise. And it wasn't a day too soon. The baby-wipes-plus-water-from-a-canteen bath was getting really old by that point. We were ordered to a public health club, kind of like a YMCA. As I was sitting on the ramp of the FIST vehicle, relaxing while I waited for my turn to shower, I noticed a rather dignified older gentleman with a small boy in hand, approaching me. I thought they were coming to barter for equipment and uniforms or for food. For the life of me I could never understand the Germans' fascination with army rations, but they absolutely loved them and would even bring homemade dishes—sauerbraten, Wiener schnitzel, *Rindsrouladen,* the most delicious bratwursts, even Black Forest cake, in exchange for an MRE. Chem lights, uniforms, and canteens were also quite popular.

As they reached me I got up and straightened my uniform.

"Guten Tag, Herr Leutnant," the old man said, extending his hand.

"Guten Tag."

"Your greeting is flawless, but your German, does it go much deeper? It seems to be the custom for Americans to eschew learning other languages," he said, smoothly and matter-of-factly, without any disrespect in his voice, at least none that I could detect.

"Yes, well," I said, "I'm afraid you're right. I don't speak German yet, but I am reasonably fluent in Spanish, so I guess I am an exception."

We looked at each other. What was most striking about him was his ramrod-straight bearing and his bright blue eyes, which appeared almost icy. His voice was quite low and raspy, the product, I imagined, of a lifetime of cigarettes. His mouth began to turn up into either a smirk or a smile, I couldn't tell which. I chose to keep it light and see it as a smile.

"What is your unit, if you don't mind my asking?" the older man asked.

"Alpha Company, Three-Five Cavalry, part of the Third Armored Division."

"Indeed," he said with a flourish. "I brought my grandson out to meet the Americans, so that he can see for himself who is defending him against the Russians."

"Well, I'm glad you came out. What is your grandson's name?" I looked down into the boy's face.

"Jorg, say hello to . . . Leutnant . . . ?"

"Lieutenant McGowan." I extended my hand to the boy, who was surely no more than eight or nine, and apparently very shy, but he reached up nonetheless and took my hand with a diffident grin.

"I served also," the man said, "during the war."

"Really? Whom did you serve with?"

"I was with the Waffen-SS." With that he rolled up his sleeve and showed me the tattooed runes on his inner forearm. I didn't know how to respond to the sight of the runes.

"That's uhh . . . very interesting, where did you serve?"

"I fought on the Eastern Front all the way out and all the way back."

"Wow, that is impressive."

"Ya, I was even wounded." He opened his coat and pulled up his shirt to reveal a long, deep scar that zigzagged across his abdomen.

"When did that happen?"

"During an attack in the Ukraine on our march to Leningrad. I lay in a bed for six months to recover, and then they sent me out again to fight in the retreat."

"I hope you don't mind my asking you this," I said. I couldn't help myself; I had to ask. "But could you clarify something for me? I always thought that the SS was very . . ." I stopped, thinking he'd rush in and relieve me from the burden of having to ask, but he remained silent, waiting, looking directly into my face, his steely blue eyes catching bits of afternoon sun. "I thought the SS was very involved in the killing of Jews?"

He continued to look at me steadily and then let out a small sigh.

"Certain units were responsible for the crimes," he said, in a way that sounded rehearsed and a little tired, as if he'd been saying it all his life, "and that was just bad soldiering, horrible, not soldiering at all, really. My unit was strictly a fighting unit. We were all good soldiers. We did our duty. We played by the rules."

"I see," I said, anxious to move away from the subject.

"You know," he said, somewhat relieved, it seemed, that the SS question had been put to rest, "at the end of the war I walked seventeen miles to surrender to the Americans."

"Really, why?"

"Because I knew that the Americans are not animals like the Russians. I want you to know that I appreciate you Americans being here. We would have a horrible life without you. The hatred is very deep between us." He said this with a finality that startled me.

Unsure how to respond I said, simply, "Well, it certainly was a tough war, for everyone involved."

Mercifully, one of the guys from my section returned from the showers at that point to let me know it was my group's turn to go in. As I reached for my gear and extended my hand to him to say good-bye, he tightened his grip and held me in place.

"Remember your duty always," the deep, raspy voice came at me forcefully, while his eyes seemed to grow even brighter for an instant, like two lasers firing simultaneously, and then to soften and dim.

Then he said, "And may I also trouble you for an MRE for my grandson? He also likes the chem lights."

CHAPTER TEN

Brawling Outside the Bulldog; Gustav in the Morning?

When we weren't doing exercises or training at Grafenwohr and Hohenfels, my officer buddies and I would often hang out in Frankfurt. We also made a lot of day trips together and occasionally an extended trip for four or five days. Usually it was four of us—John Lostrapo, Dave Bariglia, Jeff Brooks, and me. Dave had dated an au pair whose father was a high-ranking police officer in Amsterdam. When we found out that she'd be able to get us cheap accommodations at the hotel in Slotermeelaan where cops from all over the world stayed, we jumped at the chance to travel to the Netherlands for a few days. We figured we'd check out the Rijksmuseum and maybe make a pilgrimage to the Heineken brewery. It was a great trip (the Rembrandts made a big impression on me), largely uneventful, except that on our second night we ended up, oddly enough, out front of the McDonald's across the street from the Bulldog bar, fighting a half-dozen Turks, I think, at two in the morning.

It had been a long day. We'd spent the afternoon at the museum, looking at the Rembrandts and Vermeers, and then we'd hung out at the Bulldog all night, drinking and talking to various good-looking Dutch women. We were having a terrific time.

Upon leaving the bar at around one-thirty, we decided to grab some McDonald's before heading back to the hotel. I always felt kind of stupid eating in a McDonald's when I was in Europe. But that night I was a little bit too drunk to care, plus I was starving. It was a warm night, so the entire front of the McDonald's was open to the street. You just walked up a couple steps that ran the entire width of the place. The four of us stepped up into the restaurant, laughing loudly about Dave's failed attempt to pick up some girl at the bar. The place was packed, which seemed unusual since it was so late. As we took our place in line in walked six guys who we thought were Turkish. To this day I'm not sure where they were from. Apparently they'd also been out drinking, and they were laughing and yelling in their own language, in Turkish, I think, and, like us, they were kind of oblivious to what was going on around them. Unlike us, though, they didn't seem to feel it necessary to wait their turn in line. The six of them pushed straight through to the front and started shouting orders to the clerks. We all looked incensed, though no one said anything, as the two clerks tried to calm these six guys down and explain to them that they had to go to the back of the line.

After a few minutes of going back and forth—loud broken English mixed with rants in Turkish and rants in Dutch—it looked as though the clerks were giving in. And that's when Lostrapo erupted. John Lostrapo was six feet three inches tall and weighed at least 260 pounds; his biceps were easily eighteen inches. He'd been an offensive lineman at West Point. The most striking feature about him, however, was his enormous nose, which earned him the nickname Rhinoceros. I'd gotten to know him well enough by this point to understand that, despite his size, he was really a gentle giant who was generous and kind and fiercely loyal to his friends. He was also particularly sensitive to unfairness, however it might present itself in the world.

Suddenly, without any sort of warning, he marched to the front of the line and, in one deft motion, reached out and corralled all six of the Turks in his arms and pushed them out of line. They started yelling at John, and John yelled back, and this went on the whole time we waited in line. When we reached the front of the line, Lostrapo yelled over, "Two Macs, two fries, two pies, and a big Coke, thanks, McGowan," and then he turned back and continued yelling at the six Turks.

"Fuck you, too," I could hear Lostrapo shouting now. "What was that? What was that, gerbil dick? I'll kick your fuckin' ass," he shouted, almost smiling.

Our food came, and Brooks yelled over at him, "Hey, Rhino, knock it off, will you? We got the food. Let's go." The three of us sat down, and I was happily buzzed and totally focused on my Quarter Pounder and fries. But Lostrapo wouldn't give it up.

Finally, Bariglia got pissed. "Jesus Christ, what the fuck is he doing?" he said, standing up and looking over at Lostrapo and the Turks. "Oh, for fuck's sake," he said, moving out from behind the table, "it looks like it's getting serious. Come on, let's get over there."

The three of us walked over and got between the Turks and the Rhino and stood there trying to look menacing. This didn't have the deterrent effect we'd hoped for. The Turks just kept shouting what I figured were Turkish obscenities and trying to reach the Rhino. I was standing my ground and trying to convince the Rhino to back down when suddenly one of the Turks started waving his hands too close to my face. I have a rule—call it the doctrine of preemptive street fighting, if you like—if it feels as if I'm going to get hit, I always hit first. It was a lesson I learned early on in the school yards of St. Joan of Arc and Archbishop Malloy and on the streets of Jackson Heights. So I struck hard and fast and landed a nice haymaker in the center of the young Turk's not-bad-looking face. He had a salad in his hands, I think, since after I hit him a cloud of lettuce let loose around him like so much confetti.

Pandemonium broke out. The little battle surged backward toward the front door. And before we knew it the whole battle was down the steps and out on the street. A crowd quickly gathered to watch, occasionally cheering at a good shot delivered by one side or the other. Though we were outnumbered by two, we were much bigger and stronger, and soon the two smallest Turks seemed to disappear. The Rhino was truly amazing as he pounded away at anything that got in his way.

After a few minutes of good toe-to-toe fighting with my guy—the one who'd originally waved his hands in front of my face, he pulled out a knife, lunged at me, and tried to stab me with it. Luckily, he overextended himself and lost his balance, which gave me the chance to knock the knife out of his hand. It went flying, I don't know where, and just as he'd regained his balance and starting coming at me again, the Rhino, whose own Turk had had enough and run away, came charging at him. When the man saw the Rhino's huge frame barreling down on him, he let out a cluck and sprinted off. Bariglia and Brooks had taken care of their guys, both of whom were gone, and so the four of us were left alone in the center of the crowd, bloodied and sweaty and breathing hard.

"Thanks, Nocerous," I said, patting Lostrapo on the back.

"No problem, bud," he said, a big grin on his face.

Now, I don't want you to get the wrong impression here. It wasn't as if we were always getting into fights. This was a pretty rare occasion. In fact, I think it happened only one other time. In a way, I think it's almost unavoidable. A group of big, young guys traveling around together will just naturally get into a brawl or two, even if they're not looking for it. The truth is, we were a pretty mellow group of guys, though I have to say this brawl did enhance our reputation in the battalion as a being a tough group of hard-charging officers, which was, after all, not such a bad way to be perceived.

★   ★

All the way back to the hotel and then for the rest of the night, almost until dawn, we rehashed the fight, laughing, highlighting our heroics literally blow-by-blow, analyzing the cheers and boos of the crowd. The victory had bonded us together in a way we hadn't been before. The night kept refueling itself on the periodic adrenaline rushes we'd get from recalling certain moves: a tough body blow, a swift duck away from a Turk's fist, and my penultimate move when I knocked the knife from the good-looking Turk's hand and it went flying and disappeared, and then the Rhino's big charge right afterward.

After this event I felt more comfortable with the idea of going into combat with these guys. It was gratifying to know that we'd stick together, that we could count on one another when the going got tough, and that no one would leave anyone else behind. I would have done anything for those guys, and I was happy to show it. Granted, it was only a (some might say childish) street brawl, but in our line of work you could never know when you might be called upon to make a sacrifice for another soldier.

But the incident raised a question for me, one that became ever more persistent as the years passed and I became less willing to keep my sexual orientation hidden. Where was the breakdown of social cohesion that was supposed to take place when a gay man was in a unit? Hadn't I played a valuable role in all of this? I was a highly skilled, well-trained, highly disciplined, well-liked, loyal, responsible soldier in the U.S. Army, one who would be a threat to any foreign enemy. How was I a threat to my unit? How was I a threat to the very institution I'd devoted my whole life to preserving and protecting? What threat did I, 2LT Jeffrey McGowan, pose to the integrity of the U.S. military? I wouldn't be able to fully answer that question until the very end, until after I'd served in more than a just street brawl in Amsterdam, until I'd actually served in combat, in the Gulf War, and I'd reached my decision to end my career. And the answer was, of course, none. I posed no threat. And the gay men and women fighting and dying in Iraq today pose no threat as well, except of course to the enemies they've sworn to vanquish.

★   ★

Some nights I'd go exploring on my own. I'd take the train into Frankfurt and go to a jazz club in Alt-Sachsenhausen or just walk around and check cut the city. I never went to gay bars since it would've been too risky. But the bars in Europe aren't quite as segregated as those here in the States, so it's not unusual to find gay men in what we might normally think of as a straight bar. Occasionally I'd hook up with one of these guys, though I never planned to; it often just fell in my lap, so to speak. I guess the thought of hooking up was usually in the back of my mind when I decided to go out alone, without my buddies from the post, but I never really admitted it to myself.

These nights were infrequent. Most of the time I truly enjoyed the company of the guys from the post; we'd bonded in a real way, and the truth is I kind of had to do it on the sly since they would've thought it strange that I was going into the city alone.

And so it was that I was bound for Frankfurt one summer night during my second year in Germany. I was tired, badly in need of some real R & R, having spent nearly two months in Grafenwohr and Hohenfels, but the last thing I wanted was to hang out back at the post and watch TV, which is what all my friends were doing.

Outside the Hauptbahnhof, I decided to walk for a little bit, get some air. I wasn't sure if I wanted to take a cab to Alt-Sachsenhausen or just hang around in the city center. After walking a few blocks I came across a cool-looking bar. I realized I had to piss, so I figured I'd go in and check the place out.

It was smoky and dark inside. I quickly went to the bathroom and washed my hands, checking out my face in the smoky mirror above the sink. When I walked out of the bathroom, I noticed a guy sitting at the bar, drinking what looked like a Weizen beer, judging by the dark color and thick foam head. Like nearly everyone else in the little bar, he was smoking a cigarette and staring off into space. A little cloud of smoke plumed above his head and then disappeared into the breeze caused by the ceiling fan revolving wearily overheard. Well, I thought, maybe I'll have a Weizen beer myself. I'll have a Weizen beer or two and then catch a cab to Alt-Sachsenhausen. As I began walking toward the bar he turned and looked at me, stopping the hand holding the cigarette midway to his mouth. Our eyes locked, and he raised his eyebrows and pursed his lips in acknowledgment. When he didn't look away, I felt emboldened and made my way directly toward the bar stool next to his.

He looked to be roughly my age, somewhere in his mid-twenties, and he was good-looking and slender. He had reddish-brown hair, straight and long (over his ears), which he parted neatly on the right side. He wore a shiny, dark blue shirt with the collar open, under a gray pinstripe jacket. He gave the impression of the kind of casual elegance only the very rich can pull off.

As I sat down and ordered a drink, I realized, now that he'd stopped looking at me and turned away, that I had no idea how to start up a conversation, let alone a conversation in a language I could barely understand. I tended to forget about this until I found myself already deep into a situation. The bartender set down my beer in front of me, and I paid him; then, seeing in my peripheral vision, the redhead tap out a fresh cigarette from his pack, I suddenly regretted having ordered the beer. I regretted having stopped in this bar. I regretted having come to Frankfurt. I regretted not having stayed back at the post to watch *Cheers* and *L.A. Law* with my friends. I took a deep, weary swing of the beer. One beer, I told myself. One beer and then I'd move on, catch the cab to Alt-Sachsenhausen, or maybe just take the train back to the post.

But then suddenly I heard German being spoken at me, and I turned to face the redhead next to me. Our eyes locked again, and I told him in German that I didn't speak the language very well. Before I'd even finished my sentence he switched to English.

"Your first time?" he said, lighting his cigarette with a silver butane lighter that flamed higher than necessary. "Here at this bar, I mean. You're an American, no?"

"Yes," I said, "first time, and I am; I am American. A New Yorker."

"Ah . . ." he said, looking pleased, "Are you a soldier?" he asked, clicking the lid of the lighter shut.

"No, no, I'm here visiting friends."

"I see. Do they live in the city?"

"No, Giessen, they live in Giessen," I said. And then, hoping to change the subject, "Can I bum a cigarette?"

I didn't want to say I was a soldier because I didn't want to deal with the whole American military question, since young Germans tended to resent our presence. Mostly though, I knew, now that I was on the other side of my denial, so to speak, that my main reason for coming to Frankfurt was to stop being a soldier for a night in order to simply be a man.

"Sure," he said, lifting the pack and tapping the bottom so that one cigarette pushed up higher than the others.

"I don't usually smoke. Only in bars when I'm drinking," I said. I put the cigarette to my lips, and he lit it for me. "Thanks," I said. I took a deep drag.

"I know it well—Giessen, I mean. I have an aunt who lives near the center of the town. I visit her fairly frequently. So how long are you here for?"

"Another two weeks or so." The nicotine hit, and I got a little dizzy.

"Or so?"

"Well, I'm not sure when I'm leaving." That didn't make much sense, I knew. God, how I hated all this lying. Everything would just snowball and snowball until I didn't know what I was talking about anymore. Sometimes I felt like one big walking lie. I lied to my friends on the post about these nights in Frankfurt, about the fictitious girlfriend stateside; and I lied to the men I met occasionally here in the city. I was lying now to this man I'd just met in the cool little bar not far from the Hauptbahnhof. It seemed that there was no place where I was allowed to be fully myself.

"Well, I hope you enjoy your visit. Any special plans for tonight?" He leaned forward slightly and stared directly into my face.

I smiled. I liked this guy. "Well, I thought I would just explore the city a little and see what happens."

"An explorer!" he said, laughing a little. "That's exciting!"

And then we lifted our pints of Weizen beer and clinked them together.

"To exploration," he said.

"To exploration," I said, and we both drank.

I introduced myself after that, giving him, for some strange reason, my real first name. I usually told guys my name was Jack. His name was Gustav, and we spent the next few hours at the bar together, drinking, sharing his cigarettes, and talking. Toward midnight he told me he was glad I wasn't a soldier. He'd been seeing an American sergeant, and it had been difficult. He said he was swearing off army guys. And then I told him that I had been a soldier but that I'd finished my obligation about a year before. Though this was still a lie, it felt good to say it. Something about Gustav made me want to get closer to the truth. He put on a mock-weary face when I told him and then laughed, and said, "Once a soldier, always a soldier, I've heard. But maybe I can make an exception for you. You want to come back to my place for a nightcap?"

I said I did, and before I knew it we were back in his apartment having passionate sex.

In the morning Gustav made coffee, and at one point I felt so at ease that I almost told him the whole truth about my life. But something held me back, though I promised myself that when I saw him again I'd tell him everything.

Walking back to the train station, I pulled out the card he'd given me and looked at it. The few times I'd done this before I had tossed the card or the matchbook cover or slip of paper with the phone number; I had gotten rid of it even before reaching the station, convinced that it would be used as some kind of evidence, that it would bring about my downfall. This time felt different, and I decided to hold on to Gustav's card, stuffing it back into my pocket. But by the time I reached the station all the old concerns had returned; it was as if I'd crossed back over to the other side, so when I entered the Hauptbahnhof, I pulled out the card and tossed it into the first litter box I came upon. I never saw Gustav again.

★   ★

On the train ride back to the post I started replaying the night with Gustav in my head. On the one hand, I felt guilty and told myself, as I did every time it happened, that I'd never do it again. On the other hand, I felt good about the night and frustrated that I'd not be able to see Gustav again. It occurred to me that I'd learned to approach every relationship with a man like a raid: identify the target, attack, and then get out as quickly as possible so as not to be caught. I grew anxious thinking how I'd entertained the idea of letting Gustav know the truth; I knew that letting anyone too far into my life would involve taking a huge risk, one that I wasn't yet prepared to make. And so I pushed Gustav out of my mind and put my "straight" hat back on, managing once again to stuff the weary genie back deep inside the bottle.

CHAPTER ELEVEN

The Second Spotlight

Early in June of 1990, a few months before I got my first big promotion, I was selected to be a fire direction officer for one of the gun batteries. I was still a second lieutenant, but the move was a big deal because I would be one of fourteen officers competing for a single slot. I saw it as a vote of confidence. I also knew that it meant I'd probably be selected for a platoon leader position in a year or so if I kept my nose clean.

That I was moving ahead in my career, that the army seemed to be placing its mark of approval on my forehead with increasing regularity, served only to exacerbate the conflict in myself over my sexuality. I'd proven them wrong and in the process proved to myself that a gay man could be a valuable asset in the armed forces. For so long I'd believed that these two things were mutually exclusive. And they seemed to remain that way as long as I insisted on trying to squeeze my gay self into a straight mold in order to fit my preconceived notions of what it was to be a soldier. Once it became clear that I was succeeding despite failing to straitjacket my sexuality, it became clear to me that they weren't, in fact, mutually exclusive at all. Phrases like "fine gay soldier" and "outstanding gay officer," and "excellent gay major" no longer seemed oxymoronic. They were becoming phrases that might, in fact, apply to me.

But this all came slowly. And I knew that my own private enlight-enment, while it might make my life a little more bearable, wouldn't change anything in the U.S. Army. And I also knew that, as things stood, I simply wasn't going to be able to have everything I wanted. Unlike my straight comrades, I'd have to choose between my work life and my private life. And this realization often left me feeling lonely and empty. In quiet moments, when I was unable to focus on anything else, I'd often experience a yearning that was so palpable, so real, it hurt. I wanted to open myself up to someone else and let down my defenses; I wanted to be vulnerable, to be loved and to love, intimately. But no matter how obvious it became, no matter how much I knew deep in my heart that I wasn't straight, a part of me still believed that I could simply overcome it by focusing on other things or by simply ig-noring it. I'd manage for a few weeks, but the quiet moment would al-ways, always return, that whisper of accusation, Greg's calling me a hypocrite, and there it would be, staring back at me, plain as day. I'd rush to compartmentalize. And I became expert at compartmentaliz-ing nearly every single aspect of my life, each separate part sealed tight in its own little box. If I wanted to have sex, I'd opt for an im-personal encounter, which at the time was an act of world-class stu-pidity, considering that the AIDS epidemic was in full swing and we were still years away from the big drugs that would change the face of the disease in the mid-to-late nineties. An impersonal encounter was preferable to the Gustav-like encounter, though, which had scared me: the box was too big, too loosely sealed; I feared if I had another encounter like I'd had with Gustav, I'd lose not just the battle, but the war itself. I was just about to learn how easily all the compartments could break apart and get blended together.

To celebrate my selection as a fire direction officer, a bunch of us decided to go to Alt-Sachsanhausen. Our favorite place was Kyalami's, a South African bar located catty-corner to the Irish pub that drew a young, upscale mix of Americans and Europeans. We went to the Irish pub, too, sometimes, but that was just about pounding beers, and it was always pretty loud and raucous. Kyalami's was more subdued; you could actually hear what the person next to you was saying. The decor was cool: zebra skins and Zulu regalia. And there were little private nooks set apart from the main room that made things more intimate and allowed for good conversation.

That night we drank quite a bit and talked shop endlessly, as we always did. I remember thinking early on, We had this exact conversation three weeks ago. We were all dressed the same, in jeans and polo shirts, with the same clean buzz cuts, and Bariglia was complaining about the same guy he was always complaining about; it felt as if we existed in some perfectly sealed bubble in which our work lives and social lives were so seamlessly connected that sometimes I really just wanted to scream, crash straight through, and get the hell away from these guys and army life in general.

And the truth was we were, in a very real sense, in that perfectly sealed bubble. The army at that point, American military culture in general, was the only place left where LBJ's Great Society had been allowed to flourish fully and take hold. The army provided everything, literally everything—housing, food, clothing, health care, entertainment, recreation—all the basic human needs and more. It acted as a massive safety net for those who were a part of it. But it often felt less like a net stretched out beneath you and more like a net strung up all around you, like a cage, restricting your every move.

In the United States the army was a separate culture. This separation was even more pronounced in Germany and, I imagine, Korea and elsewhere around the world where the United States had army bases, since we were a distinct military culture within a foreign culture. Not only were we military, we were foreign military. As a result we were even more insular than any post in the States. This is why my leaving the post alone to go to Frankfurt was such a big deal. Not only was it a red flag to those on post, but being the lone American among Germans made me stick out even more.

So this was definitely one of those times when I wanted to break through the bubble of army life. I was basically just going through the motions that night at Kyalami's, nursing my Weizen beer, nodding my head occasionally at whoever was talking to let him know I was listening. I knew what they were saying, after all. I'd heard it all before. To pass the time I looked at the other people in the bar, watched the door as people came and went, wondered about their varied civilian lives outside the bubble.

At one point a group of four walked in, two men and two women, two Americans and two Europeans, it looked like. I'd quickly developed an eye for this—distinguishing the Americans from the Europeans. It had to do with dress and manner, mostly, and it wasn't a science, but after you spent enough time in Europe it became almost second nature. The last person in the group was an American guy, and when I saw him, I literally almost dropped my drink.

I'd seen good-looking men before, of course, and just like anyone else I'd been impressed by the especially good-looking guys, but this was completely different, something I'd never experienced before. It was as if the room had narrowed to just this one person, this one face, this one body, as if the restroom had suddenly gone black and a spotlight had been turned on this one stunning individual. I saw him immediately with such clarity that even to this day I can remember the smallest details of the features of his face, his body, his bearing.

He was about my height (six feet three inches), with thick blond hair parted on the left and fairly short, two inches long, tops. He had a high, high forehead, and a very straight nose with a small indentation at the top that traveled effortlessly down the center, creating a perfect symmetry with a full set of moist, pink, sensual lips. His cheekbones were high and firm and set just above them were a pair of deep blue eyes from which an unusual warmth emanated, not the usual iciness that often comes with such clarity of color. He wore a red button-down shirt and a pair of very dark blue jeans with a nice pair of loafers. His face gave the impression of a vague cruelty that was somehow pardoned, or perhaps enhanced, by his beauty and his youth.

I was finding it a little hard to breathe, looking over at him. My mind was racing. When I could finally form a clear thought, I instinctively recoiled from him (a defensive move, no doubt), telling myself that he wasn't really my type, that he was probably totally self-absorbed, a shallow pretty boy. But this struck me as hollow right away, the defensive reaction of one who had just been literally struck dumb by another man's beauty. And I never looked away. I kept staring at him, as if the room had remained dark and he was now doing a solo performance in the spotlight. There was nowhere else to look.

"What the fuck is wrong with you?" Roger, a tall (six feet five inches) officer, newly arrived in the battalion, asked me, nudging me hard with his shoulder and causing me to spill much of my beer down the front of my jeans.

"Nothing, dickhead!" I snapped, too loudly. "Damn—fuck—look at this fuckface—you made me spill my brew! I gotta go to the head now and dry this shit off!"

The front of my jeans were covered so that it looked like I'd pissed myself.

Normally this wouldn't have been such a big deal, and everyone knew it. That's why they all looked at me as if I'd lost a nut or something.

"Whoa, chill, dude," Roger said, as I pushed him out of the way.

It felt as if he'd caught me with my pants down or something, the way his voice had popped into my fantasy, and then the beer all over my pants, and the newly arrived pretty boy going out of my view. I felt so raw all of a sudden. Normally I would've just laughed it off and probably popped Roger on the shoulder or something, but this wasn't normal, and the bathroom break was a much-needed respite. I felt a little dizzy when I walked in. I splashed some water on my face, tried to get my bearings, then wet a paper towel and wiped the beer off the front of my pants. I knew this would only make the stain worse, but I wanted to get the smell out. I tried to figure out what had just happened to me, but nothing made sense in light of what I'd just experienced. All sense had been trumped for a moment by something far greater, and I was still vaguely in the throes of it.

I took a few deep breaths, and things began returning to normal. I reminded myself that I would not give in to this, that I couldn't give in to it. It simply wouldn't do to be so obvious about it. Don't fuck things up, I told myself. You want to get married, right? You want to be an officer, right? I looked at my face in the bathroom mirror, searching for any remaining signs of the awe I'd just felt. Had they all seen it? Did they all know? And then I saw the guy's face again, that perfect nose and those perfect cheekbones, those deep blue eyes. He couldn't possibly be a fag, I told myself. I mean, he's perfect, he's probably got a girlfriend, probably had a 4.0 at school, probably captain of the baseball team, right? Probably an asshole anyway, right? But Christ, why are you acting like a love-struck cheerleader? Geez, get a hold of yourself, stop being an idiot and go out there and order yourself another beer and get yourself hammered good.

With my composure somewhat regained, I walked out of the bathroom and rejoined the group.

"Didums Jeffy change his diaper okay?" Lostrapo said in his level-best imitation of a concerned, doting mother.

"Shut—your—fucking—head—you!" I replied, hoping I could just cut the whole thing off right away.

But by now everyone had turned toward me and was laughing about the stain on my jeans. And for the next ten minutes or so they all felt the need to pile on in classic army/frat-boy fashion. Finally, somebody put a fresh beer in my hand and the razzing subsided, and I had a chance to look around the bar again. I found him immediately, standing on the opposite side of the bar. I kept him in my vision as I started talking and laughing with the guys again, and then slowly, as the night moved forward, I felt a deep melancholy creep over me like a thick fog. I wanted so desperately to go over and talk to the guy, but

I just couldn't bring myself to do it. And so, in order to dispel the fog of sadness, I opted instead to concentrate on getting seriously hammered.

A bit later on I was listening to Lostrapo, who was a platoon leader over in Charlie Battery, tell me about a new shotgun he'd just bought. Then, as he joked about buying a pistol grip to pimp out, one of the women from the group of four walked over and broke into our conversation. She was a lieutenant from a support battalion in Hanau, and she and Lostrapo knew each other. We talked to her for a while. She was cool, had a wicked sense of humor, and I liked her right away. For the first time since the group of four had entered, I was able to put her friend out of my mind and focus entirely on something else. But not for long. A few minutes later he appeared directly in front of me, seemingly out of nowhere, with a huge smile on his face and his hand extended. The look on my face must have been priceless. I blinked like an owl, switched my beer to my left hand, and put my right hand in his.

"Hi, I'm Paul," he said simply.

It felt as if my hand had disappeared. I worried about the wetness of my palms, which had turned clammy the moment he'd appeared before me.

"Jeff, uh—my name's Jeff," I stammered, realizing immediately that I'd not heard his name. It was as if I'd gone deaf; I could only see his face, watch his lips move, but I couldn't hear the words coming out of them. "I—I didn't catch your name?"

"Paul," he said again, still smiling, then "Paul," again, as if I were a slow schoolchild learning something for the first time, but smiling, still, as if he understood perfectly why I was having trouble hearing him, the language of flirtation being universal, gay or straight, and instantly recognizable by those engaged in it.

"Paul? Okay man, sorry, it's kind of loud. It's loud in here. I couldn't hear you." I felt like a supreme idiot.

There was a brief moment when we didn't speak, and he looked

at me steadily without blinking until finally his friend, the female lieutenant from Hanau, asked him a question and he answered her, still
keeping his eyes on me until Lostrapo said something in response and
he blinked again and looked away. I tried to focus on Lostrapo and the
girl from Hanau, tried to follow the conversation the three of them
were having, but I found myself unable to concentrate for very long,
distracted by his face and the sound of his voice, and suddenly so intensely self-conscious about the way my own voice sounded and the
way I looked, the way my hands moved when I spoke, the way I was
standing, and intensely aware again of the stain, just about dry,
though still slightly visible, on the crotch of my jeans.

At one point I gave up trying to talk and just stood silently and listened, occasionally sneaking a covert glance at him. My feelings were
all over the map. Not only was he perfect, he was also in the army.
And not only was he in the army, he was an officer as well. I couldn't
believe it. I had to keep reassuring myself that I had on a kind of
poker face; my feelings were so strong that it seemed impossible they
weren't showing all over my face. I considered leaving, going out to get
some air, going to the bathroom, anything to extricate myself from
this uncomfortable situation, but I couldn't, my attraction to him was
so severe that I could barely move. The desire I felt seemed appropriate for a cheesy romance novel; it wasn't the kind of thing I imagined
I'd ever feel myself. I mean like huge waves of desire crashing against
the White Cliffs of Dover, that kind of thing. I felt helpless in his presence; all prior restraints had suddenly been cast off, and my entire life
had suddenly been recalculated as a new equation, one that had been
inconceivable until the moment this new variable was introduced.

At the same time I felt an inchoate sadness building up that soon
began to make me feel as if I were being smothered.

"Dude, what's wrong?" I heard Lostrapo's voice coming at me
suddenly. "You look like shit. Need another diaper change, Jeffy boy?"

"Nah," I said, "I'm just beat. You want to call it a night?" I tried
to keep my eyes focused on Lostrapo and not look at Paul.

"Yeah, sure," he said. He shook Paul's hand and said good-bye to the female lieutenant from Hanau.

After saying good-bye to the female lieutenant I put my hand out to Paul, and he took it with a big smile, and like clockwork, I swear, fireworks went off in my head—Fourth of July fireworks, and New York fireworks, too, high up over the East River, not some little hick-town excuse for a fireworks show.

"Nice meeting you," he said.

"Yeah," trying to sound cool, "same here. Maybe . . ." Suddenly I realized that I might never see him again. "Maybe we'll see each other—you know, around—have a couple of beers, or something."

"That'd be cool," he said.

I turned my body to leave, though my head stayed in place as he held my gaze for a split second longer than normal, adding fuel to my suspicion that the attraction might not be entirely one-sided. This really didn't seem possible, though. I was blinded by his good looks, that's all, I told myself. For a few days afterward I pined privately but ferociously over him, and soon, when it seemed clear I wasn't going to see him again, I began to let the image of him slip from my mind.

About three weeks later I was sent to the Unit Nuclear, Biological, and Chemical officer course in Hanau, the purpose of which, as the name suggested, was to teach army personnel about the various chemical and biological munitions we might face and to explain how to plot the direction of fallout from nuclear weapons. Since all mechanized Artillery units at the time were nuclear capable, it was very important to have a few people in every unit trained regarding such matters. Despite the serious nature of this particular course, the experience felt—as did most of the classes we were periodically compelled to take—kind of like a little vacation. And rather than commute back and forth I was allowed to stay in the BOQ in Fliegerhorst Kaserne.

I reported for class on the first day at seven forty-five A.M. and took a seat in the back of the classroom. I was tired and wished I could remain invisible. The other students, mostly NCOs and lieutenants, filed in during the next fifteen minutes. A lot of them seemed to be from the same nearby unit, so they were all talking to one another. Occasionally one of them would nod or say hello to me, and I'd return the nod and then go back to doodling in my notebook. I wasn't interested in talking to anyone that morning. Finally, the instructor walked in with a large white binder and was just about to begin when Paul walked briskly through the door and headed right toward me. We made eye contact, and he smiled and sat down next to me.

"What's up?" he said quietly, leaning over and extending his hand.

"How's it going?" I whispered, bursting, though trying my best once again to remain visibly cool. We shook hands, and I got goose flesh instantly.

The instructor cleared his throat. "We'll just wait until these two gentlemen have gotten to know one another sufficiently," he said.

The rest of the class laughed a little bit, Paul and I faced front, and the class began. Instead of a nice little vacation, I thought to myself, sitting next to Paul, smelling him (yes, there was a scent that drove me crazy), this week away from the battalion was going to be a week's worth of exquisite torture.

The portly sergeant first class with the Coke-bottle glasses droned on and on about VX and sarin gas, and I kept thinking that an ice pick jammed deep into my eye would have been more fun. But Paul was there. And every hour or so the portly sergeant first class gave us a ten-minute break. I tried to appear aloof and indifferent, but during every one of these breaks Paul sought me out and struck up a conversation.

That night he called me and asked if I wanted to go out to grab a bite to eat. I said yes immediately. We drove into Frankfurt to eat at a Turkish place he'd discovered several months before. I got to know him pretty well that first day. He was a really nice guy. I could tell that right away—on our first break during class—down to earth, easygoing, with a sharp sense of humor, sometimes cutting and sarcastic but never in a mean way. We were very different. He grew up in Washington State with his parents and several brothers and sisters, the very epitome of bourgeois respectability. He had a girlfriend back home, and they'd been together since high school. He was really into sports, including hunting and fishing. The only thing I'd ever fished for was a subway token at the bottom of my jeans pocket.

And so for the next five days we spent pretty much every available minute together. The time took on a magical quality. I'd never experienced anything like it before, never having known the sheer pleasure of being in the company of another person whom I liked so much.

It was a kind of relief when the week was finally over and we had to separate. That kind of intensity is exhausting. And besides, he'd said he had a girlfriend, so the relationship was never going to go in the direction I wanted it to.

As time went by and I gained some perspective on that magical first week, I was a little stunned by just how pure and right my passion for Paul seemed to be. It had caught me completely off guard, and I was overwhelmed by the suddenness with which it came on and by its sheer intensity and unqualified authenticity. I'm not sure I'd ever in my life been more certain of an emotion than I was about my feeling for Paul. This alone was cause, I assumed, for private celebration, but also, I was sure, for alarm.

Indeed, once my passion for Paul became clear to me, I found myself getting extremely paranoid. The thrill I had when contemplating a relationship with him was more than counterbalanced by a terrible sense of dread, knowing exactly what the consequences of that relationship might be. I knew with absolute certainty that should the relationship ever be discovered, my career would be over in a heartbeat. No excuses, no apologies, no benefit of the doubt, no understanding or turning a blind eye, nothing but pure, cold dismissal and professional ruin. With a stroke of a pen it could happen instantly. All the hard work and dedication, all the mental stress and physical strain, would instantly mean nothing. It would all be null and void. I would have broken the rules, and the punishment would be swift and sure.

The saddest thing about this was just how much I'd accepted it, and how perfectly incapable I was of seeing it any other way. What a failure of imagination! What a victim of a kind of cultural tyranny I was! So much so that I couldn't even see it. I was a slave to the word *normal*, as defined by the UCMJ. And I was still convinced that I belonged in the culture of the military, that it was my home, which meant making the personal sacrifice and denying myself what any heterosexual would never, in a million years, even dream of giving up.

After I got back to the unit I decided I was going to keep it light and not let myself get into a situation like that again. In my heart I knew that there was something very special about my attraction to Paul and that I probably would not fall that hard again for anybody anytime soon. I reasoned that it made no sense to put pressure on myself and focus on something that I had a snowball's chance in hell of changing. It boiled down to an old West Point maxim, "Go along and get along." That's what I'd have to do. Very few of the lieutenants in the battalion had steady girlfriends or were married, so it would be easy for me to blend in, which is what I wanted to do.

But Paul wasn't interested in taking it light, and "Go along and get along" may have meant something different to him. He called me almost every weekend. And every time I heard his voice, all my reasoned resistance seemed to drop away, making me once again helpless. I'd travel down to Hanau and then to Frankfurt with him. If I tried to come up with some reason to say no, he pressed me and I'd give in immediately. In Frankfurt one night, a few months later, he told me that his unit was deploying to the field and that he'd be away for a forty-five-day rotation. I didn't say anything, and he got a weird look on his face, as if he was expecting me to say how much I'd miss him or something; when I remained silent, he quickly changed the subject. I felt guilty about this since I knew that I would, in fact, miss him terribly, but I was still unsure just how much of that feeling was mutual. The whole thing still made me so paranoid. Though I was upset, I was kind of relieved that we'd be able to bring an end to things gracefully and could just get on with our careers. Little did I know that this was merely the beginning of the relationship and, far from coming to a graceful end, it would be the catalyst that would ultimately lead to my departure from the army.

CHAPTER TWELVE

Desert Shield

As spring turned to summer we began to prepare for the annual fall exercises. We'd be doing a massive computer exercise to test communications and help us develop standard operating procedures. Some units would deploy their command posts to the field, where they would receive situation reports from the simulation center. Even though the Berlin Wall had just fallen and the enemy as we knew it for forty-odd years was no more, I was assigned to the OPFOR (opposition forces), which meant I got to play the part of the Soviets. Little did we know just how short-lived our lack of a traditional foe would turn out to be, for as we planned this simulation Saddam Hussein was beginning to threaten Kuwait.

During the simulation planning I was sitting in the office with a few of the guys talking about going to Switzerland to see a jazz festival when the boss walked in and told us the battalion commander had called a meeting of all officers in two hours. He wouldn't tell us what it was about. Two hours later we all filed into the battalion classroom and sat down until the adjutant appeared in the doorway and announced the commander.

"Gentlemen, the battalion commander."

As one, the whole group of us stood at attention until he told us to take our seats.

"Gentlemen," he started, in a formal voice I'd never heard him use before, "the president of the United States has just ordered elements of the Eighty-second Airborne to Saudi Arabia in response to the invasion of Kuwait by Iraq. We are there to ensure that the president of Iraq does not attempt to invade the kingdom as well. The operation is called Desert Shield, and it is very, very serious. We may end up fighting a war in the Middle East for the first time ever, and for those of you who do not know, Iraq's army is the fourth largest in the world, so it would be a tough fight.

"I called you all here to let you know about the situation and to inform you that we must be ready to deploy as well. The word has come down that we will be called upon to backfill units if casualties occur, and we may even go ourselves. Right now there is nothing but a thin green line of paratroopers standing in the way of a mechanized force that is equipped with Soviet weapons. The focus of the entire army is to build up to combat power as quickly as possible in order to handle whatever comes next. We must be focused and ready to do whatever we are asked to do. As more information flows to me, I will pass what is not classified down to you. At this point I will take some questions. The S-Two will—Deuce, where are you?—okay, the Deuce will help me out answering your questions since he's been doing his homework over the last several hours."

The Virgin Mary herself could have walked into the room at that point, and to a man we would have completely ignored her. Iraq? I'd heard of it but wasn't sure how big the border with Saudi Arabia was; as for Kuwait, all I knew was that it was jammed somewhere among the Arab Emirates in the Gulf. My first instinct was to think we were interested in protecting Kuwait because of the oil, but then I remembered that the United States had a policy stating that any alteration of existing borders in the region would be viewed as a threat to the interests of the United States. This was one of the few times my political science degree from Fordham came in handy. I'd taken a course in

Middle Eastern politics and so was pretty familiar with the geography and the issues.

After the initial shock had subsided somewhat, the room began to come to life and hands shot up with questions for the commander. The questions were all over the place, from the basics like where these two countries were and what languages were spoken, to the weapons they had and who ruled them. It wouldn't be the last time we'd discuss this, obviously, but it seemed as if everyone was straining at the very limits of his comprehension in order to process what was happening.

The possibility of our going to war was the most exciting thing I'd ever heard. Images of glory, of being tested in combat—not just winning in a training exercise, but fighting against an actual enemy—is what every real soldier dreams of. Finally, we'd have the chance to cut our teeth, to test ourselves in the ultimate arena. There was no doubt in anyone's mind that with the fourth-largest army in the world, the Iraqis had all the toys to give as good as they got. It had been twenty years since our army had engaged in a conflict of similar size and scope. Panama, which had occurred just months before, had been too small to be of any major note. It was only when mechanized forces were in play that a conflict took on a certain grandeur, if you will. The brute power of even one mechanized brigade is truly awe-inspiring. The entire mechanized force of the greatest army in history on a rampage would be something beyond words, and surely something that would warrant more than a footnote in the history books. I had no doubt we'd be victorious, none at all.

But beneath this élan and sense of invincibility there was the more thoughtful and questioning part of myself, one that even then began to think about casualties and to wonder, too, if the lessons that Vietnam had taught us would be applied. But this would be a question for the generals and the historians. Just then, all I knew for certain was that the undertaking would be enormous and that we were about to begin a brutal couple of months preparing for battle.

Looking around the room at my fellow officers, I couldn't help but see them in a new light. Up until now they were simply young men like me, little more than college kids, really, but now, as the reality of the news sunk in, they seemed to age before my eyes. No longer simply the fun-loving, hard-drinking knuckleheads I'd bonded with, they began to look like soldiers, serious professionals who'd heard the call and were now prepared to do whatever it took to make sure the United States came out on top.

We all knew what war meant in theory. We'd all studied the battles and walked the sites where they'd been fought, but now we'd be experiencing the real thing. And we all seemed to realize instantly that the mental process of steeling oneself against the prospect of whatever was thrown up at us had to begin right away. Blanks, computer simulations, and referees had done what they could to keep us as prepared as possible in peacetime, but now the real training would begin in earnest. We had to know our jobs cold and be able to act effectively in any and all situations in which we found ourselves.

I knew that one of the big things hanging heavy in my fellow officers' minds was the prospect of chemical weapons. The commander had mentioned that the Iraqis were known to have them and to have actually used them against their own people. He tried to reassure us that our equipment could handle anything they threw at us, but it was clear that few were convinced. NBC (nuclear, biological, chemical) training was one of the things that officers blew off regularly, for two reasons, I think. The main reason was just the sheer unpleasantness of the training. Imagine gardening, in the middle of one of the hottest afternoons in August, wearing a heavily padded coat, with a dozen layers of cellophane plastered across your face. Imagine so much sand getting caught inside the mask that you end up feeling it in your teeth for days. The second reason was, I think, the knowledge that one wrong move and all these elaborate precautions would prove to be futile. There was something particularly dreadful about imagining it, too, something just so qualitatively different from imagining, say, bullets and shrapnel, that some soldiers just weren't willing to face it.

The commander took questions for about an hour, and when it appeared that we were all talked out, he dismissed us, instructing us to keep the troops informed and to let them know that more information would be forthcoming. As we got up to leave, my buddy Duncan came alongside of me and said, "Dude, you know we'll never go. They would never pull troops out of Europe." Normally I would have agreed with him, but somehow I felt that this time was different, this time all bets were off.

Over the weeks that followed, the situation worsened. The president used every means, short of combat itself, to signal to Saddam Hussein that the invasion would not stand. Preparations were fast and furious as the machinery of war went into high gear, moving forces halfway around the world to reinforce the thin green line in the sand.

Finally, about a month later, when it became clear that only a lot of body bags filled with Iraqi soldiers would convince Saddam to pull back from Kuwait, word came down that we were going in. My friend Duncan had been wrong, and my hunch had proved correct. The Pentagon decided to deploy an entire corps into the theater to provide the coalition with a credible offensive punch. After we found out our unit would be going, everyone had a newfound spring in his step, and morale was very high. We were going to kick ass! Differences dropped away as we bonded over the higher purpose of deploying, fighting, and bringing everyone home safely. In an effort to reduce stress and keep morale high, the chain of command made sure soldiers' families were included whenever possible. Married officers went out of their way to invite single officers like myself over for dinner as often as possible, a gesture that was deeply comforting to me at the time.

★   ★

The next few months were like taking a dozen rides back-to-back on the Cyclone at Coney Island. There was so much to do that it was hard to find time to sit down and examine all the feelings swirling around inside me. I decided it was time to do just that when, one day, as I was watching my driver perform maintenance checks on the Hummer, I suddenly wondered what I would do if his head were blown off right in front of me. Talk about wanting to be prepared for every single scenario. Some things were just unknowable, I realized. Some things you just couldn't be prepared for. Like the boy on the rock, like the young German dead in his Mercedes, there would always be things that didn't make sense, that fell outside the narrative— horrible loose ends, tragedies that you'd discover your reaction to only after they'd occurred.

And, I realized, the only antidote, the only salve for this strain of senseless tragedy that so often infects the world, is love, family. And even that treats only the symptoms; it's never a cure, for these things are, by definition, incurable. Still, they're made bearable by love and family and that may be as good as it gets. Where was the love in my life? I asked myself. Whose arms would hold me when I returned from the war? Naturally, I thought of Paul during these moments. But even as his face materialized in my mind, even as his arms reached out to embrace me in some imaginary homecoming, I realized what pure fantasy the whole thing was. And, realizing this, I became overwhelmed with a sadness that seemed to reach into the very core of my being. In an ideal world I would have been able to have a relationship. But the world I'd chosen to live in, the world of the U.S. military, strictly forbade the use of my particular antidote; the love I wanted was against the rules. I was, in fact, a criminal. The irony of my situation was so incredibly galling to me! Here I was, ready to put it all on the line in the service of my country, willing to pledge my blood and breath for the United States, and yet I faced dying, I faced meeting that pledge a liar, a cheat, a criminal. Even if I had a lover, even if Paul and I had been together for years, all our communication would still have to be camouflaged in the most bland and platonic terms. If I was killed, he'd have no rights, receive no benefits, be handed no crisp widower's flag. I could earn ten thousand Purple Hearts, but still there'd be no Paul standing on the tarmac, waving a little flag, waiting to embrace me, to kiss me hard on the lips, when I returned home from the war. Why did it have to be this way?

Did it have to be this way? Everything I'd been taught, from St. Joan of Arc through Archbishop Malloy, every Catholic pronouncement on the subject, every faggot joke I'd had to endure by a straight man who couldn't imagine that a gay man was actually standing next to him, all of this told me that if you had to ask the question there was something wrong with you. But still, there it was. I was off to war, and there the question was. It was so simple and so powerful, so replete with common sense, why on earth could no one in the Pentagon see it? I could meet the standard, I was popular, I was accepted by my peers; my blood would shed as red and as easily as the straight soldier's fighting next to me. Why was I forbidden to be the person I am? Why could I be a soldier but not a man?

CHAPTER THIRTEEN

War for Love

By the time my birthday rolled around in November, the stress of anticipating our departure was beginning to take its toll. The flow of troops into the theater was a twenty-four/seven operation, but it was constantly changing as new information became available to airlift command and priorities and strategies were suddenly reshuffled and shifted. We were given departure dates and times only to have them changed at the last minute. Wives and children, having made their tearful good-byes, would be told suddenly that the soldier would have another three days, or a week. I'm sure that everyone was relived to have a little more time, but it was also emotionally wrenching to have the departure date shift so arbitrarily.

The initial rush over the news had slowly been replaced by a kind of measured anxiety, as—in our minds—the war became less like a state championship game or the Super Bowl and more of a reality. We were going to war. None of us had done that before. Feelings of invincibility had gradually given way to an anxious confidence that tried to take into account all possibilities. And there were so many— so many more contingencies, it seemed to us—that soldiers in previous wars hadn't had to consider, most notably the threat of chemical warfare.

Indeed, this question of the chemical-weapons threat posed by

the Iraqis was the main source of the anxiety many of us were feeling. It seemed that no matter how much training we endured, how
many contingencies we planned for, it would never be enough. Like I
said before, the threat of chemical attack produced a level of dread in
us that I think was simply of a whole different degree from the kind
of anxiety caused by old-fashioned bullets and artillery. We tried our
best, however, to keep that anxiety under control and to bear in mind
the fact that we were still the most advanced and powerful army in
history.

As the day of my own departure drew near, the swelling numbers
in the desert became increasingly impressive. This would be, we knew,
a major conflict. Some in the unit were predicting that we'd see epic
battles on the level of Kursk in World War II.

Weekends it was the four of us, mostly—Lostrapo, Barigilia,
Brooks, and me—Friday nights at Der Speckmaus, and Saturdays at
some place in Alt-Sachsenhausen, maybe, or in the city center. We'd
all become very close, like brothers, really, and the Iraq situation had
only intensified our bond. I was certain that I'd do anything for those
guys, no matter what.

The weekend after Thanksgiving I got a call from Paul. I was
overjoyed. Just hearing his voice again sent my morale totally through
the roof. He filled me in on what he'd been doing over the summer
and then let me know that his unit would be deploying a few days before mine, supposedly in the next few days. He suggested we get together before he got the word to report for departure, and I said yes
without even thinking. We agreed to meet at Kyalami's since it was the
place we'd first met. When I let the guys know that I wouldn't be
around for our usual Friday-night session at Der Speckmaus, I caught
a rash of shit for it but was able to get away nonetheless.

I was so excited about seeing Paul that I drove to Frankfurt directly from work to make sure I wouldn't be late. As a result, I found
myself in Frankfurt two hours early, unsure how to pass the time. The
waiting was excruciating. I figured I should put something in my

stomach, so I went to a café and tried to enjoy a *pilzraum schnitzel* and Weizen beer. But I couldn't stop thinking about him, couldn't stop hearing his voice on the phone, imagining his face and body in front of me at the bar. But he has a girlfriend, an accusing voice would suddenly pop into my head, and then I'd measure this against the look I'd seen in his eyes, the feel of his handshake, a particular turn of phrase he'd used, and I'd find myself flummoxed once again, right back where I'd started from, that is, as confused as ever, and if not in love, then, at the very least, immensely infatuated.

Leaving the café, walking out into the brisk Frankfurt evening, the accusing voice would morph from pointing out Paul's supposed girlfriend to pointing out the threat our relationship posed to our respective careers as army officers. It was so doomed, I thought, trying to walk off the heavy German beer and failing to be inspired by the high Christmas spirit filling the narrow streets.

And then, all at once, the streets came alive; they'd sparkle and shine with silver bulbs and bright-colored lights, with the smiles of happy Germans strolling arm in arm—a Christmas card, honestly— as all my feelings for Paul would erupt unbounded by the lies of imaginary girlfriends and by the threat of expulsion and ruin. Love triumphant buoyed me up and carried me in its arms, stupid with desire, all the way to Kyalamis.

Paul was late, forty-five minutes late, in fact, so I had the chance, sitting at the bar, nursing a Weizen beer, to go through this whole process a few more times: up and down, hope then doubt, terror then relief and joy—again and again. What a mess in love I was!

And finally around eight forty-five, just when I was about to give up, not just on seeing him that night but on him completely, his absence the final proof, I was sure, of his straight indifference, there he was, bursting through the door, rushing briskly toward me, looking contrite, eager to explain. His face was flush with exertion, and he was bright-eyed and smiling big, all perfect white teeth ear to ear, as he pushed past my clammy extended hand, to hug me hard, like a long-lost brother.

"Heeeey, buddy, what's up!" he enthused. "Sorry I'm late, but my unit was doing some last-minute stuff before we fly, and we had to work late. I'm so sorry, really, bud," he went on, pulling out of the hug and backing slightly away and looking into my face intently.

"I'm great," I said, too loudly I thought. "What about you?"

"Good, good," he said, still breathing a little hard. He pointed to one of the unoccupied private nooks. "Let's sit down and get a beer."

We didn't miss a beat. It felt as if we'd seen each other only yesterday. He told me he'd moved up in his unit, having been given an executive officer position, and that a few times, in the absence of his bosses, he'd briefly commanded. Commanding is always an honor and is especially good for your promotion prospects when you're a lieutenant. I was truly happy for him. The conversation came so easily and seemed just so right that I felt completely relaxed and open.

After a few beers it started to feel as if we'd left the army far behind. There was a moment, when he got up to get us the third round and I was left alone at the table, when I felt the whole unwieldy burden of the military just lift from my shoulders, as easily as an overcoat, and suddenly, but only briefly, it was just the two of us, Paul and me, having beers in a bar in Europe, two young Americans far away from home, *on a date*, I thought to myself. How simple it all was when you removed the army from the equation, removed its antiquated bias and all the wasteful and unnecessary hand-wringing and drama that came along with it.

But as Paul loped back toward me, through the smoke and red light of Kyalami's, bearing two fresh Weizen beers, all I could think of was the war. And suddenly, that's all there was. There was only the war. Only the military. And I think in the few seconds it took for him to reach me, as I watched what I couldn't have move closer to me while at the same time receding from possibility, I understood, for the first time in my life, what it might be like to have a broken heart. I think I aged a decade in those few seconds, and I grew up right then and there. I understood that I was, after all, just like everyone else, a man who can be hurt, who can be vulnerable; I understood that I, too, was a man who bleeds.

I almost spoke up at that point. I almost shouted, "Wait, I have to tell you something!" thinking I could save us. I almost told him everything. I almost said it all. But as he put down the two beers and settled himself into the booth, he started talking about his girlfriend for some reason, and the moment was gone. He might as well have slapped me across the face.

All hope wasn't lost, however, because it became plain to me right away that he was talking about the stateside girlfriend out of some sense of obligation, the excitement that had lit up his eyes just a few minutes before disappeared, and his easygoing manner became clipped and a bit curt, as if she was an unwanted, though necessary, intrusion at this point.

For my part, as much to cover my own ass, I think, as to put him at ease, to let him know we were playing the same game, I told him about a girl I'd met through a friend at Speckmaus. Her name was Annette, and she had a huge crush on me. I liked her well enough that I'd decided to date her somewhat casually. Paul reacted to this coolly. He was smooth and noncommittal, though he did seem distant for a moment, and the reaction seemed just a little bit off, as if he'd slightly miscalculated his response and had, as a result, underplayed the role. He was too cool, too indifferent. And I could see this. And to complicate matters even more, I think he saw that I saw.

Suddenly we broke into laughter, sharing the unspoken inside joke, and I think within that laughter and that split second of self-conscious acknowledgment, we inadvertently managed to look at each other with unguarded honesty for the very first time. But neither of us had the courage to make a move, neither of us had the balls to say what needed to be said, so the laughter petered out and the moment vanished.

After another round of beers I was sporting a pretty good buzz and beginning to feel increasingly less guarded about my feelings. I was edging gradually closer to an all-out confession as I became filled with a deep, deep yearning just to stop the bullshit and talk straight. It was the whole, long process at the café and during my walk to Kyalami's to meet him, but speeded up so that it moved through me in miniature waves.

I'd look at his face, hear his voice, sense his body across the table from me, and all the desire would just well up in me; with each successive wave, I felt the barriers in my mind straining hard to hold on, yet beginning to loosen under the pressure. My carefully crafted life plan, my false ideal of what it was to be a soldier, seemed so utterly trivial in the wake of this desire. I kept trying to figure out something to ask, some coded way of inquiry, that would help me determine if there was even the slightest possibility my suspicions and instincts were correct. But then something would pull me back from the brink, fear mostly, I suppose, but common sense as well, since I knew I wasn't prepared to be booted out of the army and forced to build a whole new life in the civilian world.

But then, damn, another wave would come crashing down on me, and I'd think, Maybe, just maybe. His signals were so subtle and guarded that it was hard to tell, but there was something there, I just knew it. How could I figure it out for sure? I couldn't. The risk was too great. And in addition to the big risk of exposure and professional ruin in the army, there was, too, the added normal risk of basic vulnerability, of admitting that you were attracted to someone only to discover he didn't share your feelings. What if Paul was gay but simply not attracted to me? That seemed impossible. I knew it didn't make any sense. But that possibility made it feel as if the cliff I was standing on had suddenly doubled in size: the drop would be twice as

long, the impact twice as hard. All at once the risk of admitting my attraction to Paul had been magnified twofold.

But then another wave hit me, a bigger wave, fueled by a slightly
higher buzz from the Weizen beer, and I was pushing all that aside
again, feeling bold, my heart screaming: *This is it! Take a chance! Trust
your heart!*

"Paul," I said abruptly, interrupting his story about a dog he'd had
when he was in grade school, "I need to ask you something." His face
turned a little pale, and there was something close to terror in his eyes,
though a terror laced with hope, I'd think later on. He'd seen something in my face. I'd scared him. The look in his eyes was too much
for me, and I couldn't bring myself to continue. I hated myself for
being so cowardly, but it didn't seem as if I had a choice. It just wasn't
in me yet.

"Nothing, nothing," I said, trying to laugh. "I was just thinking
that I should probably get going." I'd had enough. It was close to one
now, and I still had the drive back home to my apartment in Cleeberg.

"What? You gotta be kiddin' me; crash at my place, it's much
closer."

"That's really nice, Paul, but it's, what, almost one now, and I have
to work in the morning, so . . ."

Paul looked visibly disappointed, as if his perception of me had
suddenly proved unworkable and he'd have to start all over again. I
wanted so much to go back to his apartment, to spend the night with
him, but I was feeling so frustrated and a little sorry for myself. The
thought of being alone with him in his apartment was almost too
much to bear. And the idea of being in the apartment and being unable to touch him, to have to sleep on the couch, or on the floor, when
he'd be only a few feet away from me, seemed impossible. I decided
just to slink home.

"All right, man," Paul said, a little too casually, I thought, considering the expression that had just been on his face. "Maybe I'll have
one more and then head home." He was again trying too hard to ap-

pear indifferent. But then he said, kind of abruptly, "So, when do I see you again? We're going to fly pretty soon. Could be any day now." This didn't seem indifferent at all, and I started to feel a little bit hopeful and a little less sorry for myself.

"Give me a call later this week," I said, starting to smile, "and we'll set something up." I moved to shake his hand, but just like when he arrived he moved right past my outstretched hand and gave me a big hug, even harder and longer this time, now that both of us had had a few beers.

As I walked out into the cold night air, my head began to clear from all the smoke and beer, and I figured I'd be okay for the drive home. I wasn't feeling too bad, all things considered, and when I reached the car I thought about going back and taking Paul up on his offer. I flashed on his face, tried to imagine his fit young body naked beneath the T-shirt and jeans, tried to imagine a kiss, how we'd wrestle and fumble to pull off clothes, frantic to get at each other, but then all the questions and doubts returned, clouding over my fantasy, and I reminded myself that I did have to get up early for work after all, so it really wasn't possible tonight.

But would it ever be? Would it ever be possible? I liked Paul even more now that I was getting to know him better. He was a very good-looking man, beautiful, in fact, one of those people you wonder about, about how someone that beautiful gets to move through the world. But he was also smart and funny and modest and easy to talk to, and it just felt so damn good to be around him. On one level I was absolutely certain that what had just happened was a kind of date, that I'd just walked away from a four-hour flirtation. On another level, that notion certainly collapsed in light of the tremendous risk and all my other doubts. And it was this dilemma that nearly drove me crazy with Paul.

Driving home to my apartment in Cleeberg, I tried to imagine a perfect world where I could express myself however I liked without fear of losing my job and destroying my professional reputation and being humiliated in the process. A world in which I could say, "Paul, I like you. I'm attracted to you," and he'd be able to say, "Thanks, I like you too, Jeff," or "Thanks, Jeff, I'm flattered, but I see you more as a good friend," the world in which my straight peers lived. Later on, I would realize that that world did, in fact, exist, with some limitations. It was the civilian gay world in which Greg lived, the world that I was unable to find credible for a very long time. If either one of us could have spoken the truth that night in Kyalami's like Greg had spoken to me on that first night we went out drinking way back in 1985—the ease with which he came forward and said so simply and so forthrightly, *I like you so much, Jeff. I'm really attracted to you*—it would have made things so easy, so simple, we would've avoided so much unnecessary pain. But Paul and I had given up that freedom; we'd given up access to the burgeoning gay civilian world to be soldiers and now found ourselves trapped in a kind of lunacy in which all desire had to fit neatly into a prescribed formula, a formula that excluded us lock, stock, and barrel.

And why couldn't I find the gay civilian world that Greg inhabited credible? To put it simply, I'd been taught that it could never be credible, that it was deviant (yes, *deviant* was the word that still ran through my head at that time), that it stood in direct opposition to and was mutually exclusive of the set of values I'd inherited from my aging, old-world grandparents, and from the aging and increasingly out-of-touch and sexually conflicted Catholic Church. In addition, I could never be a "real man" and give in to these impulses. It was all pretty typical stuff, though stuff with tremendous power, stuff that, once ingrained, is still, even in this relatively liberal age, very hard to undo.

Because of all this I was blind to the increasing visibility of the civilian gay culture, and as a result I failed to find gay role models or any kind of guidelines that could have helped me along. It might as well have been 1950 (and in the military it often *felt* like 1950) as far as gay culture was concerned. The gay movement could have screamed at me through a dozen megaphones, and I still would've been deaf to the idea of freedom they were offering.

Still, despite my stubborn belief that the military and the church had it right on the issue of homosexuality, I could not deny the positive feelings that Paul brought up in me—I couldn't deny the positive nature of love itself.

Over the next week I tried to keep my mind off Paul by throwing myself back into work as the preparations for our unit's departure became a little more hectic. The workload was increasing daily, and the vehicle departure date was fast approaching. Our equipment would be shipped down to the theater in the Gulf, and we would link up with it at a later date. The holidays made the whole thing seem only more dramatic. The closer we got to Christmas, the harder it seemed to become for the families with whom I'd occasionally have dinner. Many of the wives were already emotionally brittle, and now they had the added pressure of dealing with all the trappings of the holiday and putting on the good face of Christmas cheer. I often felt awkward because it seemed obvious to me that the wives would have preferred spending every available second with their husbands alone, rather than entertaining bachelor lieutenants like myself. But they knew that officers like me had no real family in Germany, so they opened their homes and hearts to us all the same.

About a week after my night with Paul I got back to my apartment and found a plate of food from my landlady, Marlies, on my doorstep. She was a sweet lady who often left cookies and other things for me whenever she could. Like the wives who had me over for dinner, Marlies apparently felt some sort of obligation to take care of me, and I appreciated it mightily. As I started to take off my boots I listened to the one message I had on my answering machine. It was from Paul.

"Hey, bud," he started in that light, bouncy voice he always used, as if nothing could upset him, "I was hoping to talk with you before I left, but since you're not around I'll have to leave a message and maybe try again a little later, too." He paused, cleared his throat. "We're leaving tonight from Rhein-Main, and it looks like it's going to be a nightmare. The plane schedule is all fucked up again; it's like the Keystone Kops are running the base, I swear, but that doesn't matter. I wanted you to know that—ever since I met you—I just knew we would—ahhhh—that we would always be friends. We're going to war now, and I don't want to—get too mushy, but I—just wanted you to know that I would miss you and all—so—stay safe, bud, stay safe, Jeff, and maybe, hopefully, we'll see each other over there. If not, we'll definitely have to get together when it's all over. Okay then, so—bye for now."

I lay there on the bed, one boot on, one boot off, playing the message over again, three or four times, staring at the ceiling. Yes, I thought, we were going off to war, and yes, the only thing we were sure of was that we'd do our duty as we'd been trained to do.

But none of that mattered too much in light of the message. All I could hear was his voice. This was the last piece of evidence I needed. Add this to every conversation we'd ever had, all the signals he'd sent, the lingering glances after some double entendre, the times I'd caught him secretly staring at me, the heat that so often seemed to rise off his body when we were together (his body was one that seemed to have been specifically designed for sex, as if his beauty was his evolutionary trump card)—take all this into account, and you could arrive at only one conclusion: Paul liked me, was attracted to me. And I was thrilled. The girlfriend was just a front, I thought, and suddenly the sheer ardor with which he'd pursued our friendship became crystal clear to me; it was so telling, it was all the evidence one needed, really.

Still, damn it, still, I thought, pulling myself up and finally taking off my other boot and throwing it against the wall, how can I be sure? I played the message over one more time and found myself hearing the voice of a friend, not the voice of a lover, and everything was up in the air again. This wasn't fair! I quickly changed my clothes and went to the fridge to grab a beer. Here we were, I thought, on the eve of war, facing the great abyss of uncertainty that comes with every war, in which the possibility of death, of mutilation, of unspeakable horror, is very real, and we are denying ourselves the comfort of shared affection, the knowledge that the other waits for us, no matter where we are, and is thinking of us, hoping for us, praying for us. Damn it, if there could be something between Paul and me I wanted to know, I wanted to be able to have hope for the future, to know that there might be something wonderful to live for after the war. And this knowledge would be a refuge when the going got tough, a private place of comfort. I wanted to be able to pull out a picture of someone I loved, or to send him a letter—to be connected to another individual in a way that might make the war, and my whole life, more meaningful and valuable. What is it that we defend in war, after all, but the tranquillity of our domesticity? We fight for the right to live in peace and to love. We fight war to defend love.

Yes, there was my grandmother back in Jackson Heights, hoping for me, praying for me, sending me letters; she was a great comfort, but it was the potentially intimate connection with Paul that would have given me even greater comfort. I wanted to be able to share my whole being with another person, and I was pretty sure that's what Paul wanted as well. I thought of all those soldiers' wives who had been so generous to me, taking me in and feeding me, and how thoroughly they took for granted their right to love and hope and pray for the safe return of their soldier husbands. My God, so often I felt as if I were standing behind a piece of glass, watching other people who were in every way just like me go about their lives, and all I could do was look, never touch. How long could I live like this without going completely insane?

Listening to Paul's voice on the machine again, I suddenly felt a powerful urge to throw all caution to the wind, making a promise to myself that the next time I saw him I would just do it, I would just come out and say it, *What is going on between us, Paul? What is this?* But why wait? I could simply pick up the phone right now and call him and ask him, I thought, and the fact that I couldn't bring myself to do it made me realize just how cowardly the promise to myself really was. What if something happened to him? How would I live with myself knowing that I'd failed to take the risk and that he'd died in the war not realizing that he was loved by me? The truth was, it was probably too late to call him now, anyway, since he'd likely already boarded a plane and was now on his way to the kingdom where our fate would be determined in the coming months. I wanted to cry but couldn't; I was too angry. In that moment, everything that I ever loved about the army and about being a soldier seemed to be just one big, tremendous, stupendous lie. What was the point? What would all the glory and all the medals mean if I had no one with whom to share them? Nothing. Nothing at all. For so long I thought we were special, soldiers, and that I was particularly unique, being an officer in the greatest army in the history of the world, but I was quickly learning that I was just like everybody else; I needed to love and to be loved, and there was just no getting around it, no matter how much idealistic furor I used to try to cover it up. For the first time in my life I realized that it was entirely beyond my control. And that something that I couldn't control, like, say, my height, or the color of my eyes, could be used against me, could be justification enough to end my career in a heartbeat, rendering meaningless all the years of hard work and good intentions I'd put into it, was just plain wrong, un-American, even.

"Fuck the army!" I shouted at the walls of my empty apartment. "Fuck America!" I shouted again. For making me feel as if my life didn't matter, for making me feel as if my life was worthless. The words rang out in the silence, and it felt so good, but then it stung; it felt as if someone had just thrown a glass of cold water in my face. I felt guilty. I knew right away that I didn't mean it. But truly, I thought to myself, sitting down now on the edge of my bed, pressing the button to play Paul's message one more time, could I really live like this for the rest of my professional life, say, another eighteen years? Was that even remotely possible? "Hey, bud," his voice again . . . and I knew right then that the answer to my question was no; then I lay back and enjoyed the sound of Paul's voice one last time.

CHAPTER FOURTEEN

Daddy, I'll Be Good

The following afternoon we were told that our date of departure would be December 24, Christmas Eve, which meant, of course, that no one would be spending the holidays with family. Those final days before the war were a blur as we completed training and hurriedly closed down the post. There were several other units in front of us in the queue, and we got regular briefings on their progress through the system. We noticed it was rare for a unit to get off at the appointed time. They'd arrive at the airport for the scheduled flight, but then the plane would get diverted or the flight would be canceled for maintenance, so they'd end up having to wait for a day or two. Based on this, we were prepared for a nightmare at the airport.

On the twenty-fourth I went down to board one of the buses that would be taking us to Rhein-Main. The farewell scene was like a funeral, all pretense of dignity and restraint thrown to the wind, as wives and children wailed and soldiers did their best to appear strong, though many broke down and cried along with their families. Little girls clung to their father's legs, wives clung desperately to their husbands' necks, holding on for dear life, pouring a lifetime of emotion into those final hugs and kisses. Watching the more emotional couples—the younger, childless soldiers and their women, mostly—it looked to me as if they were actually trying to merge, as if by holding

on to each other long enough and hard enough they'd become inseparable, one would disappear into the other, and they'd both go off to
war, or they'd both remain in Germany. It was a sobering scene, a
hard reminder, just in case anyone still needed one, that what we were
about to embark on was serious business indeed. The children were
the hardest to look at, because they seemed not quite to understand
what was going on. All they knew was that their world had been
turned upside down and that Daddy was leaving. I was holding together pretty well myself until I looked over and saw a little boy grasp-
ing a soldier's knee, his small head turned up toward his tall soldier of
a father, his face streaked with tears; he said, "Daddy, don't go. I
promise I'll never be bad again if you stay."

I burst into tears, watching the young father gently lift his son up
into his arms and reassure him that it wasn't his fault and that he
would be back as soon as he could. No, I thought angrily, it isn't your
fault, little boy, the person at fault is a shithead dictator from the Middle East who's about to get his due.

One of the officer's wives who had had me over for dinner several
times saw my tears and came over to hug me and tell me she'd be
thinking of me; then the other wives came over and did the same,
hugging and kissing me on the cheek and telling me they'd write and
send care packages. Those big-hearted women were really my heroes
that day. I wasn't expecting such an outpouring, and it came as a relief since it allowed me to believe that I wasn't quite so alone. The
bachelor officers, myself included, were a part of the family, too, and
we'd be taken care of.

The bus pulled away and I watched through the window as the
wives and children waved good-bye to their men, uncertain when, or
whether, they would ever see the men again; I couldn't help thinking
of Paul and the possibility that we, too, might never be reunited. All
the hurt began to well up in me again, and I felt as though I might be
consumed by it. The only thing that brought me back was the thought
that everybody around me was experiencing a terrible loss as well,

and, in that moment, I made the conscious decision just to let it go. My relationship, or lack thereof, with Paul would be dealt with after the war was over. For now, I had an obligation to be fully engaged as a soldier and a leader, and I had to be focused on the task at hand. It was now about killing the enemy, winning at all costs, and bringing my troops back in one piece. As I looked around at the glum faces on the bus, I knew this war would bind us to one another in a way that families and civilians could never truly understand. For now, these brave men were my family, and I knew that I'd give my life for any one of them.

True to form, we spent the next two days at the airport terminal camping out waiting for our plane. The gloom had dissipated somewhat once we'd gotten away from the post. There were a few officers' meetings, and we kept busy playing cards—endless rounds of spades, mostly—and a lot of guys just napped while the air force people rushed around us, grappling with the constantly changing situation.

Around six P.M. on the second day our plane was finally ready. Unfortunately it was a C-41, not one of the many civilian planes that the government had commandeered to make up for SAC's (Strategic Air Command) shortfall, and it was cramped and uncomfortable. The engines were very loud, and the constant odor of plane fuel made us all cranky and groggy. We spent the trip in silence, pretty much, since it was hard to hear over the roar of the engines, plus I believe everyone welcomed the chance to be alone with his thoughts before any real action began. A lot of guys just slept, something soldiers often do when away from the garrison since they can never be quite sure when the next opportunity for sleep might present itself.

Six hours later, we landed at an airfield somewhere in Saudi Arabia. Our descent had been quite bumpy, so when the plane finally came to a halt there was a slight groan of relief and then everyone began to move around and stretch stiff arms and legs. The load masters lowered the back ramp of the plane, and we began to file out in an orderly manner. At the base of the ramp there was an air force sergeant speaking to us through a bullhorn. He seemed to be repeating something that he had said many times before, and this repetitive, singsong quality was comforting, though parts of his message weren't comforting at all.

"Welcome to the Kingdom of Saudi Arabia! On behalf of the Air Command, I hope you had a wonderful flight and will fly with us again." There was a kind of grumbling laughter among the troops at his lame attempt at a joke. "Place all duffel bags on the pallets that are available to the left of the ramp; they will link up with you when you arrive at your inprocessing center. Once you have accomplished this, you will be taken to the buses that will get you to where your unit will stay. The threatcon is alpha, and there have been drive-by shootings over the last several weeks. Stay alert and report anything that is unusual. Thanks, and have a nice night."

We were all pretty beat after the frustrating days spent at Rhein-Main trying to get out of Germany and then the long, uncomfortable flight. Everyone was eager just to get to a cot and a pillow and then collapse. It was a beautiful night: clear, warm, the stars shining bright above us. The NCOs began the process of getting everyone in order and accounting for all the weapons. This becomes a major obsession for the chain of command on any deployment. The last thing you want is for one of your troops to leave a weapon somewhere, because everything stops until it's found.

We boarded the ancient white school buses they had waiting for us there. I tried to get comfortable, thinking I'd sleep a little, but as we pulled out it was immediately clear that that wasn't going to be possible. The bus seemed to lack shocks of any kind, and the seats had no springs. So I simply sat and stared out the window into the foreign darkness, lost in my fatigue, feeling a little bit lonely, and longing for the comfort of my apartment in Cleeberg, all the war whoop having been drained out of me by the long flight.

The world outside my window seemed forbidding and joyless. The lights of the old school bus revealed a terribly bleak landscape made up of nothing but a series of plain concrete buildings, one after another, with no decoration or style whatsoever. "Bare necessities" was the expression that went through my head as I squinted into the dark, expecting, for some reason, to see rabid attack dogs rushing out from behind every new building we passed. I'd thought, considering all the oil money, that we'd come across towns and villages that evoked the mythical richness of *The Arabian Nights*—fanciful minarets and colorful, lavishly intricate, inlaid tile work with bits of the Koran artfully represented. As flashy as the Arabs were abroad, I thought the kingdom would be replete with the magnificence that only unlimited money can make possible. Instead, we'd been dropped into what looked like the most despairing of slums. We were, in fact, on our way to what was called Cement City, home of a cement plant near Dhahran that was providing space for American operations here.

When we arrived inside the actual compound, a kind of tent city built on sand and cement dust, a sense of relief overtook me upon seeing the familiar sight of U.S. troops manning a heavily guarded post. After a few perfunctory checks, we were waived through and taken to our bivouac area, where we got off the ancient buses and were allowed to go directly to our tents, pick a cot, and crash, letting our weary minds and bodies finally give in to the merciful oblivion of a well-earned sleep.

In the morning, daylight revealed just how bleak the place really was. Long, straight rows of olive-drab tents covered in sand and cement dust and bleaching fast under the merciless Saudi sun served as the interim home for a few thousand soldiers waiting to be linked up with their equipment. A virtual hive of nonstop activity, Cement City was the last piece of civilization one saw before moving to the deep desert staging areas. Our stay lasted several weeks, the days bleeding one into the other with little distinction. It was hard duty that often left us bored and frustrated. We had no idea when our equipment would arrive, so we worked on individual skills and did our best to keep from going stir-crazy, practically an impossible task considering the environment—nothing but sand and cement dust, a scraggly palm tree here and there, the occasional camel ambling by in search of food. In an effort to brighten things up and bring some Christmas cheer to the drab tent city, a group of guys had constructed a Christmas tree out of empty water bottles filled with sand and stacked up in the shape of a tree and covered with green canvas, garlanded with toilet paper and decorated sparsely with the tops of water bottles. When the first vehicles from our battalion began to arrive, it actually felt a little like Christmas morning as we rushed out in anticipation, thrilled finally to have something important to take care of.

A few days after the equipment began to arrive, while a bunch of us were in the dining facility for dinner, I got quite a surprise. We always tried to arrive early for meals in order to avoid the huge lines that would form later on. The place had just opened, so we waltzed right in, got our food, and sat down. The food was the same tasteless crap we had been eating and would be eating for the foreseeable future, but mealtimes were about camaraderie, not cuisine. I was halfway through my chicken cacciatore when I looked over at the sign-in desk and saw, much to my astonishment, Paul standing there with several officers from his unit. My whole world just lit up. All the olive drab vanished in that instant, and Cement City suddenly seemed like the most beautiful place on earth. I tried not to look too excited, although inside I was fairly bursting, while I quickly wolfed down the rest of my meal in order to break free from my friends. Finished, I pushed my tray away and stood up.

"Hey, where the hell are you going?" Duncan said to me in his heavy Brooklyn accent, looking at me quizzically. "Whaddya gotta date or somethin'?"

"Nah, he's just lookin' for a place ta jerk off, right dick beater," said Dave, the crooked scar on his face twisting into a smirk.

"Yeah whatever, assholes, I got business to take care of. I'll see you guys later." The irony of Dave's remark was that, from the first moment I'd met Paul that night in Kyalami's, merely being in his presence, merely seeing him from across the room, was enough to get me excited. There were times when I didn't even see him, I just sensed him (maybe his scent preceded him), before he emerged from a room, say, where I was waiting for him, and I'd get so hard it was nearly painful. My desire for Paul was a certainty that astounded me at times. And there were times when it was the *only* thing I was certain about.

"Seriously, where are you going?" Roger asked.

"See that lieutenant over there?" I said, thinking fast. "I know him. He's in one of the support battalions, and I want to see if I can get stuff from him." By stuff I meant anything, really. It is a long-standing tradition in the army that you have to be able to scrounge supplies and equipment outside the normal channels, and for that you need contacts.

My legs suddenly felt a little rubbery as I walked over to the table where he and his friends had sat down. My heart was racing, and I had to keep myself from breaking into a run to get over there sooner. Remain calm, I told myself, anything else will look weird. I adjusted my pants casually, worried that the tent city starting to rise in my crotch area would be apparent to everyone in the dining hall. Paul was covered in a thick layer of dust and had a rag tied around his neck, something we all did to keep the sand out of our faces. He'd probably been out driving around. I came up behind him and put my hand on his shoulder. He jumped a little, and, before I could say anything, he'd turned around and stood up to greet me. I worried that he was going to hug me the way he always did, though in a way I hoped for it, too, despite how strange it might have looked, but he knew the score and so opted for an exuberant handshake instead, while clasping my shoulder with his other hand as tightly as possible, as if the clasp contained all the emotion he wasn't allowed to express: the secret, miniature hug of a lover.

"Hey, buddy, howya been?" he said, beaming, still holding on to my hand and shoulder. "Did ya get my call? I tried to hook up with you before I left, but it got overwhelming. Come on, sit down a minute . . . oh yeah, let me introduce you."

After the introductions were out of the way, I sat down in the space they made for me at the table. For the next few minutes Paul and I disappeared into the bubble of our own private world. He did most of the talking, filling me in on just about everything that had happened to him since we'd last seen each other. I was happy simply to listen to him talk. Truth was, I was hardly paying attention to the actual words coming out of his mouth, I was so thrilled just to be in his presence again, to look at his face again. I smiled and nodded occasionally, feeling so complete in the moment—I didn't need to speak. I felt such relief! All the stress and strain of the last several weeks melted away in an instant, and I worried that the moment would end too soon, before I'd had time to savor it properly, before I'd had time to get the image of his face and body fixed in my memory so firmly that it would last a very long time, a lifetime, if need be.

After he finished, he stood up and motioned for me to follow him, and we left the dining hall together. A Hummer was waiting outside. Apparently he'd come back to Cement City to check on some equipment that had arrived late and would be in the rear for only a couple of hours. He stood talking to me with one foot resting up in the passenger's side, holding on to the windshield frame since the Hummer had no tarp for cover. The driver was sitting on the other side, waiting, so our conversation was a lot less animated than it normally might've been. Not only did we have to conceal our excitement (at least I knew I had to conceal mine, at that point), but we also had to behave like officers, so there were certain limitations.

We finished our conversation, and he extended his hand to me; I shook it firmly. He didn't squeeze me on the shoulder. There was no hint that he'd even considered hugging me good-bye, which couldn't have happened anyway, considering the circumstances. No, it was just a formal, soldierly handshake, executed in a bit of a hurry, and then he was gone, speeding off toward the gate and back out to his unit in the desert.

Walking back the short distance to my tent, I felt as if I were glowing. Our conversation had been, by any standard, just friendly, innocuous banter, not the dialogue of a great romance, but that didn't matter to me. I thought about the impassioned promise I'd made to myself prior to our departure, that if I saw him again I'd tell him how I felt. But somehow that didn't seem so important right now. Just seeing him had been enough. Seeing him had healed everything, had set the narrative straight: we had connected one last time before combat, and that was good enough. We were at war now, in theater, waiting to commence operations against the enemy; now simply wasn't the time to be distracted by some vague longing for a fellow officer who may or may not be gay. I was here to do a job, plain and simple. And it would no doubt be the toughest job of my life, requiring my undivided attention every step of the way. Paul had a job to do, too, and for the next few months he would be focused on nothing else as well.

It was clear now. The conflict between my dedication as a soldier and the longings of my heart had now tipped decisively in favor of our roles as soldiers. I would worry about him. But I also knew and respected his commitment and that we shared a bond of sacrifice for a greater good: what we were doing was right, and it was far more important than either one of us alone, even more important than the two of us together.

Over the next several weeks all the equipment arrived in good order, and we were finally prepared for movement into the desert. We moved out and headed for the port of Dammam, where everything was being marshaled for the final push to our assembly area. UN Resolution 678 had condemned Iraq's invasion of Kuwait and called for withdrawal of all troops and influence by January 15. Just two days after the passing of the deadline, on January 17, aerial bombardment of Iraq and occupied positions in Kuwait began. Fearing Iraqi retaliation with chemical weapons, we were put on threat condition DELTA.

We were awakened by the shriek of sirens indicating a chemical threat. The war had begun, and with a bang.

We scrambled to pull on our masks and gloves, fear causing many of us to shake, making the task more difficult. All you have is seconds, literally, with no margin for error, and when the sirens are for real, not the sirens of a drill, those seconds seem like hours. Every sense goes into hyperdrive, every move counts. Your life is at its most meaningful, in a way, since during those moments *everything* is consequential.

Once everyone was suited up and communicating, I began to take in the scene around us. The port was bathed in the eerie glow of floodlights. The light cast huge ominous shadows out of the exposed steel girders that composed the guts of our maintenance bays. Bradley fighting vehicles raced up and down the streets of the compound, turrets spinning madly. The gloves were finally off, and we were going to do it to them before they did it to us. As we sat there immobilized by the stifling layers of charcoal-impregnated cloth and rubber, we gazed up at the sky and watched the flickering lights of hundreds of planes streaking north on their first mission, knights of the air thundering across the sky to engage the enemy and reduce their defenses to ashes. Soon after the initial wave of planes had passed overhead, the thud of exploding munitions could be heard from hundreds of miles away as we unleashed on them the full fury of our might.

I felt a strange evil glee as another wave of planes flew by, knowing that their mission was to annihilate the Iraqis. The overflight of planes signaled for me the final break from civilized behavior, a move from the politics of diplomacy and reason to the politics of war, which has its own set of rules that more closely resemble the rules of brute strength and force as opposed to the rules of mind and spirit that normally guide our everyday civilized lives. We'd stepped outside that world now and were locked in a titanic struggle from which only one could emerge victorious. Watching the power of our assault unfold, I knew that we were nearly invincible, and I was vaguely thrilled by the great jolt of energy that comes with witnessing the logic of pure ag-

gression played out in real time. There was something immensely sat-
isfying about experiencing in such a visceral way the deep connection
to our animal ancestry, the brutal instinct to survive and triumph. All
the impulses that polite society reviles were now not only laudable but
indispensable—though still tamed, in a way, being wrapped up in the
specific boundaries of organized warfare. It was like watching a great
ball of fire harnessed and made useful. And to be a soldier was like
being a part of that blaze. The enemy wanted me dead, and I wanted
the enemy dead. It was either fight or die. And we were now fighting
for our lives.

★ ★

After those initial heady moments, the chatter of the radios began to
die down as we waited for the NBC folks to give the word that all was
clear. It seemed like an eternity, waiting in those hot, bulky suits,
shrouded like moon men. Indeed, to find ourselves thrust into an environment where the very air we breathed might prove fatal was like
finding ourselves suddenly catapulted to the moon. The minutes
ticked away, and no word came. We listened to ourselves breathe. It
was two A.M., and I was beginning to get drowsy, my body urging me
back to the sleep from which I'd been awakened. Just as I began to
nod off, Mike, a lieutenant from Alpha Battery, reached over
abruptly and tapped the shoulders of Tom, the other officer in my
unit, and me. I caught myself and began frantically gulping for air in
the claustrophobic confines of the heavy mask. I thought he wanted
to tell us something about the situation, but he only wanted to ask a
question.

"Hey, you awake?" he said.

"Now I am."

"Tom, you up?"

"Yeah, what's up?" Tom said through the mask.

"Um . . . I gotta take a dump, what should I do?"

There was a moment of silence as we all considered this. We were in full chemical gear, and there was still no way of knowing if anything had happened, if the air was safe.

"What about the diaper they issued us? Didn't you put it on?" Tom said without missing a beat.

"Diaper? What fucking diaper? What are you talking about. Are you outta your mind?" He looked to me for support. I played along with Tom.

"You didn't get one?" I asked, trying to keep from smiling.

"What? Fuck you, I'm serious. I gotta go, whaddaya think I should do?"

"Can't you wait?" I said. "It won't be that much longer."

"What did I just say? No, I can't wait."

Welcome to war at the end of the twentieth century. All the training in the world wouldn't have prepared us for this.

"Just try to find a private spot and seal it off as much as possible and don't take off your mask," Tom said.

"I agree," I said.

Mike got up and left the area to find a private spot to take care of business. We simply sat there in silence, waiting for the situation to change, lost in our own thoughts, sweating profusely from the rubber seals against our skin. After about twenty minutes the radios crackled to life and the word came down to go to MOPP (mission-oriented protective picture) 2, which meant chemical suit but no mask and gloves. I pulled the mask off and let the fresh air flood over my face, then took my sleeve and wiped the sweat and grime off my face and off the mask's interior. Tom was doing the same when Mike walked in, still decked out in full chemical gear. He quickly pulled off his mask and gulped for air.

"So did everything come out all right?" Tom asked.

"Yeah, but some raghead is going to have the surprise of his life in the morning."

"Whaddaya mean?" I asked.

"Well, I couldn't find a bathroom, so I barricaded myself in one of the offices and used a trash pail."

Tom and I looked at each other, horrified, and then we broke out laughing.

"You idiot, the bathroom is two doors down that way." Tom pointed, laughing.

"I just want you to know that it is moments like this that you establish yourself as a national treasure," I said.

"Which office was it?" Tom asked, still smiling.

"That one." Mike pointed in the direction of a small building some distance away.

"Jesus, Mike, that's one of ours, Americans are using that one. Didn't you see all the paperwork there? I can't believe it wasn't locked. Thank God we're leaving tomorrow."

Tom and I both just shook our heads and stared at Mike incredulously.

After that first incredible night, with the jackhammering of the Iraqis nicely under way, things took on a predictability that we could not have anticipated just three weeks before. The Iraqis were unable to counter the massive air strikes, so we were able to conduct operations unopposed and largely in stealth. We moved our unit to a desert staging area and in doing so became part of the largest armored assault since World War II, all the new weapons systems of the 1980s proving their worth and then some.

★ ★

One special note from those eventful days was the fact that the New York Giants were in the Super Bowl. On game day it was raining pretty heavily, as it does very often during the winter in the kingdom. Several other football junkies and I stood at the foot of one of the Hummers with a small radio that could pick up the game and listened as the Giants kicked the winning field goal. It was a great boost to our morale, and we took it as an omen that the fighting would go well. The outcome of the war would be clear in a matter of days, and we'd have control of the ball the whole time.

CHAPTER FIFTEEN

Desert Storm

Iraq in January; rainy season in the desert. I know to some that may sound fabulously exotic, enchanting almost. You imagine stunning gold-and-jewel-encrusted mosques jutting up from low-lying clouds; a morning mist gently rising above bone-white sand dunes; dramatic snow-capped mountains to the north; the twin rivers, Tigris and Euphrates (the names alone evoke a kind of magic), which flow unencumbered southward like azure-colored ribbons; partridges and wild geese perched atop miles and miles of date palms and poplar trees effortlessly swaying in the soft temperate air, the birds flying off, then disappearing beyond the endless horizon.

But no, I'm afraid that's not the Iraq we found ourselves in. There was no temperate air, and it wasn't soft. It was muggy, wet, and hot, and it often changed to wet and very cold in what seemed like an instant. There were no jewel-encrusted mosques where we were. The only architecture we were privy to was the ugly gun-metal oil wells that shot up incongruously from the dirty gray sand like petrified fistulas. We saw no exotic animals or birds—only the occasional lost and tired camel; the ever-present scavenger buzzards that, if given the chance, would peck out your eyeballs while you slept; and hideous swarms of giant bats the size of 155mm projectiles. The Iraqi desert was entirely unexotic, unenchanting, unfriendly. It was goddamned uninhabitable.

We were on the move in the southernmost part of this hellhole somewhere along the 33rd parallel, stealthily positioning our troops and precision-readying them so that when the word came to unleash hell on Saddam's army, we'd be able to do just that with surgical accuracy. I was commanding a group of five men out of an impossibly small M577 personnel carrier. It was approximately seven feet wide and nine feet deep, and that was with nothing in it. Once it was filled with the computers, communications equipment, chairs, and platforms, as well as the actual personnel it was meant to carry, available space shrank considerably. Working inside that thing I often felt like a one-hundred-pound sausage living in a ten-pound bag.

The interior of this very ugly, very expensive armored sardine can was drab olive green and black. Thick black cables coiled around everything, and there were big chunky bolts and hard angles every place you moved. We considered ourselves especially blessed if we managed to avoid jabbing ourselves at least once over the course of the day. The worst was getting jabbed in the groin by one of Uncle Sam's little wake-me-ups. Needless to say, the working environment in this highly necessary communications node was tight, charmless, and cruel.

Working in such a small space with four other men really makes you appreciate the value of personal space, however tiny that actual personal space may be. And a lot of barriers are broken down as well. For instance, in most working environments you wouldn't expect to be present while one of your colleagues is having a bowel movement. And if you were, you probably wouldn't expect said colleague to describe the deed in perfect detail for anyone within earshot—probably just to counteract the absolute lack of privacy. Good manners and other niceties that have been deeply ingrained in you your whole civilian life are tossed aside during the extreme circumstances that often come with deployment. But when you realize that the colleague describing the bowel movement is a fresh-faced, eighteen-year-old enlisted boy, who could be reduced to mere vapor by a stray RPG (rocket-propelled grenade) in a nanosecond, you suddenly understand how trivial all your hang-ups are. Humor, comingled with the stark realism of the prospect of serious injury and death, has a funny way of cold-slapping you into reality.

In this close environment, where there's zero visual stimulus, it's very important, if you want to avoid going stark-raving mad, to develop a level of comfort and trust with the men you're working with. And, primarily, this translates into talking. It's important to talk. So the guys talked first about their sports teams back home, then the girls they'd known, then the miserable, unpredictable weather, and then maybe the last book they'd read or the last movie they'd seen; gradually, it was only a matter of time, everyone became a little more personal, and soon enough the whole scene took on the feel of informal group therapy. Of course, for me it was different. I couldn't be totally honest with these men. God knows I wanted to be. But that would have been professional suicide and might've easily led to a total breakdown in morale. So, for the sake of my career and for these men whom I was leading into battle, men whom I was convinced I'd die for and who would die for me, I chose to continue living the lie.

★ ★

I had to create a series of sex stories in order to fit in, to show that I was just one of the guys and that I was willing to open up. Lying so blatantly to these men always made me feel more stressed. The more lies I told, the more I'd have to keep track of.

I definitely felt the pressure to fit in whenever the talk turned to sex. Once we were conducting dry-fire missions, an exercise in which you compute all the acquired data on certain hard targets without actually firing on them. It's an excellent means of getting the processing time down and remaining frosty before actually having to uncork hell. Specialist McCarty was the computer operator that day. McCarty looked as if he was just a couple of years past puberty. I swear, if he'd told me he was nineteen, I'd have been shocked. He was rail-thin, and his uniform was too big for his slender frame, giving him a gaunt, almost sickly look. He did, however, have a great knack for making us all laugh—no small talent in circumstances like these—and he never had a problem being the brunt of his own jokes. He was well liked by everyone, and, quite honestly, the tour wouldn't have been the same without him. As he was applying dabs of Clearasil onto to his thin, pimply face, he looked up from the standard-issue metal mirror and said, "Anyone heard from home lately?"

No one answered. There was no e-mail then, during this first Gulf War, so "hearing from home" meant a letter, usually, and it carried a kind of weight and meaning that I imagine e-mail doesn't provide in quite the same way for soldiers being deployed today, if only because a letter actually exists as a physical object the lover or friend or family member has actually created and touched and sealed themselves, something tangible. It was probably a combination of nerves and sadness, anxiety and homesickness, that prevented the men from answering McCarty's simple question. No one really wanted to think about home because it was a special category, something to be cherished during happier times. As things now stood, we were just days, maybe hours, away from literally scorching the earth and killing Iraqi soldiers, and we needed to be game-face ready. Our main focus at that point was simply to kill with great precision while absorbing little or no collateral damage. We had been privy to most of the intelligence gathered on Saddam's army: seven hundred thousand strong, well equipped with heavy armament and chemical weapons, willing to die for their cause. We all knew it wasn't quite going to be a cakewalk.

But McCarty, always unruffled and unfazed and ready to talk and laugh, said, while replacing the cap on his near-empty tube of Clearasil, "My girl just wrote me a letter. She's worried about the ground phase. She thinks we're going to take massive casualties. Imagine that. Where'd she get that kind of information?"

"Real loyal bitch you got there, McCarty. What's she look like under her veil?" said Private First Class Moore, a twenty-year-old homeboy from the Bronx. I had a soft spot for him, despite his being a pain in the ass at times, because my memories of home were good, and it was thoughts of New York that often kept me balanced during times of anxious calm like this one, when there was too much silence and too much space to think.

"Fuck you, Moore!" McCarty parlayed back, "my bitch is prime corn-fed, red-blooded son. How else she gonna handle"—he became suddenly animated, grabbing his crotch and pumping his hips into a frenzied gyration—"Big Daddy's python? She gots to be all woman to handle some a this!"

Everyone laughed, and he kept pumping his hips, occasionally slapping his ass, and then he pulled on one of the extension cords, taking the slack and wrapping it around the imaginary neck of his girl, and whispered through clenched teeth, "Whose python is that? Who's your daddy? Who's giving you the monster fuck of a lifetime? Who? Tell me who!?"

And then, in a high-pitched falsetto, he responded as the girl. "Why, you are, Daddy! Oh—give it to me harder! Yes, you are, Daddy!" fluttering his eyelashes and swishing his hips.

"Okay, McCarty, finish up now," I broke in. I was afraid that if I'd let him go on, we would've been privy to the *really* dark side of an eighteen-year-old mind, one that had way too much time and testosterone on its hands. But everyone was still laughing, and the men seemed visibly more relaxed. They always got a kick out of watching one of McCarty's outbursts. It broke the tension, so I allowed it, within reason.

Staff Sergeant White, my sergeant, slid his chair away from the computer terminal, looked up into the nothingness of the drab metal ceiling, and said, "Goddamn, I miss pussy. Been too damn long." White was a devoted father of two with a third on the way. He was as straight as an arrow and generally very mild-mannered, always impeccably uniformed, and almost obsessed with cleanliness. And he was a highly valued tool in my arsenal, since I knew that when it was time to do the job, he'd be a virtual killing machine. He was indispensable to me in other ways as well. The younger soldiers had a lot of respect for him, so he often served as a buffer between the men and me. Any problem that arose in the field would go to him first. He would then filter out all the bullshit and give it to me straight. He saved me hours of effort. Now he was turning toward me with an expectant look on his face. I tried to busy myself in order to derail the conversation before we got to where I knew we were headed, but it was too late.

"What about you, LT," White said. "You have anyone at home you keeping company with?"

Keeping company with—I had to smile at the phrase. My grandmother used to ask me if I was keeping company with any girls, and my answer was always the same: no. I looked up from my terminal, tried to deflect the question by doing my best imitation New York cool.

"Nope, no one special at the moment," I said, smiling a little.

Moore jumped all over that. "Sucks to be you, sir," he said.

Now Moore knew he had a slight tilt with me, but he also knew he was dancing on a very thin sheet of ice. I leaned in, only half serious, and tipped my head at him. "Come again, *Private*?" I said.

The track was suddenly quiet. Moore quickly resumed his job of capturing coordinates. He laughed when he finally spoke. "I was just saying, *sir*," he said, slowly, "how totally fucked up it must be that the last piece of pussy McCarty got was in this very track just thirty seconds ago . . . *sir*."

Specialist Ranklin was a twenty-two-year-old fresh-faced kid from Kentucky, just six months removed from a trailer park. He was checking the chemical-warfare suits. He looked to White at this point and smiled, said, "No offense, Sarge, but when was the last time you got laid?"

"No offense taken, Ranklin," the courteous sergeant said. "Just before I left we put the kids to bed early. My wife made us a great steak dinner with some broccoli and potatoes. We had a little wine, put on some easy listening. . . ."

His face was filled with a sad kind of pleasure, remembering the night with his wife. Looking at him, I suddenly understood in a way I hadn't before just why the men respected him so much. He was just so honest and good, a good father, a loving husband; he was everything you saw right in front of you, no deception. How I admired that and how I wished I could be more like him! But how could I be? Was it even possible? Not in this army, I thought, not in this war. But maybe in the next?

"We lit some candles," White continued his reverie, "got in the bath together, and made love all night long."

"Check out the sarge getting all Barry White on us and shit . . ." Moore said, breaking up the soft moment with his own brand of New Yorkese. He started to sing in a big sultry baritone, doing his best Barry White imitation, and there was more laughter all around. The sarge was a good sport and took it all in stride. There was a warmth to the moment that was very special. These were good men I was living with, and I was proud to lead them into battle.

"What'd you do before we flew, Moore?" White asked then.

"Went down to Kstrasse with one a my homies from Charlie Company," Moore said, referring to the red-light district in Frankfurt.

He stopped what he was doing and looked up to the ceiling as if he were savoring the experience. I wasn't sure I wanted to hear about his night in a Kstrasse brothel. I told myself it was because I was twenty-six and Moore was only still a kid, just twenty, and I was way beyond this kind of thing. I realize now that it made me uncomfortable because it was somewhat transgressive, like my own sexuality, outside the accepted norms represented by Sergeant White's perfectly respectable sex-in-wedlock-with-children, making-love-by-candlelight-in-the-tub-all-night story. He could've told the story on *Oprah*, for God's sake, word for word. Despite my discomfort, though, I let Moore continue with his brothel story. It was a morale booster, after all, and everyone needed to feel comfortable enough to be open with the other men. That is, everyone but me. But I was leading these men, I told myself, so I had to make certain sacrifices, I couldn't afford to be quite as open. Which was true, to an extent. All differences of sexuality aside, I still had to maintain a certain distance as the unit leader. And I wasn't so naive as to think that I or anyone else for that matter would be able to tell a same-sex story among a group of men like this—in the army or otherwise—anytime soon. But still, still, did I have to be this isolated? Did I have to remain this hidden? We might all die together, for Christ's sake, and soon; yet I still had to lie, in the face of death I had to keep on lying.

"Asian bitch from . . . from . . ."

Moore couldn't remember where his Kstrasse prostitute had been from.

"Was she Asian, Moore?" Sergeant White said, not looking up from his terminal, but trying to be helpful to the now-stuttering Bronx boy.

"Yeah, yeah," Moore said. "Mos def, bitch was Asian. She pulled out all the toys, too, son. Had this red leather mask with this wild bra thing."

"Bra thing?" Ranklin asked, sitting up now.

"You know that shit with all the laces running up to her titties."

"Bustier," I said.

Moore looked at me, confused. "Bustier, yeah, I guess. I didn't know it was a French thing. She let us take turns on her. My shit was rock hard behind that French shit she was wearin', too, you can believe that. Bitch was fine, son, she was talkin' some a that Chinese shit, you know, lovin' it and whatnot. I got all up into the guts, know what I'm sayin'?" He laughed and high-fived the men.

"Then the bitch started to play with her shit, nasty man, nastiness. She had meat curtains. They hung down to her thighs, man, looked like ma fuckin' car doors all opened up and shit, waitin' for some Asian mafucker to drive his Toyota out."

The men laughed, and there was a slight lull in the track. I knew the conversation was inevitably going to swing my way again. I could cut it off now, if I wanted to, but it was always a balancing act. I didn't want to cause any friction between the troops and me. In combat the troops need to respect the officer leading them, but they need to respect the individual beneath the officer's bars as well. I decided the best thing to do would be to make a quick joke to show that I was part of the group but then get out of the track as quickly as possible to avoid any follow-up. So I stood up and grabbed my crotch. "Have to shoot off some missiles," I said, smiling wide and moving toward the door. The men laughed hard. I think they liked feeling that I could be as raw and out there as they could be. But before I could make my exit, Ranklin asked the question.

"LT, you married?"

The whole section was watching and listening closely. I felt so self-conscious I could barely move. Were they catching come unconscious vibe I was giving off? I wondered. Did they know; could they see? How much gaydar were they equipped with? My lie was going to have to be a good one, with details. But the prospect of telling it made me tired. Wouldn't the truth be simpler? I was LT Jeffrey McGowan, patriot and gay man, ha! Sure, that would go over well! But I knew better, of course, so I smiled wearily and said, "Never married, Ranklin, but was close as hell last year with a girl I met at Speckmaus in Langgons with some buddies a mine. Almost tied the knot but hey . . . whaddya gonna do?"

I shrugged my shoulders, put out my open palms, and raised my eyebrows in the classic New York shrug, then closed my eyes and let out a small laugh. All the men saw was a guy remembering his ex-girlfriend, but what I saw was a man having all his self-respect slowly drained out of him as the lie factory in his head went into overdrive and the fresh lies spiraled and blossomed out of his mouth. "She was perfect," I lied, "blonde, five feet ten inches, thin, gorgeous, went to Bryn Mawr, had rich parents with a house on Martha's Vineyard, and she had gorgeous tits, too, she was perfect . . . except—"

"Except what, LT?" Moore asked.

"Except for the meat curtains which looked like fuckin' car doors—she'd been busy before I met her!"

The men howled. I was off the hook for now. I rushed out of the track, smiling, relieved. My steps were so quick I was almost running, fleeing the track and the men with whom I would be slinging bullets in just a few short hours. And then I found myself actually running. I was full out running in the darkness now, all by myself, deep into the desert night.

The farther I got from the track the easier it was for me to get some perspective on the situation, which I was convinced now wasn't all that unique. I reminded myself that I'd made a choice. I chose to be a soldier and I was going to be a goddamned good soldier even if it killed me (and it might, I thought, if not from enemy fire then surely from the stress of living a double life). But no, I had a job to do, and I was going to measure up; there was no question about that. In a perfect world that's all that should matter, really. One standard for all. You either meet the standard or you don't meet the standard; it's as simple as that. And I was going to meet the standard. I was meeting the standard already, dammit! I'd get beyond these feelings just the way I always had, just the way I'd done my whole life. But I was wrong. I was wrong still, again. And the desert night was silent.

★   ★

A few hours later we were on the move, searching out to destroy. We had not yet made contact with the enemy and this was always the most difficult part of the mission. The anxiety of not making contact was rocketing through me like a misguided RPG. We were maneuvering through the Wadi al Batin, attempting to do an end run around and catch them unawares as they retreated to the north out of Kuwait. This was part of an elaborate plan of deception designed to separate the enemy from his command, control, and then destroy his forces down to the last man—divide and conquer, basically. The strategy went as far back as Sun Tzu and his oft-quoted *The Art of War.*

Then suddenly, out of the desert stillness—*pop-pop-pop*—I heard small arms fire. All my anxiety was immediately transformed into a powerful hit of adrenaline. We had already been at MOPP 2, so we were wearing our chemical suits with gas masks affixed to our waists. The second we made contact we'd been upgraded to MOPP 4, so then everything went on—the masks, the hoods, the rubber gloves— and we were a virtual track full of bubble boys.

A few minutes later, we found ourselves in the middle of a *shamal,* a violent sandstorm. Ranklin was acquiring target positions, and White was receiving and prioritizing the "gift list." The gifts were two tons of molten steel and shrapnel. I was coordinating the whole thing, and it was hell doing it at MOPP 4. The weather had turned unbearably hot and humid, and the chemical suits were lined with charcoal, so our bodies were quickly becoming covered in a thick grimy layer of soot and sweat. Despite the heat and the chemical suit, I worked my best to coordinate us into the field of battle quickly and smoothly. I was tense, but fully alive and alert in a way I don't think I'd ever been before or since. This was it; this was what it was all about. As we feverishly processed the missions, we heard an unmistakable roaring sound overhead. Two low-flying A10s came in to bombard a path for us so that we could then systematically destroy the point of origin of the enemy fire. Again there was more enemy fire, but then the relentless sound of 30mm bullets began raking the earth not far ahead. The sound was that of a giant, muffled chain saw. It was a cruel, raw display of power, certain death heard clearly though not visible at all.

The radios went crazy. Commanders were now into the horrific ground phase ass-deep. They were stepping over one another on the radio, barking commands. We were now into the second phase of our assault. Observers in the field were giving out calls for fire. My job was to calculate their distance and direction and choose which type of ammunition would be used to engage and ultimately kill the enemy. Once all the guns were set up, I then gave the command to fire. My men were agile and deft as we dumped massive amounts of fire onto the enemy. The more we delivered, the mighty thunder and lightning of Desert Storm, the more frenzied the calls for fire became. Occasionally I could hear the fear in a kid's voice, and it was heartbreaking, but not one of them cried out or was killed during this ground phase. These young men were scared, but they didn't let that get in the way of their doing their duty honorably, and of being men before the enemy.

Every so often there would be a sudden void in communications, the radio would cut dead, and I'd get a horrible, sinking feeling in my gut. These guys were my friends, and I didn't want to see any of them injured or killed or captured. Silence was ominous; there was almost a kind of negative sound that would ring in the air the moment the radios would go dead, as if echoes of the last set of voices were vibrating all around us. But then the radios would suddenly fire back up, and there those voices would be again, breathless with anticipation, ready to get the next series of rounds downrange. This went on nonstop for hours. We had no time to think about how exhausted, hot, tired, and hungry we were. The conflict that seemed to be ripping me apart just a few hours before as I ran out alone into the desert darkness now seemed like just one small speck on a very large canvas.

I turned to look out the track and there were men, asses and elbows working urgently, completely focused on defeating the enemy. That was hands-down my proudest moment of the war. If God had chosen for my life to end at that point, it would've been all right by me; in my heart I knew that we were righting a wrong, and that all the rest would be sorted out by him.

The cordite was thick in the air. The darkness seemed to magnify everything. Planes swooped in to drop their payloads after receiving my coordinates, and the sky would then light up ten miles deep in-country. The concussive force that we felt immediately after was that of a solid roundhouse to the chest. It was so impressive that it scared the living shit out of me, though I have to say again that I've never felt so totally and completely alive. We were the most lethal killing machine this earth had ever seen. We were *invincible*. All the rules of society were suspended. This was the thrill, the fantastic jolt, of pure aggression. Our job was to defeat the foe, grind him into dust, no questions asked, and that is exactly what we were doing. During training they used to talk about the lethality of the modern battlefield. Well, I'm here to tell you that nothing you can imagine comes close to the reality. Nothing you've seen in real life, nothing you've seen on a video screen or in the movies, can begin even to approximate the tremendous sound and the sheer, overwhelming force and power of this relentless onslaught. Why this is such a thrill, why destruction even has the potential to thrill, is a question for the philosophers, and one I didn't even ask myself until many, many years later.

And just when I thought I'd seen it all, the lethality intensified. The tanks in my brigade changed formation to mass their guns. This spectacle was the most awesome and evil sight I have ever seen. The guns looked like nuclear-fueled pistons slamming back and forth in their turrets; their precision was superb. We were acquiring targets, and they were engaging them from two and a half miles away and subsequently killing them by firing right through solid fortifications. At this point I almost pitied the Iraqis. These guys could never have known this was coming; they were eviscerated, vaporized, swept away like butterflies in an F5 tornado. They tried to fire back but were so quickly overwhelmed that they simply died in place.

We moved several more times over the course of the next twenty hours. By early the following morning, the men were covered in the thick black powder from the 110-pound rounds, and they were beginning to look exhausted. With all my energy nearly spent, I simply crashed and dozed for a minute or so before suddenly being jolted awake by a massive explosion. I grabbed my weapon and looked out. Apparently, an enemy tank thought to be unoccupied had been bypassed when suddenly it had come to life in an attempt to ambush our track. Fortunately, one of our M1s nearby had seen it swing into life behind us and had blasted it. We moved to check out what was left of the tank. There was a gaping, burning hole where the M1 had blasted through. Through the stink of cordite and burning oil, I could smell the distinctive odor of burning flesh and hair and nails. It's a smell I'll remember for the rest of my life.

I pulled my binoculars out and observed a few commanders from the Third Battalion and Fifth Cavalry, conducting tact meetings. It was oddly comical, seeing all these men, each with the same black ring around his right eye, from peering out of the gun sight of his Bradley. Wondering how I was able to retain a sense of humor in a time like this, I understood the phrase "gallows humor" in a way I never had before. The men looked grim. It was clear they knew we had plenty more fighting ahead of us, and I felt it in myself, the grimness, the starkness of what we were actually doing. In this moment of haggard realism, of heightened mindfulness, with the odor of cordite and death all around me, I realized why every veteran I'd ever spoken to was so reticent about talking about his war experiences. There is nothing glorious about killing to someone who actually has had to do it. There is nothing thrilling about the results of pure aggression left unchecked. We had done our job, performed excellently and were victorious, but there was a price to pay. We had stepped outside society's protective norms to do our duty. Stepping back in, we would never be quite the same.

I searched my track to make sure all my men were safe and accounted for. They were, and I was pleased. One by one, they looked at me and gave me the thumbs-up, without a word. Nothing needed to be said. We knew what the black-eyed commanders knew: there was far more to do. We were not out of harm's way by a long shot.

Sitting back, I let some of the tension ease out of my body and began to process what had occurred over the last two days of nonstop combat. Each thumbs-up I'd received from my men was ineffably pre-

cious. Still, there was an emptiness inside me. These men, who gal-
lantly went into battle for me, who listened to every word I said and
obeyed it to the letter, who treated me as their teacher, their leader,
sometimes their friend, would never really know who I was. I'd just led
them into victory. Would I ever be able to be honest with them? More
important, I wondered, would I ever be able to be honest with myself?
But there wasn't time to ponder this now. The radio had crackled to
life once again, and we were suddenly back on the move. My men
needed my support and command. I had my job to do.

CHAPTER SIXTEEN

The Stirrup Modification Kits (Caissons) Go Rolling Along

We could hardly believe it when we got word that all hostilities were about to cease. It felt like coitus interruptus, and we were baffled. With our hands firmly around the neck of the Iraqi army, we were well on our way to finishing the job and removing the threat of a loose cannon in the Middle East. Removing Saddam would be left for another time and another army, the unfinished work of the moderate father would be left for the radical son, who'd exploit the worst attack on our nation's soil in order to defeat his father's foe and to do the bidding of his father's former cronies. Removing Saddam was always a good idea. What was *never* a good idea was trying to do it unilaterally, especially when the UN sanctions were actually working and the rest of the world (and more than a few here in the United States, as well) was in such opposition to it.

But back in 1990, the moderate father had us stop on a dime and adjust to the new orders. We would impose peace now and stabilize Kuwait as it licked its wounds from the horrible mauling it had received from Saddam's army. The scenario was completely unexpected, and it seemed surreal. As more recent history has shown, winning the peace is often much harder than winning the war itself, and it's never been one of our strong suits. It requires employing a touchy-feely approach to the very people you were just days or weeks or months before trying to kill and conquer. Shifting from aggression to patient coaching is easier said than done. We worked hard at improving this part of our job in the 1990s, and I think we got much better at it. We were ill prepared for what awaited us in Iraq in 2003, but our failures weren't from lack of trying, rather from a great deal of bad and misleading information and from the myopic hubris of an inexperienced commander in chief and his neoconservative handlers.

★ ★

In the days after the fighting, we were given time to rest and recuperate. The focus was on getting our positions along the demilitarized zone up to snuff and then rotating troops to the United Arab Emirates for a little R & R. We were stranded in the deep desert for about two weeks and then were ordered to redeploy to the Safwan area, which is where the peace talks would occur. I couldn't wait to get back to civilization, any civilization, it didn't matter; all my senses craved the fresh stimulation of a city. We had spent almost a month in a place where there was nothing at all but sand and sky—everywhere you looked, in every single direction. It had been almost impossible to maintain any sense of place in this formless desert landscape, and it left you feeling lost, unmoored, entirely out of context, a random dot within the vastness of infinity.

For several months I had slept in this formless infinity on the front cover of my Hummer or on a cot, and I longed now for the feel of a real bed and clean sheets against my sand- and sunburned skin. For months the only entertainment I'd had was talking to other people and eating with them. Meals were hands-down the highlight of every day, and they served as milestones, too, a way of measuring the passing of time, and of keeping track of how close we were to finishing the ordeal. That's not to say we ate well. We ate MREs and T-rations (vacuum-packed meals designed to last a half a century—yes, fifty years). And not only was the food bad, but occasional distribution problems sometimes caused disruptions in supply, and we ended up eating the same thing several days in a row. In February, we ate vacuum-packed chicken breasts and sweet potatoes the whole month straight, three meals a day, because of a distribution problem in the rear.

With much time on our hands and little to do, our energies turned to amusing ourselves at one another's expense, and doing a bit of sightseeing. We had all been brought up on the war stories of our fathers or grandfathers or both, almost all of which were associated with some souvenir that often acted as the touchstone of the tale. And so we figured we'd try to find some souvenirs for ourselves. The lure of souvenirs was very powerful, despite the dangers inherent in looking for them. Battlefields are extremely dangerous, even after the fighting stops, on account of unexploded ordnance and traps that may have been left undetected.

What was truly amazing was the sheer amount of destruction. The pictures on CNN didn't even begin to represent the devastation. Everywhere we went we saw hastily abandoned bunker complexes, many of them completely destroyed; mile after mile of charred vehicles, some of them unrecognizable, all evidence of just how completely overwhelmed the Iraqis had been, how they'd been caught by surprise at every turn. They just hadn't known what hit them. There were tanks with turrets blown straight off, personnel carriers with blast marks and bullet holes, mangled Jeeps with charred bodies still in them.

When we entered the bunkers that housed the chain of command, we were stunned to discover that the Iraqi army, the army the whole world thought was so formidable, was, in fact, at least ten years behind us in quality and compatibility of communications and weapons systems. It was not unlike the more recent miscalculation of Saddam's strength, though that miscalculation had far more serious consequences because it was the rationale (well, one of the rationales) for the war itself. It was the very reason we went to war, unlike August 1990, when the actual invasion of another country was the reason the United States, with a broad-based UN-sanctioned coalition, went in to oust Saddam from Kuwait. Fool me once, shame on you; fool me twice, shame on me. Seeing what the Iraqis really had we could only conclude that we had prepared for an enemy that didn't quite exist. It was like the 1990 New York Giants playing all out with a local high school football team, and it made me believe, arrogantly although the 2003 offensive would prove me right, that to go on to Baghdad would have been a cakewalk.

As for souvenirs, there were all manner of weapons lying around that soldiers snapped up and shipped home to be displayed on trophy walls all across America. A short time later new rules were instituted to restrict what could be shipped home; soldiers had been trying to send things like AK47s and presumed duds from cluster bombs, the latter of which caused several deaths when they turned out still to be live.

In addition to collecting souvenirs from along what became known as "the highway of death," the road the Iraqi army used to retreat into southern Iraq, and where the air force had destroyed several thousand vehicles, soldiers made the remnants of these ruined vehicles and bunkers that sat abandoned all along the road into what might be called "the gloating graffiti wall."

"Your army and a quarter won't buy you a cup of coffee, Saddam."

"What were you thinking?"

"Need a battalion destroyed, call B Company, Two/Sixty-seven Armor." It was funny but brutal, I thought, particularly in spots where some of the remains of Iraqi soldiers had yet to be removed, easy to locate by the swarms of flies and the horrible smell rising up from the wreckage.

As for amusing ourselves at one another's expense, literally a nonstop stream of jokes and pranks occurred throughout the day. We'd just come out of an extreme situation, after all, and the adrenaline still ran high. One of my favorites involved the service battery commander, Ron Vasquez. Ron was a good man and a dedicated officer who worked hard. He was also a little too trusting on occasion, which made him the perfect target for pranks.

One day I was sitting in my command post carrier with some of the other lieutenants, who had come by to visit.

As we were sitting there talking about the latest care packages and letters we'd gotten from home, Paul Duggan said to me: "Listen, I gotta go, one of my ammo carriers is down, and we need to get it up by tomorrow. I gotta get the parts."

"What's wrong with it?" asked Mike, who was sitting on the ramp.

"It just needs a new length of track and servicing."

"Oh, I wonder what they did before we had ammo carriers," he mused, while lying on his back staring up at the sky. "I mean, did they use special harnesses for the horses or something? You could call them stirrup modification kits maybe."

John, Paul, Dave, and I marveled at the fact that Mike didn't know the army had originally used caissons. It's practically the first thing they mention when teaching the history of the Artillery. "The Caissons Go Rolling Along" is actually the field artillery song.

"Mike, look at me, please . . . are you focused?" Paul said. Mike looked at him innocently. "Good. Now, Mikie, they say there's no such thing as a stupid question, but you, sir, have just proven them wrong. You, sir, have just asked the stupidest question I have ever heard."

Dave started to sing. " 'Over hill, over dale, as we hit the dusty trail, and those caissons go rolling along.' Sound familiar?" he asked, looking at Mike.

"Caissons, Mikie, caissons! They called them *caissons*! What, were you out sick the first day of Artillery One-oh-one or something? Geez."

"Oh, right, right," Mike said. "Caissons. I remember from the song."

"Duh . . . good, Mike, very good," Paul said, laughing. "But you know what? Now you got me thinking. We shouldn't let this opportunity go to waste," he said, and raised one finger in the air as his face lit up with malicious joy. "We should see if our esteemed service battery commander will in fact, order some . . . let's say . . . 'M109A3 stirrup modification kits,' whaddya say?"

I loved a good practical joke, so I reached for a hand microphone from one of the radios and said, "Kiowa Six, this is Gunner Six, over." Kiowa and Gunner were our Hollywood call signs. Every unit had its own call sign so that you could identify who was calling on the radio. For instance, our brigade was known as "ready first combat team." The brigade commander was known as "Ready 6," the number 6 designating the speaker's status as a commander.

"This is Kiowa Six, over," a voice crackled out of the radio.

I said, as quickly and professionally as I could without laughing, "Kiowa Six, this is Gunner Six; the new stirrup modification kits for the howitzers are in at division, and I want us to make sure that we got ours signed over before anyone else does. This is a top priority; get on it now."

"Gunner Six, Kiowa Six, roger, over."

"Gunner Six, roger, out."

And then we all burst out laughing.

"Listen," Paul said, gasping, "we gotta keep the pressure on, give him a call later and check up on him." He was holding his side from laughing so hard. Then, to John, Dave, and Mike, he said, "Come back at around four o'clock, and whatever you do keep it close hold; the commanders can't know or we'll get in trouble." He looked at me. "I hope you didn't use the command net, did you?"

"No, I used A/L," I said. A/L stands for Administrative/Logistics. If I had used the command net, the battalion commander would have known instantly and come down on all of us.

With that, Paul turned on his heel and started off, whistling the caissons song. John and Dave joined in, too, and soon Mike joined them grudgingly as they walked off, in mock seriousness. I couldn't believe they knew the words.

Then it's hi! hi! hee!
In the field artillery,
Shout out your numbers loud and strong,
For where e'er you go,
You will always know
That the caissons go rolling along.

The four of them looked hilarious marching across the sand singing this old song, John and Dave arm in arm, Paul and Mike shadowboxing back and forth behind them.

At four o'clock, not only did my original four co-conspirators show up, but also seven more lieutenants from various nooks and crannies of the battalion. I was lucky that my boss was off attending a meeting at headquarters. Had he been around, he would have surely noticed the large group of Hummers parked next to my track.

Once everybody was in place I picked up the radio again.

"Kioiwa Six, this is Gunner Six, over."

There was a long silence, and some of the guys started laughing. Finally, he answered, "Kiowa Six, over," but he seemed a little tentative. I worried that he was on to us and was now just trying to figure out who was tormenting him.

"This is Gunner Six," I said loudly, trying to sound brisk and impatient. "I would like an update on the stirrup modification kits, over."

There was another long pause, and Paul started whistling the caissons song again; soon most of the group joined him.

"This is Kiowa Six," I said, cracking up, placing my hand over the mouthpiece for a second to prevent the guy from hearing the whistling. Paul stopped, made a cutting motion across his neck, and the whistling stopped abruptly. I cleared my throat and then continued, "I went to division, and they didn't have the paperwork ready yet, over."

The whistling now had been replaced by hoots of laugher, and Paul was trying to get everybody to shut up. I figured this would be a good time to press him a little bit more to make sure Vasquez wasn't just playing along.

"Kiowa," I said, deepening my voice, "this is Gunner Six. I am not happy at all. My guidance to you was to get ahead of the power curve and get this done. I was talking with Thunder Six, and he says he got some of his already, so what seems to be the problem? Do I have to give this mission to someone more capable?" I had raised my voice just a little, to sound as though I was starting to get angry.

"Roger, Gunner Six . . . I'll get right on it . . . I'm sorry, over."

"This is Gunner Six . . . Okay, but I want you to give me an update at command and staff tonight. Gunner Six out."

At around seven that night, Paul and I were enjoying our MREs and talking about the upcoming NFL draft when our commander's Hummer pulled into the battery area. We'd decided not to bring up the prank, figuring it would be safer simply to wait for him to mention it. Captain Hart walked toward us, and, as he entered my vehicle, we both stood up.

"Sit, sit, guys . . . so how's it going?"

"Good, sir . . . how about with you? How was command and staff?" Paul asked brightly.

"The usual stuff . . . I have a couple of issues that I need each of you to run down over the next couple of days. I'll tell you when I get it organized."

"Sure, sir, whatever you want," I said.

"One other thing . . . something strange happened at the meeting tonight," Hart said, looking at Paul and me intently, as if searching for something.

"Sir?" I said, trying to sound as innocent as possible.

"Captain Vasquez got up to brief the battalion commander about . . . what did he call it? . . . stirrup kits . . . I don't know what he called it. Anyway, the colonel looked at him like he had a dick growing out of his forehead and asked him what he was talking about. Ron told him that he had called him and told him to find out about these kits . . . said he got pretty upset with Ron, too, because one of the other battalions got theirs before us." He stopped and waited, still watching our reactions carefully.

"Is Captain Vasquez all right? That sounds like very strange behavior," Paul said, somehow able to keep a straight face.

"Sir, I have no idea what you're talking about," I said, realizing I sounded a little defensive and strange, and hoping he hadn't picked up on my tone of my voice.

"Well, Gunner Six thinks someone may have pulled a joke on Kiowa Six. Like some of the lieutenants . . . did you hear anything?"

"No sir . . . we've been here the whole day and everything has been very quiet," Paul said flatly.

"Yes, sir, it was very quiet," I said, turning away to take a swig of my Parmalat milk.

"Okay . . . but the colonel is very interested in finding out who did this, so let me know if you hear anything." With that, he turned around and walked down the ramp and back to his tent.

Fortunately no one in command ever discovered who'd played the prank on Kiowa 6. And the phrase "stirrup modification kits" became a long-running joke for anything unimaginably stupid.

CHAPTER SEVENTEEN

Greg in Scarsdale

I returned to the States in 1992. After four years of travel and adventure—Europe, the war—I was happy and relieved to be home again, to be a foreigner no longer, to be around other Americans— New Yorkers especially—who spoke English. I hadn't quite realized just how much I'd missed it all, especially the city itself.

But the country had changed. The bonhomie and muscular confidence of the Reagan era had finally run its course, and there was a feeling of angst and frustration in the city that seemed almost palpable. A feeling of uncertainty was just beginning to grip the military as well, as the post–cold war era really got under way. The lack of an enemy meant that for the first time in fifty years the military was bereft of a specific purpose. It was clear that some major adjustments would need to be made.

While the military and the country in general may have been suffering from a lack of "the vision thing," I was returning home with my confidence at an all-time high. My four years overseas had been very successful. There was little doubt in my mind that I'd be promoted to captain. With my second tour of duty about to begin, I was bursting with confidence. But this was a major crossroads. I'd finished the debt incurred through the ROTC program, had fulfilled my obligation of four years, and now I had to decide whether or not I wanted to make a career in the army.

I didn't have to dwell on this for very long, I knew how much I still loved being a soldier. I loved getting up and going to work every day, and I was good at what I did. And though I'd been through a lot, not the least of which was a major conflict in the Persian Gulf, I still approached my job and army life in general with almost the same amount of boyish exuberance as I'd had when I first signed up. A part of me was convinced that I'd stay as long as they would have me, and that I could continue to ignore my personal feelings and desires, or at the very least, keep them safely compartmentalized, and still achieve professionally. And in my more confident moments I maintained that perhaps the ideal life I'd dreamed of, with a wife and kids and the whole bit, was still possible after all.

But another part of me was now fully convinced that that just wasn't going to happen, that my sexuality was fixed, that nothing was going to change. I was attracted to men—that's just the way it was and the way it was going to be. My sexuality was, I realized during more lucid moments, something I *was*—essentially, constitutionally—it was the unchanging background color on the canvas of my life. All manner of things could be sketched onto that canvas, but the color of the canvas itself would never alter.

And maybe it didn't matter. I think having been to war allowed me to have a bit more compassion for myself. After all, did I really have anything left to prove? I'd met the greatest test of manhood there is, fighting in combat, and I'd passed—I'd done very, very well. I had done my duty. More than anything, I'd proved it to myself, I'd passed my own test, met my own standard. Having done that, I'd begun to wonder if the sacrifices I was making needed to continue indefinitely.

The very night I returned home from Europe, my grandmother took a call for me. I was fast asleep, jet-lagged. In the morning she told me a "young man by the name of Greg" had phoned. I couldn't believe it. He hadn't left a number, so I called Doubleday and was given the number of the Scarsdale store. Apparently he was now managing that branch.

"Doubleday Bookshops. Greg speaking, how may I help you?"

"Torso!" I yelled into the receiver.

"Jeff? McGowan?"

"The one and only," I said.

"Oh, my God. How weird is that? It was totally a whim last night. I had no idea you'd just got home. I was having a few beers, and I thought about you and . . . I wasn't sure . . . I thought you might be . . ."

"Dead?"

"Well . . . I figured you'd been in the war, but—"

"I'm still kicking," I said. "But I'm surprised you called. I thought you'd never want to speak to me again, after the way I treated you."

"We were kids, Jeff; that was seven years ago," he said. I was surprised at how much I enjoyed hearing his voice again. He sounded exactly the same. It felt as if we hadn't missed a beat, as if the years apart had suddenly vanished and we'd spoken on the phone just last night, after having left work together and hanging out in Grand Central, holding hands secretly beneath the fading vaulted ceiling of the old train station.

I had nothing to do that day, so I decided to take the train up to Scarsdale to see him. My grandmother didn't drive, and I, of course, hadn't yet had the time to buy a car. A few hours later I was walking through the open door of the tiny bookstore next to the old Lord & Taylor on White Plains Road in Westchester. The store was empty but for a tiny old woman going through a stack of travel books next to the cash register. I asked for Greg, and she hurried toward the back and disappeared into a small stockroom. Greg walked out briskly, all smiles. He looked pretty much the same, maybe a little thinner, a finer pair of pants, perhaps, a more expensive tie. We shook hands and did one of those uncomfortable halfway hugs.

"You can cover for me, Rita? We'll be in the back."

"Go on," the old woman said, waving her hand dismissively.

"She's a barrel of laughs," I said, as Greg closed the sliding wooden door behind us in the little stockroom.

"She's great, actually," Greg said. "The best." He tapped out a Marlboro Light from a box of cigarettes sitting on a stack of *Millie's Book* paperbacks, the Christmastime bestseller of that year written in the voice of the First Dog, Millie. "As dictated by Barbara Bush," it said on the cover.

Lighting the cigarette, he turned and was now facing me directly. I was stunned to discover that all the chemistry was still there. We tried to get a conversation going, but we seemed to be too distracted by each other, our bodies were like magnets, and soon I had my arms wrapped around his thin frame and we were kissing.

The thin wooden door started to rattle and then slide open, and we jumped apart. Rita hurried in. "Excuse me, fellas, but all of Scarsdale seems to want *Millie* in paperback today." She picked up the small stack of the little book with Barbara Bush in blue, holding Millie, the presidential cocker spaniel, and standing on a White House balcony. "Give me a drag of that," she said, resting the stack on her hip and reaching out to take Greg's cigarette. She took a deep hit and said, "Cute dog, but honestly, it's just a little silly, in my view." Little puffs of cigarette smoke came out of her mouth with every other word.

"The perfect gift for the Scarsdale lady who has everything," Greg said.

"You know, she's a Rye girl," Rita said, referring to Rye, New York, the First Lady's hometown, which wasn't far from Scarsdale.

"Yes, I know, Rita, you've told me," Greg said.

Rita chuckled and hustled herself, the stack of *Millie* in hand, back out onto the sales floor.

Greg closed the door. He was smiling sheepishly now. "It's probably for the best that she came in, Jeff."

"And why would that be true?" I asked, moving toward him again.

It was so strange, how normal it felt for us to be doing this so soon after seeing each other again.

"Let's take a walk outside," Greg said.

★ ★

It was an unusually mild afternoon in late October. The trees in front of the white Lord & Taylor building were shining bright orange and red and yellow in the autumn sunlight. Greg seemed a little nervous. He was virtually chain-smoking. He asked me about the war and Germany and Europe and the army, and I told him all about everything I'd been going through the last few years. I'd forgotten how easy it was to talk to him, and as we walked through the winding Scarsdale streets (down one called Winding Lane, in fact, Greg made a joke about it) I couldn't help thinking about our time together seven years before.

"So why was it a good thing that your clerk came in and busted us up?" I asked him, as we reached Scarsdale Village and the Christmas-tree train station.

"I've got the virus, Jeff," Greg said quickly, looking away.

We hadn't talked about AIDS at all. I realized then that part of the feeling of angst and frustration I'd sensed upon returning to New York had to do with the fact that the epidemic had by that time cut a huge swath of devastation across the city. Especially in the gay community, of course. Add to that a crack epidemic and a crime rate setting new records daily (this was pre-Giuliani), and it's no wonder the city seemed desperate. And now Greg seemed desperate, too, and I wanted so much to be able to help him.

"Oh, Greg," I said, "I'm so—"

"It's okay, don't say anything. I'm not sick or anything now so . . . who knows . . . some people don't progress to full-blown AIDS; maybe I'll be one of the lucky ones."

"When did you find out?"

"Back in 1990," he said.

Walking back to the store, he told me all about his last few years, how hard it had been finding out, but how he'd tried to keep things in perspective and to keep on writing (he wrote short stories and was obsessive about keeping a journal). I felt terrible, but he remained so upbeat that after a while it rubbed off on me and I relaxed. When we hugged good-bye outside the store, I almost burst into tears. But he kept it fraternal, made it quick and not too close, and then kind of pushed me away, as if he couldn't bear being too close to me. We promised to stay in touch, but we didn't. After about a year I simply could not try to get back in touch with him anyway; I feared learning that he'd died. And then after a few more years I just assumed that he was dead, and I regretted never having properly apologized to him for the way I'd treated him way back in 1985, when we were both so young and had our whole lives still so much in front of us.

Seeing Greg again reaffirmed some of the changes going on inside me. And during that brief period between Germany and Fort Bragg, I managed to begin to see, for the first time in my life, the faintest glimmer of the possibility of life outside the military as an openly gay man. For the first time I didn't instantly slam the door on that idea when it presented itself to me, though I did still close it, of course. However, I had no details; the possibility was so vague as to be virtually meaningless. I didn't know how even to begin to think about my life as a gay man in an authentic way, in a way disconnected from the most typical preconceptions and stereotypes. And AIDS terrified me, of course. As a result, these fresh thoughts I had during quiet moments after my return from Europe and seeing Greg again remained strictly that—quiet and unexplored. The reality of army life still had no room for this, and I still wasn't ready to leave. Changes were coming with the new president and the new era he'd usher in, but for now things were the same as they'd always been: one bad move and you were out. For now I'd hunker down and wait. Besides, my new assignment was at Fort Bragg, so an old dream was finally about to come true.

CHAPTER EIGHTEEN

Flying Watermelons
and Platinum Blondes

I made the thirteen-hour drive down to Fort Bragg in my Toyota on the day of the 1992 presidential election. I had spent several wonderful weeks visiting my grandmother and friends, and I was ready to get back to work. I'd been assigned to the First Battalion of the 319th Airborne Field Artillery Regiment (AFAR). I'd finally get to become a paratrooper!

I already had Airborne wings, having earned them at the basic Airborne course at Fort Benning, but there's an important distinction here. Though I'd completed the course by doing five jumps successfully, and I'd been given the honorific "five-jump chump," I was not yet a paratrooper. And I say that emphatically because being a paratrooper meant being part of a very special and elite community, with a culture all its own. To be a paratrooper was to be a member of the first unit that would respond when the president dialed 911. Anybody could get the wings; not everybody could serve in an airborne unit. I was on my way to meeting the challenge of becoming a part of that unique culture.

On the drive down I-95 I listened to the election results as they came in and couldn't believe what was happening. Things weren't going all that well in the country—that I knew—but I hadn't seriously believed Bush the elder would be a one-term president. Now it looked as if that might be a real possibility.

Even as I tried to wrap my mind around the idea, I didn't have a clue, of course, just how much things would change once Clinton was elected. He seemed so radically different from any of the five presidents I'd known in my lifetime (I was only four when LBJ decided not to run in 1968). My impression of Clinton had been almost uniformly negative, though this would change over time. As the hours passed, and the polls closed, and results trickled in, it became clear that the old guard was out and a whole new show was coming to town. Little did I know how much this change would directly affect the military and my own life.

I was exhausted after the thirteen-hour drive, so when I arrived at Fort Bragg I checked in to the visiting officers' quarters, Moon Hall, and soon found myself out cold in my room. I would stay at Moon Hall for another couple of days while I found an apartment and got settled in.

Once I was all set up, the first thing I had to do was take the airborne refresher course. Basically, it was a whole week of dealing with the parachute—how to put it on and so forth, how to rig personal equipment, and a review of aircraft procedures in general. This was immediately followed by my first jump in almost five years. The first jump in the division was always a day jump as well as a "Hollywood" jump, which meant that I'd jump without a weapon or rucksack. Like my first five jumps at the basic course, it was actually a "night" jump since I closed my eyes as I exited the plane as well as for most of the way down, but I got to the ground safely.

The next major event was the propblast ceremony, an elaborate ritual that every new officer has had to go through since it was first established during World War II. It is a rite of passage that makes you a part of the family—a "made guy," if you will. Originally, the newly minted paratrooper would simply toast the Airborne with a drink specially made for the occasion, then do a parachute landing fall (PLF) from a table. A PLF is the method used to land so as to avoid breaking your back. It basically means hitting the ground and rolling, not trying to land standing up. Over time this simple toast and little mock PLF had morphed into an elaborate ritual that could take several days to complete.

The propblast was scheduled for early December, and it would be a two-day event. The first day was a written exam on Airborne history, the second day was a practical exam. I passed the written with no problem and was told to report at three-thirty the following morning at the track across from our headquarters.

From the minute we arrived, the officers in charge peppered us with verbal abuse. The first event was a PT session that involved repeated sets of push-ups, followed by pulling a sled around the field loaded up with as many of the cadre as possible, all of them showering us nonstop with insults and abuse. That was followed by a nice roll in several large mud puddles covered in ice. For good measure we then had a good forty-five-minute session of rolling up and down the hills on either side of the track. By about six A.M. we were finished with PT and about to begin the gunnery portion of the day. After we were driven out to one of the firing points on the western ranges, we began unlimbering fully rigged howitzers as part of a competition to see which team could do it faster. We then spent the morning firing rounds. All throughout, any infraction—some real, some made up—resulted instantly in a flood of extreme verbal abuse and plenty more push-ups.

By noon I was exhausted and had started to feel resentful. The whole process reminded me vaguely of some of the things we used to do at the frat house back at Fordham. Later on, after the Marine hazing incidents made headlines, the tradition of propblast along with all other hazing rituals throughout the military were banned. For now, though, I had to keep my chin up and get through the rest of this day so I'd be able to add my name to the book we all signed at the end, the book that every propblast "graduate" had signed for the last fifty years.

The afternoon's festivities were held where the Airborne refresher course had taken place, the most notable feature of which was a pair of thirty-two-foot-high towers, with cables extending from each to anchor on a fifteen-foot-high berm some one hundred feet away. Jumping from these towers while attached to a cable was supposed to mimic the feel of jumping from an airplane. If you can jump at thirty-two feet, the thinking goes, you can jump at 850 feet. Not everyone was convinced, but that was the idea.

We were to be graded on our exits. This was supposed to be a pretty straightforward process. The grader would check to see that your elbows were tight against your sides and your feet and knees were together when you landed. Of course nothing was really straightforward that day, because the graders were intent on making the whole process as difficult as possible.

I was getting it worse than most on account of one particular captain who seemed to take sadistic joy in busting my balls. Basically, he followed me closely the whole day just waiting for me to fuck up. I'd met him when I'd first arrived and was still staying in Moon Hall. One of my buddies from Germany had invited me to join him and two other people for dinner. The two other people turned out to be the sadistic captain, who had been commanding headquarters battery at the time, and his longtime girlfriend, a tall, striking platinum blonde who drove a white Corvette. What I didn't know at the time was that the sadistic captain, whose name was Ron, was on the verge of breaking up with the platinum blonde, whose name was Ruth.

We had a good time that night, at least my friend from Germany and Ruth and I did. Ron was quiet and withdrawn all night, though he watched the three of us intently all through dinner. At the end of the evening, Ruth said that she couldn't remember the last time she'd had so much fun and that she wanted both our phone numbers. Normally we would've balked at this point since she was Ron's girlfriend, but the way she asked seemed innocent enough, so we gave them to her.

About a week later, she called, said that she and Ron had broken up, and explained that her birthday was coming up and she wanted me to come to the party she was throwing the following Friday. I said sure.

So I went, expecting to do nothing other than socialize. It was a nice enough party, mostly army guys and their wives. Around eleven I figured I'd call it a night and made to leave; suddenly Ruth appeared, looking distressed.

"Why are you leaving so early?" she asked. "Aren't you having a good time?"

"Oh no, Ruth," I said. "I had a great time, thanks, just tired, that's all. Thought I'd start heading home."

"Well, okay, funny man," she said, smiling. "I . . . guess that's all right, but am I gonna see you again soon? Do you want to go to dinner, maybe next week?"

The following week we went to dinner and were having a great time until about halfway through the meal when she got very serious and started telling me about her relationship with Ron and how difficult it had been and how he hadn't been very nice to her. I suddenly felt awkward and said nothing, sensing that she just needed to talk. When it appeared she was through, I tried to lighten things up, but she wanted to know all about me and my past. I told her about my childhood in Jackson Heights, about my grandparents, about Fordham and ROTC and Germany and the war. When she asked about girlfriends, I lied and said I still had one in Frankfurt. I did this not only to conceal my sexuality but also because I had no intention of dating a fellow captain's ex just two weeks after they'd broken up. She took it pretty well, and we finished the night on a light note.

The day before the written exam, Ron walked up to me in the hall. "So I heard you went out to dinner with Ruth the other night," he said.

"Hey Ron, how's it going?" I said, kind of taken by surprise. "Yeah, she's nice. Ruth is a nice girl. We had a good time."

"I think it's fucked up," he said, and with that he walked away.

So it was actually no surprise when I realized that this guy was planning on busting my balls throughout the entire propblast ceremony. But after about ten hours of it, ten hours of his screaming at me about how weak and worthless I was, making me do things twice, three times, I was starting to get pissed. As I completed my first jump from the tower, I heard him yelling over a bullhorn.

"Blastee McGowan, that was the most fucked exit I've ever seen. Get back to the tower immediately and do it again."

He was sitting on an elevated chair that looked like the kind of lifeguard chair you'd find on Coney Island or Riis Beach, kicked back, self-consciously relaxed, looking up at me with what I imagined was a malicious gleam in his eyes. As I got out of the harness and ran back to the tower, I heard him yelling again.

"Blastee McGowan, go to the head of the line. Go to the head of the line now and wait for me there."

I did as I was told, cursing him under my breath, and by the time I was fully rigged again, he'd arrived and pulled me off to the side and started pulling at my harness.

"Well, Blastee, it looks to me like your harness is too loose. Shall we tighten it up a bit?"

He made me tighten the harness so tight that it bit into my shoulders and thighs.

"Okay, Blastee McGowan, I think that will do. It looks right now. You can't do much right, can you, fuckface? Now listen, listen up, you jump only when I am grading you, got that? Do not jump for the other graders, only me, pal, got it?"

"Whatever," I said. I felt like punching him in the face. I was really beginning to lose it with him, but the day was supposed to be about mental toughness and fighting wasn't allowed, so I bit my

tongue and did what he wanted, waiting until he was in position before getting ready to jump again.

In a few minutes there was one guy in front of me, then I was next
up. One of the captains came up to me and whispered quietly in my
ear.

"See that watermelon?" he asked.

"Yeah."

"We were going to have you guys jump with it and whoever
dropped it would have to carry it around with him for the rest of the
day, but since Ron has been such a total prick all day long, especially
to you, we've decided that you should dive-bomb him with the watermelon. Whaddya think?"

"Yeah, but won't I hurt him?" At that point I hardly cared if I
hurt him, but I thought I should ask anyway. I was fired up to do it
right away.

"I don't think so," the captain said. "Joe's there now to distract
him, and he knows it's coming."

"Cool," I said. "Done." I couldn't wait to see the expression on
that fuck's face as the watermelon exploded all over him.

He was on the bullhorn again, yelling for me to hurry up, when
Joe distracted him and the captain handed me the watermelon and I
jumped. I held on to it for a second, trying to aim it perfectly, and then
let fly. As I dropped from the tower I watched the watermelon fly
through the air in a beautiful arc, smacking dead center on the floor-
board of Ron's chair. *Splat!* Ron had just started turning his head back
from Joe when it hit. His face and body were completely splattered.
He was so startled that he slipped and nearly fell out of his seat. Hanging safely now in my harness, I looked over to see him pulling himself
up and wiping all the wet red flesh and slimy, black seeds out of his
eyes and nose. The whole unit exploded into laughter and applause;
there were whistles and shouts, and I joined along. It felt as if a huge
burden had just been lifted off everybody's shoulders. Ron tried to

maintain his dignity, collecting himself quickly, though comically, since there were still big chunks of watermelon on his uniform and in his hair. He then ran over to where I was hanging helplessly in the harness.

"What the fuck, you could've fucking killed me. I oughtta kick your fucking ass."

"Fuck you," I said, not caring about anything now. "Let me outta this harness, you dumb motherfucker, and I'll beat your ass from one end of this field to the other."

But at that moment a couple of the other captains intervened and pulled Ron away and helped me out of my harness. It was time to go. There was still the evening portion of the ceremony to prepare for. I rejoined the others. Everyone was high-fiving me, and all the energy had returned to the group. As we formed up, ready to march away, Ron trotted over and said, so that only I would hear, "Remember, I still have tonight, fuckface!"

"Fuck off," I said, and we marched away.

The final phase took place in a classroom away from the unit area. The room was draped in camouflage netting, and seats were placed in neat rows as if in a theater. In front of the seats were two tables with large cushy chairs, where the senior officers sat. This was all facing a mock-up of a C-130 chassis that had been built especially for the occasion. The idea was that the blastees would do their fake PLFs and then report to the president of the board to answer questions. If we answered all the questions correctly, we were inducted. The kicker was that the plates of the door of the mock C-130 were metal and were electrified, so as you took up a position in the door and put your hands on the plates, you would be zapped with current.

It was pretty much guaranteed that you were going to go through at least twice. It was also pretty much guaranteed that two other officers would hold your hands to the plates to make sure that you got a full dose of electric current.

As we put on the harnesses, and waited to be called forward, in walked Ron with a smug look on his face. He walked directly over to me.

"Hello, Blastee, remember me? It's going to be a long, long night for you. I hope you realize that. You got it?"

"I'll be thinking of Ruth's pussy the entire time. It was nice and tight; guess a guy like you doesn't give a girl much of a workout," I said, looking down at his crotch. I never talked this way, but I was trying to speak his language, and I think I was succeeding.

The look on his face changed instantly from smug superiority to cold, deep, unmistakable hatred. It startled me almost, the malice in it. He looked as though he was going to attack me, though I knew he couldn't. So just to piss him off more, I broke into a large grin and stood there staring right into his face. He stared back for a second, then turned and walked out of the dressing area to take up his position in the door of the mock chasis.

As he reenacted the procedures for preparing the door for exiting troops, the room filled with excited chatter as the men anticipated the next several hours of ballbusting. As the first officer went up to the door and put his hands on the electrified plates, he let out a grunt, trying hard to remain composed. After about a minute or so, he was allowed to exit the chasis and do his PLF. When he reported to the president of the board, he was asked several questions that I couldn't hear, and for a moment it looked as though he might make it. But there was a loud whoop as he crashed and burned and was sent back to us. And so it went for the next several attempts. Basically, everyone had to go through once before the process could move forward.

When my turn came, I stepped into the door and put my hands on the plates, where they were immediately held firmly in place. Being electrocuted is a hard feeling to describe; it hurts but in a very non-specific way. It also seemed that it would never end, even though it was only a minute or so It stopped as suddenly as it began, and as I regained my wits, I executed a PLF into a kiddie pool filled with water, which I could not see because of the spotlights shining from behind the board members. I slipped and fell in the water and struggled to get up quickly to report, all the while being hooted and hollered at.

Once up and standing at the position of attention, I reported to Colonel Mastrianni, who was the division artillery commander at the time. He was an interesting character if ever there was one. In his mid-forties and in superb shape, he was able to run a six-minute mile, thus outrunning the entire officer corps. He was also something of a psychopath, known for screaming like a maniac whenever he came upon something he didn't like. He made life in the DIVARTY (Division Artillery) pretty miserable, as he ruthlessly enforced his standards. He was the type of boss whom everyone hates.

In fairness, though, despite Mastrianni's harshness, I have to say that the DIVARTY and, for that matter, the Eighty-second Airborne Division as a whole were at an extremely high level of readiness and competence at the time. Commanders like Mastrianni, and many of the other brigade commanders under the exceptional leadership of Major General Hugh Shelton, challenged soldiers at every level to push themselves to the limit in training. The Eighty-second always has on standby a unit able to deploy anywhere in the world within eighteen hours, so it takes a certain unique brand of toughness and readiness to fulfill that mission.

Anyway, after I had spat out the blurb that everyone said when he reported to the board, there was a brief pause as I stared helplessly into the lights being flashed in my face.

"Good evening, Blastee McGowan," Mastrianni said. "Tell me all the brigades in the division and what their flashes are."

I began to respond, and I actually got pretty far along, but then suddenly I drew a blank. As I paused, I heard a voice coming at me from the left of Colonel Mastrianni.

"Could you sing us a song? A joke maybe?" I didn't recognize the voice.

I immediately launched into the "All American" song, which is the song of the division. Whenever it's sung, everyone must stand and join in. Toward the end of the song, the exhaustion of the long day was beginning to hit me, and I had trouble keeping up. When we finished, everyone sat down and Colonel Mastrianni spoke.

"Well, Blastee McGowan, I don't know if that will do. It appeared to me that you were lip-synching!" There was a low buzz of hisses and mock grumblings of "Shame!" and "I can't believe it!"

"Sir, may I speak?'" The officious voice of CPT Ron Pierce interjected.

"Yes, Jump Master?"

"Obviously this blastee is not prepared for this evening. May I recommend remedial jump training for him? Maybe it will jog his memory?"

"A little bit of electroshock therapy might do the trick. All right then, send him through again."

That fucking asshole Pierce. If only he knew how misplaced his anger was. If only he knew how stupid he was being! So threatened by a guy who'd never lay a hand on his big-breasted, platinum blonde, white-Corvette-driving ex-girlfriend because that guy had *zero* interest in touching any woman, big tits or otherwise. The funny thing was, though, at that moment I was so pissed off at Ron that I thought about dating Ruth and sleeping with her just to get back at him. But I knew I'd never do that.

So I simply turned, remounted the mock-up, and submitted to being electrocuted twice more, then graded on my exit and PLF. As I returned to the setup area, I was definitely wide-awake now and pretty pissed off. I would go through the door three more times before I was invited to drink from the propblast cup. Once you were offered the drink, you had to chug it down in one gulp, and then everyone congratulated you. When we were all finished, we lined up to sign the book and receive our card and coin. It was handshakes from everyone then, and pats on the back, and finally the propblast ceremony was over.

I had passed another milestone, and was now officially a part of the division with which I had wanted to serve from the time I was in college. After a very long day of bullshit, I wanted to crawl into bed and sleep for a couple of days at least, doing my best to make sure not to dream about CPT Ron Pierce or big-breasted platinum blondes.

CHAPTER NINETEEN

The Bible and Bulgogi

I had just started my new job as the battalion's logistics officer, or S-4, when I found myself visiting the headquarters on some routine piece of business. I decided to stop into the operations office to say hello to a few buddies of mine. As soon as I entered the room, I realized I'd stepped right into a heated discussion about gays in the military. At that time everyone was talking about it. President Clinton had wasted no time putting the issue on the table, but even though both the House and Senate were controlled by the Democrats, an all-out repeal of the ban didn't seem likely, especially considering the Pentagon's own extreme opposition to the idea.

"Goddamn gay guys," Captain Fred Jones was saying, "they can't serve. Somebody will end up killing one of them," he continued, as if that hadn't already happened. "And what about the shower situation? I mean, I don't know about you, but I don't want to be showering with guys who like checking out my hoohaw." Jones was speaking in his typically intense way, which I'd grown accustomed to. It was nothing by halves for Fred Jones.

Captain Andy Loughlin agreed. "Yeah, yeah," he said. "I can only imagine the nightmare it would cause. You know . . . I bet they'll end up having one of those special months, you know, like Black History Month, faggot month, right, gay guy month, and can you imagine the sensitivity training we'd have to endure? And where would they live? I mean, they wouldn't live with us, would they? They'd have to build, like, separate housing for them. And how much would that cost? Millions just to house the homos!" He kicked back and put his feet up on the desk.

Maybe "discussion" was too kind. Shooting the shit was more like it.

Fred looked up at me, "What's up, Jeff?" he said. "How's it going?"

"Good, good, what are you two meatballs up to?"

"We're talking about gays in the military." Fred sneered, twisting his face as if someone were yanking hairs from his forearm.

"I heard," I said.

"I mean, really," Andy said, exasperated, "what are they thinking? I bet most gay guys wouldn't even want to join. And what about the security risk thing?"

Fred looked at me, grinning. "What do you think, McGowan?"

I took a bite out of the apple I had with me, then said, chewing, "Hadn't really thought about it." I took another bite of the apple and said, "I don't think it'll happen, though."

"I mean how the hell do you find love in another man's asshole?" Andy asked. "It's like making love to a garbage pail. Dis-gus-ting!"

"You mind there, Andy? I'm eating," I said.

Fred laughed. "Well," he said, with an I-told-you-so tone in his voice, "that's what you get when you have somebody who never served in charge. I think all that time not inhaling twisted his way of thinking or something. Doesn't matter, though, the generals won't let it happen. My buddy up at division says his boss told him they're working the issue real close in Washington. Ole Bubba there doesn't have enough credibility to do this, especially if Powell says no. It's a safety issue. They're afraid somebody would kill 'em. If you ask me, they don't belong here. This just isn't their world." Fred said this last bit with such absolute certainty that it chilled me. Up until that point I'd been hearing "they" and "them" as if those words didn't include me.

"What's wrong with you?" Andy said, looking at me quizzically.

"Ah, I'm just tired. I had a jump last night," I said lamely, finishing the apple and tossing the core into the tin pail next to the desk.

"Where'd you jump?" Fred said.

"Camp Mackall—Rhine Luzon—it's always a bitch. Twenty-one seconds of green light I almost went into the trees."

"Now see," Andy said, leaping to his feet, "that's exactly what I'm talking about. Just imagine what some faggot would do if he got caught in the trees. Ooh, ooh . . . help me, help me. I think I broke a nail . . . ooh, ooh!" He pranced around the office like a mincing queen on Dexedrine. "See what I'm saying?" he went on, his face red now, his breath oddly labored. "I mean, what is this world coming to? Can you tell me what the fuck is going on here? They are actually thinking seriously about faggots, *faggots* in the military. Well, not in my army, Bub, not in my army! It's that damn Clinton dude. No way would this have ever happened under Reagan."

"What the hell is goin' on here? What's all this bullshit? Shouldn't you be crankin' on the training schedules?" Major Mark Crist had suddenly appeared in the doorway. He was only half serious, looking for an excuse to take a break, apparently. Crist was a West Pointer and a good guy. I liked him a lot.

"Just talking about our commander in chief's desire to let the faggots in," Fred said, chortling.

"Don't get all worked up; it isn't going to happen," Crist said confidently. "You'd have to change the UCMJ, and it takes Congress to do that. The army has a lot of friends there. Do you honestly think Helms or Strom Thurmond would even let it get a vote? They'd die before that happened. Besides, nobody wants to see homos getting beaten to death splashed all over the front page of the newspaper. Let 'em go be hairdressers and actors, no problem, but soldiers? No. I remember this one time when I was a lieutenant at Fort Hood and one of the duty officers was making his rounds and he caught two privates screwing in a trash Dumpster. We couldn't get 'em out quick enough; they must have had three or four fights each, waiting to be chaptered. Nope, no way, it's just never gonna happen."

"Damn right it isn't," Andy said. "And what about AIDS? I really think Falwell's onto something with that. It's not natural, and God's taking revenge." He leaned back with a self-satisfied look on his face. Both Major Crist and Fred were smiling sheepishly, though Crist's smile was tinged with an unmistakable discomfort.

I couldn't hold my tongue any longer. "That has to be one of the stupidest things I've ever heard. Andy, God does not give people AIDS because they're gay."

"Oh yes, he does, my friend," Andy said, taking on a serious, almost scholarly tone. "It's how he marks them for hell. It says it in the Bible. You need to read your Old Testament, McGowan."

I hadn't yet learned that trying to engage this kind of thinking is futile, that, in fact, to engage it is to dignify it in a manner it doesn't even begin to deserve. "Give me the chapter and verse, Andy," I said. "Where exactly in the Old Testament does it say that God will give you AIDS if you're gay? And besides, a lot of people sin every day, does that mean that they should get AIDS, too?"

"That sin is worse than others. It's on a whole different level. And it's in Leviticus or Judges, I'm not sure, one of those. It doesn't talk about AIDS, McGowan. Whaddya think, it's all spelled out like a rule book or something? But it's clear what the meaning is."

"So, what about someone like, say, Hitler. Should Hitler have gotten AIDS, Andy?"

"Maybe he did. How the hell do I know what the freak did with that Eva Braun chick in the bunker."

"What about the people in Africa with AIDS? What about the starving people in Africa and India? Have they done something wrong, Andy, that God has made them suffer with starvation and get

AIDS, too? Are people dying of starvation in Somalia because they've displeased the Lord, Andy? Huh? Tell me."

"Well, I'm not saying anything, but Jeff, those aren't exactly Christian nations, if you get my drift. But let me get this straight, are you defending the homos?"

"I'm just defending clear thinking, Andy. I think you're smarter than this, and I know you're better educated than this. It's ridiculous to say shit like that. God does not hate groups of people, Andy. God doesn't hate, period."

"Are you calling me stupid, McGowan?"

Fred broke in, with a slightly bemused look on his face. "You can see them serving in the military? I mean, is that what you're saying?"

"I think that it will happen eventually, no matter what we want or think. Look at women and blacks," I said.

"Women and blacks?" Andy erupted. "Are you out of your fucking mind, McGowan? And you call *me* stupid! Women in the army is a complete and total *mess*. Should have *never* happened. Just look at how many pregnancies there are."

"Really, Andy, is that so? Tell me, what are the numbers? I haven't read anything recently."

"You know what, McGowan, I don't know the numbers, okay? I think I read it somewhere. But it doesn't matter. You know what I'm talking about. Look at all the sensitivity-training bullshit. And God forbid you should correct or discipline one of them and they're out there quicker than you can say 'cock tease,' screaming, 'Oh, sexual harassment! Oh, his tone was inappropriate. Oh, he stood too close to me!'" Andy was prancing around again in mock hysteria, speaking in the same voice as the queen on Dexedrine. "At least we don't have them in the line units; that's all I have to say," he added, taking a seat again.

"Listen," I said, hoping to put an end to the whole thing. "I don't really know what it's like in the other units with women. Never been in one. What I do know is that we win every war we go to, no matter who's in the lineup. So we must be doing something right. As for fags, I used to work with them when I was in college at a big bookstore in the city. They weren't all that bad, just people, really. It's not such a big fucking deal." As the words came out of my mouth I knew I was skating on very thin ice. I worried that I'd misjudged the whole situation, and that what I thought was just standard common sense was, in fact, only the common sense of a gay man—that a straight guy could never really have the opinions I was expressing—that I'd somehow inadvertently outed myself.

"You hung around with fags in college?" Fred said, incredulous. "What, like, were you in the Communist Party, too? I thought you went to Fordham. Those Jesuits put up with all that homo shit?" He had a big smile on his face. This was just good-natured ribbing now.

"Take it easy, nimrod. I didn't say I hung around with them, but I knew them. They were pretty normal really. I didn't actually know they were . . . homos. The bookstore had nothing to do with Fordham. And don't say anything about the Jesuits, Jones, the Jesuits know what they're doing." I was backtracking a little, and lying, of course. The image of Greg's face when he said he had HIV popped into my head. *I have the virus.*

"Listen, I say again, the only good faggot is a dead faggot," Andy said brutally, with a finality that left no doubt I'd wasted my time in trying to reason with him.

"Listen," I said, "someone once told me that fear of the unknown is usually fear of the *all too well* known."

"Are you calling me a faggot?" Andy said. His back straightened, and he pulled himself to the edge of his chair.

"Well . . . now that you mention it, I just happened to be over here yesterday and I needed a pen so I went into your desk to find one and whaddya know I found one right next to a bottle of bright pink nail polish and lipstick. I mean, Andy, it's your business after all; it's none of mine. I don't want to get personal, but I'm beginning to get the distinct impression that you're at least a half a fagola if not a whole one." I tried to inject the word *fagola* with as much Archie Bunker as I could muster. Everyone broke out laughing then, even Andy himself, and the subject was finally dropped.

Alone at home that night I couldn't help mulling over the conversation. President Clinton really had balls taking this on, I thought, but was it even remotely possible politically? I didn't think so. Still, I was learning that things could change in the most surprising ways. The cold war, for instance, and the Soviet Union, and the Berlin Wall— these were things that had seemed unchangeable, fixed forever. If in, say, 1985 someone had told me that by 1992 all three would be consigned to the dustbin of history, I would've said they were out of their minds. And remember, too, I thought, just how different things were culturally in the not-too-distant past, the 1950s, say, for women and blacks especially, and how things changed so dramatically in the 1960s and 1970s. Maybe it was possible, after all. And suddenly I could see it, or at least the possibility of it. Like a small, faint ray of light at the end of a long tunnel, the vision of a military that included every qualified American, even gay Americans, became visible to me for the first time.

But I still felt slimy from the conversation with Fred and Andy and Major Crist. In my heart, I knew I'd done my best. I'd done what could be done, under the circumstances. I'd said what could be said. But a part of me still felt cowardly, a part of me still felt that I hadn't done enough, I hadn't defended myself more vigorously and openly. But they weren't attacking me, I told myself. I was no mincing queen on Dexedrine, after all—that's who they meant, not me, but then, no, I thought, I'm wrong. It was me, too. They were attacking me as well. They just didn't know it.

I'd been in the military for a while now. And I'd pledged a fraternity in college. So it's not as if I wasn't used to run-of-the-mill faggot jokes. I'd learned how to hear those jokes in such a way that the proverbial "faggot" in each could never be me. I simply wasn't that type of gay man. The jokes were about the typical, swishy gay guy; he was the target, not me.

But what I'd listened to today was different. In the back of my mind I think I knew that Andy and Fred, and maybe Crist, too, held these strong feelings about gay men, but I'd never been confronted with them quite so viscerally before. Seeing it laid out so baldly was strange and kind of chilling. The sheer intensity of their animosity was truly astounding. Where did that come from? How much of it was fear, as so many people claimed, how much of it was truly homophobia, and how much of it was just plain old hatred? *Some* of it was just showboating for the other guys, professing a hatred of gay men in this case (*gay* is interchangeable with *weak*—the argument is almost not about sex at all, simply about a perceived lack of strength and a degree of vulnerability) as a way to kind of prove your mettle as a man. What was most interesting to me was that otherwise these three guys were pretty much perfect examples of a kind of moderate, easygoing, American male. This Jekyll-and-Hyde bit was more than a little unnerving.

They were talking about me, after all, and, I realized, though I didn't want to admit it to myself, I was hurt. It hurt me to hear them talking that way, all that mean spirit, all that bile, all that blanket rage aimed at something perceived to be weaker yet predatory at the same time. It was the strangest thing, so hard to comprehend fully. But more than anything it was just personally hurtful. I was hurt because I had been welcomed into their homes; I'd eaten dinner with their families. I was a trusted friend and colleague, and now it appeared that all of that would change if they learned the truth. But why should it? Wasn't the friend they'd come to know really me? I thought it was. And I would have done anything for those guys. I would have stood by them. In combat I had been ready to lay down my life for the men I was serving with. Would these guys do the same for me if they knew I was gay? See, Andy, I wanted to say, I didn't fall out of the tree! I didn't complain about breaking a nail! I'm *not* that kind of gay guy! I'm a man just like you! I imagined taking the three of them out for beers and coming out to them.

"Andy, Fred, Major Crist, thanks for coming and cheers." I'd start, raising my bottle of beer. "I've asked you here today to let you know something. I like men. Now, save your protestations, you shall not sway me from my preordained path. There's nothing you can say." And they'd be supportive. "No big deal, McGowan," Crist would say, "you're not one of those obvious ones, so it doesn't matter. Live and let live, that's what I say."

Who was I kidding? Andy and Fred would be shocked, that's for certain, and Major Crist would be, too, no doubt. They'd never see me in the same way again. Right before their eyes I would instantly transform into something else, something unfamiliar and strange, something they feared and hated. All the good I'd done for the unit, for the army, and for them personally as friends, would be immediately wiped away by this one revelation.

And I'd thought the war in the Gulf was a major conflict! The question was, still, How could I do what I loved and still be the person I am? I wondered then if I'd actually been a kind of traitor up until this point, collaborating to survive, so anxious to fulfill my dream of being a soldier that I'd been willing to work with people who'd actually hate me if they discovered who I truly was. "Go along and get along" was a powerful expression, and it had begun to represent for me a certain cringing mediocrity from which only the small-minded derive comfort. It is the box *inside* which every bureaucrat, every company man, and, as it turns out, every soldier ends up being forced to think. I had begun to feel like a small-minded, hypocritical bureaucrat with his head stuck firmly and deeply in the sand. "It's like a disease," Greg had warned, of hypocrisy, back in 1985. "It's like a cancer," he'd said. "It's insidious, it's going to eat you up until you're empty." I could feel it eating me up now. And what if there was a point of no return, a point at which my long years of denial would render me incapable of ever actively engaging that part of myself? Would I die a soldier, perhaps a hero, but still unloved and alone?

I reminded myself that we all have to make sacrifices, that we all have our unique cross to bear, and that I, as one man, was certainly not going to change an unjust military policy, let alone the world. What I didn't realize at the time is that change often occurs when individuals *do* take a stand. Through a simple, straightforward act, a complete nobody can make the world sit up and take notice. And even if that one person doesn't succeed, whatever he does accomplish will almost certainly make the effort easier for the next person who tries.

The conversation with Andy and Fred and Crist pushed along a process within me that had already been well under way for quite some time, and would subsequently speed up as the issue grew more pressing once the new policy was in place. My thinking was changing dramatically. That I was experiencing regret at having failed to stand up for myself adequately was evidence enough that I was growing in a wholly unexpected direction.

There was a time when I would have given barely a second thought to the conversation. Like I said, a part of me had learned to think of the "faggot" in those discussions as referring to someone other than me; the "faggot" was the stereotypical gay guy you still saw all too frequently on television and in the movies. I had never associated that guy with myself.

But now, the consciousness-raising that had started with Greg was moving forward, seemingly on its own. I'd never expected to feel so differently, but here I was. It happened so gradually, like the way the flow of water in a river shapes a stone, that I didn't notice the changes until the major moment of stumbling upon those guys discussing Clinton's policy and hearing their antigay feelings expressed so baldly. I no longer feared being sidelined or failing in my career because it just hadn't happened; I'd advanced and succeeded. I'd done well. Maybe it was time, I thought, to start taking care of myself, to start tending to my own personal needs as rigorously as I'd worked at being a good soldier.

But I wasn't yet prepared for the big leap. My identity was so wrapped up in being a soldier that I couldn't find room there for my sexuality. I still was failing to understand that a person is more than his work, that a person's identity goes far past what he does for a living, what his title is, how people address him. Change would come, but not yet. The next day I would get up and go to work, and I would interact with everyone as I always had. I would go along and get along, not making a fuss, swallowing my pride, not making waves, just so that I could continue being a soldier, so that I could continue fulfilling the dream of that little boy from Jackson Heights, Queens. That I had fulfilled that dream I had no doubt now. No one could take that from me. But I wasn't a boy any longer. I was a man, and life was complicated.

And so "Don't Ask, Don't Tell" was instituted, and I watched along with everyone else as courageous soldiers and sailors and airmen came forward to proclaim who they were on all the talk shows, only to be summarily cashiered—rejected, dishonorably discharged. It reminded me of what happened to the resistance fighters as the Germans pulled back across Eastern Europe. Thinking that a new day had dawned, they emerged only to be ruthlessly annihilated. For some reason, everyone thought the new policy would usher in a new era of freedom and openness. Nothing could have been further from the truth.

It was true that, after a considerable struggle, a compromise of sorts had been struck. It sounded somewhat promising on paper. Theoretically, it guaranteed that a soldier's private life was now off limits to a degree never seen before. But the policy was virtually meaningless in the face of the entrenched antigay culture within the military itself. Laws and rules don't change people, only people change people.

Couple this with the new realities of the post–cold war era, and you have a recipe for the discharge of massive numbers of gay people. Instead of making the military *safer* for gay service members, the new policy actually made it worse. Things were changing in major ways.

The contrast with the 1980s could not have been greater. Instead of being like a football player on steroids, to whom every wish was granted, we were now asked to slim down and make do with far less. People were dropping like flies as we were forced to shrink to a ten-division force—from just under a million to a little more than half a million. The dreaded mentality of the zero-defects army began to creep back into military culture. Being gay was decidedly a defect, no matter what the new president said. One could stick to the letter of the new gay policy, but totally disregard the spirit, and gay men and women were thrown out in record numbers as a result.

★ ★

Andy and Fred and I often had lunch together. The day after our conversation with Major Crist, we went to one of the local Korean restaurants. You could get a great, cheap (five or six bucks) meal at these places. We'd usually order the *bulgogi* and kimchee, and that day was no exception. Just when our food was being served Andy started in again on the gay issue.

"I was reading in the newspaper that the policy is going to be called 'Don't Ask, Don't Tell,' " he said. "What the fuck is that? I mean, we gotta know. How the hell is this gonna work? What if you see someone, like, going into a fag bar or something? Maybe we should just set up snipers to deal with it."

I decided I wanted to be a little more aggressive in dealing with this today, so that maybe when I went home I'd still feel as if I had some self-respect.

"Hey, Andy, the Gestapo called and wants your résumé. The CQ has the number. Looks like the concentration camp should be open soon and it will be busy," I said with a smile on my face.

"Listen, McGowan, I am not a Nazi. Just because I hate fags and want to see them dead doesn't make me a fucking Nazi. I happen to be a moral guy. I wouldn't just kill people because of their religion. We're talking about *faggots* here. Faggots are sick, pure and simple. It's like child molesters. They're total perverts and child molesters, and there's no way in fucking hell they could cut it in the Eighty-second or anywhere else, for that matter."

"Okay, help me out here," I said. "You tell me one religion or philosophy, whatever, that says hating people is good or that killing them is okay." I had little chance of reaching this idiot, but I was entirely in the moment now and not thinking about being cautious.

"Islam," he said simply.

"You moron, Islam doesn't advocate that. Religion is strictly about peace and love.'

"It's also about morals and standards, right and wrong." He was getting excited again, and had turned red. "Faggots are wrong, end of story." He said it flatly and with the same conviction as he might say that the world is round or that two plus two equals four.

"What they *do* is wrong," Fred said. "Hate the sin, not the sinner."

"What are you, the fuckin' chaplain? Eat your fuckin' kimchee, Jones," Andy said.

"You know, you're just killin' me here, Andy. Fred's right, by the way, but let's get back to the basics. One, we are all human beings. Two, you can't go around advocating killing people or hating them just because they're different. Blacks are different, and you don't wanna kill *them*, do you? You don't have to like other people, Andy, but you do have to refrain from killing them or hurting them. They have the right to exist and pursue happiness just like the rest of us. Nobody is saying that you have to hang around anybody you don't want to, but they do have a right to be there."

"No, no, McGowan, that is where you're wrong. They do *not* have that right. Most Americans think that what faggots do is immoral and disgusting, and you know what, the majority rules, dude. If you got the votes, you can restrict what those immoral fuckers do."

"Oh, Christ, I don't know why I'm even talking to you," I said.

"Actually, Andy," Fred said, "I think it's kind of one of the things about America that the government is supposed to protect the majority from, like hurting the minority, right, Jeff? I mean it's not like I'm saying homos have rights or anything, but that's the way it is, I think."

"He's right, Andy. What you're saying is actually un-American. Your vision is a zero-sum game."

"No," Andy said, "that shit's for, like, the Irish and the blacks. It's not for fags. You're wrong."

"Christ almighty, Andy, you don't know how fucking stupid you sound when you talk like that."

"If you call me stupid one more time, McGowan, I'm going to pop you," Andy said, smiling a little. "Don't get so excited."

"Look, Andy, I just can't stand narrow-minded crap like that, okay? You don't fucking hate people, it's as simple as that. Didn't you go to Sunday school? It's like the major thing that Jesus was saying. And especially if you're educated, *and you are, Andy*, you should be more open-minded. That's how you learn and grow, by trying to see the world through other people's eyes."

"That's a New Yorker for ya," Fred said suddenly, trying to lighten things up. "Always trying to make us southerners feel like yokels, with yo ha'falutin' intellects."

"Ah, fuck it. Let's just eat," I said with a disgust, only slightly tempered by Fred's stab at lightheartedness. But still, I felt good at having said something. I knew Andy was an idiot, but at the same time I knew that a lot of guys felt exactly the same way. The fact that I wouldn't let him get away with that kind of talk anymore was a small step, but a significant one, nonetheless. I was finally beginning to face the fact that I wasn't going to change and that I'd have to learn to live at peace with myself. I'd always believed that being a man meant being tough and responsible and steady. I was learning that it also meant having the integrity to accept who I was. I was moving toward a scary place now, because I didn't know what to expect. But I was excited about the prospect of perhaps finally becoming not just a soldier, but a soldier who was also a man.

CHAPTER TWENTY

Heartbreak and Liberation

The old site, where the PX (post exchange) opened temporarily while the new facility was under construction, was conveniently located at the end of Ardennes Street, where all the units of the Eighty-second and Special Forces are located. After the PX moved, the military clothing store moved in along with a nice food court and a few other shops. What drew me there on a frequent basis was a coffee stand that made these really sweet coffees with whipped cream and caramel on top, sort of like the caramel macchiato at Starbucks. I would go alone or with a group, two or three times a week, if business took me that way.

One day in the early spring of 1995, I was enjoying a coffee after picking up a new set of uniforms for All-American Week, the annual celebration of the Eighty-second Airborne. It's a weeklong smorgasbord of competitions, parades, and plenty of parties. The week begins with the entire division lining up for a four-mile run. It's a pretty impressive sight. The division Artillery places cannons along the route and fires a salute as each brigade commander runs by with his flag. All the bigwigs turn out, from the corps commander on down. One of the highlights of the run when I was there was this one WWII paratrooper in his late seventies. They'd put him in a Hummer and drive him past the formation while he'd wave to all the troops and we'd applaud and cheer back at him. He had a lot of energy and would yell at the formations, especially when he saw a good-looking female soldier. "Hey good lockin', what's cookin'?" he'd shout, or "You're breakin' my heart!" Sometimes he'd jokingly ask for their phone numbers. It was hilarious, and nobody minded because he really was such a sweet old man.

After the run, the division would go to All-American field, which is near the original WWII barracks, and practice marching for the review at the end of the week. This final big parade usually included a guest speaker of some prominence. Of course it would be incredibly hot all week long, and we'd sweat like pigs the whole time. When we weren't practicing for the end-of-the-week parade, we'd take part in athletic competitions, which included everything from softball to my favorite, pushball. Pushball is simple enough, kind of a combination of soccer and football, two teams fight to move a large inflated ball down the field and through the opposing team's goalposts. Other than that, there aren't many rules, at least there weren't in the version of the game we played, so it got pretty rough, so rough that a few times limbs were actually broken. We all loved it.

I stood at one of the tables near the coffee concession, drinking my caramel-flavored coffee. All-American Week falls at the end of May every year, so it was getting hot. I found myself sweating as I sipped the hot concoction, wondering if maybe I should have had an iced coffee instead. I watched as soldiers and their families passed by, loaded up with bags, browsing the various kiosks that seemed to change as often as the seasons. In a way it was a pretty depressing sight. Cheap and tacky. There was a shop loaded with souvenirs and other crap no one really needs, and lots of T-shirts with Airborne-related slogans printed on them: KILL 'EM ALL AND LET GOD SORT 'EM OUT and ON THE 8TH DAY, GOD MADE THE AIRBORNE. There was a trophy shop where just about every unit on post bought plaques for departing officers and NCOs, a shop that sold African masks and kente cloth clothing, and a few no-name hot dog and burger stands thrown into the mix. It was, like so many other aspects of military life, a place that catered to a very narrow set of tastes.

Finishing up my coffee, I remembered that I had an afternoon meeting at headquarters and that the air conditioner there wasn't working. I need a break, I thought to myself. I was making my way to the exit when I noticed a tall, blond soldier in front of me who looked familiar, even though he had his back to me. The shape of his head, the back of his neck, the way he held his body, it all looked strikingly familiar. Suddenly it dawned on me. Could it be? God, I hoped it was. My footsteps quickened a bit to catch up with him. He stopped to look in the window of the trophy shop to his right and I got a clear view of his profile. It was Paul.

A thousand thoughts exploded in my mind all at once, and I felt as if I were going to burst. I wasn't sure what to do as I approached. Should I shake his hand, hug him? Would he remember me? After all, we hadn't spoken since that one brief episode in Cement City right before the war.

Reaching him, I managed to quiet the trumpets in my head and keep myself from tackling him. I was even able to muster up the presence of mind to decide on a more jocular approach by positioning myself behind him and giving him a good shot in his right arm. He was completely taken by surprise, and I almost knocked him over. But as he turned and saw that it was me standing there, grinning ear to ear, his eyes lit up, and he threw his arms up in the air and moved toward me. I took a short step forward, and we gave each other a heart-felt embrace that we ended almost instantly, as if we had collided and bumped off each other, so self-conscious were we both, I think, of the true import of the embrace. I think we both knew that had we held the hug any longer we would've ended up with our tongues in each other's mouth.

"Jeffrey, Jeffrey, I can't believe it. My God, what is goin' on, brother? How ya been, big guy?"

"Not too shabby what about you? Where the hell've you been, buddy!"

The words were mere conduits through which our excitement flowed. I had no idea what I was saying. It felt as if a huge burden had just been lifted off my shoulders and at any moment my feet would lift off the ground in defiance of gravity. I kept smacking him on the shoulder, just so that a part of my body could make contact with a part of his.

"Uh, well," Paul said, "I left Cement City pretty quickly because of my orders. What about you? Where're you at? Are you in the division?" Then he did what everybody does at Fort Bragg. He swayed lightly to check out the patch on my left shoulder and then gave my uniform a once-over to see the badges I had. Simple Airborne wings are not enough. To have credibility, you must have a star or a star with a wreath around it, signifying either senior or master parachutist status. Sometimes when somebody achieved master parachutist, they'd say he got an "afro on his wings."

"First of the Three hundred nineteenth," I said. "What about you?"

"I'm at COSCOM [Corps Support Command], in the G-3 shop. Writing orders and doing slides, you know the drill, same as every other post command captain."

"Cool. So . . . maybe we . . . could go out to dinner or something and catch up on old times." My heart was racing as I waited for his response. I was pretty sure that he would say yes, but I wanted him to say it with the kind of enthusiasm that matched my own, that wouldn't leave me guessing.

"Are you kidding me?" he said, actually looking a little confused, far surpassing my enthusiasm requirement. "What are you doing tonight? Let's go to Bennigan's or the Outback," he said.

"Tonight," I said, thinking I was gushing, though I'm pretty sure I wasn't. I was worried, however, that my face would split open from smiling so big. I'd never experienced this kind of joy at seeing another person. There was something spectacular about this feeling. All of the yearning would be fulfilled, and the thrill of it far outweighed any fear I still had about being discovered. "Yes, tonight."

"Let me give you my number," he said.

Just before I was about to take the slip of paper from his hand, he pulled it back a little and looked into my eyes and said very simply and quietly, "Wait, promise me, Jeff, that you'll never lose it, okay?"

"No, I won't. I promise," I said.

"So, whaddya say, Bennigan's then, at seven?"

"I'm there, Paul."

"Okay, see you then." And he walked off.

Heading back to my car, I was floating on air; I was defying gravity. It didn't seem real. The whole thing felt almost scripted. I just couldn't believe that he was back in my life again. Suddenly, I was in a different world. The tacky shops, the drab T-shirt stands, the whole dull mediocrity that so often infects army life had been transformed into something endlessly fascinating and meaningful. How love supplies meaning! It's truly amazing.

That day was an agony of waiting. I went through the motions of my day, playing in my mind this scenario, then that one, confident here, then unsure there, bursting with hope, then crushed with uncertainty. It was, I think, in some respects, a kind of adolescent experience of love and desire, but it made sense in a way since I'd been denied the experience during my real, chronological adolescence. Like other gay men who come out later in life, I had some catching up to do.

Once again Paul had me entirely in his thrall. His presence made me feel helpless and vulnerable; it had the power to break through all of my delusions and defenses. I was no longer in control when he was around, and what a relief that was, to relinquish some control, to relax into a kind of easy abandon! Seeing him could literally silence me, and I'd become incapable of resistance. He was, in every sense of the word, irresistible. Physically, emotionally, mentally, I wanted all of him. He made me reckless and hopeful for the first time in my life. Indeed, that proverbial light switch had once again been flipped on, but this time it felt more like a whole wall of switches, an entire bank of them capable of lighting a skyscraper, or even a whole city.

I was at Bennigan's a half hour early because I couldn't stand sitting in my apartment any longer. I was nervous and figured I would have a Guinness or two to loosen up and take the edge off. As I sat at the bar, watching a basketball game on the television behind the bar, the door opened and in walked Paul. I was surprised to see him so early, and when he saw me he looked a little sheepish. The moment felt terribly awkward, as if we'd caught each other doing something wrong.

"Great minds think alike, I guess," he said. "We're both early!" He pulled up a bar stool and sat down next to me.

"Yeah, wanna drink or something? I don't think there's a table yet."

"Great, uh," he said, as the bartender stepped in front of him, "a Rolling Rock, please."

We chatted mostly about work, filling each other in on the different assignments we'd had. By all accounts it seemed as if he'd been successful by getting an early command. We felt a little bit exposed, I think, sitting up at the bar like that, in plain view, so we were both kind of stiff, more like coworkers than anything else. We were relieved when they finally seated us in a booth. It felt more private, plus the beers had loosened us up a little.

"So how come you never called me and told me where you were?" I asked quietly.

"Well, when I got back from the desert, it was hectic because I had orders that were put on hold so I could deploy. I got back and literally had to outprocess almost immediately."

"Yeah, but you could have sent a letter or a card or smoke signals," I said, laughing a little. "It's like you just dropped off the face of the earth, Paul, like you died or something. I didn't know what happened. I was worried." Was this too obvious? I wondered. But I hardly cared anymore.

"That's nice, Jeff, but . . ." He smiled, though he looked a little nervous, too. "Well . . . I came back to the States and went to the Advanced Course and got caught up in my life here. I mean, it wasn't like I didn't think of all of my friends and you in Germany, but you know I just don't call anybody, really."

The way he said "all of my friends and you" was a classic example of how he often spoke in phrases that required careful interpretation. Did he mean he thought of me differently from everyone else, or was he signaling that he thought my question was weird and he wanted me to back off? I played the phrase over in my head, trying to remember the tone of his voice when he'd said "and you." Had there been a hint of sarcasm in the phrase, or had it sounded like almost everything else he said, light and simple? I decided it had been the latter because his face had remained so open and he seemed so obviously happy to see me. I couldn't remember his ever being sarcastic about anything. I pushed all the doubts from my mind and simply tried to savor being with him again. He'd not changed at all, except his body seemed a little more toned, the result of his newfound passion: sprint distance triathlons.

"Come to think of it, though," he said, "I have to admit, out of everybody, I really wanted to call you the most. I mean . . . I just had the best times hanging around with you."

"Yeah, me, too," I said. There it was. No doubt about it. I thought I'd burst.

"So I promise, now that I have your info, I won't disappear again."

Both convinced, now, that we were back on the same page, we felt at ease to simply enjoy each other's company again. We ordered the Bennigan's margaritas and a couple burgers. We talked about the war, of course, but also about our childhoods again and our favorite foods and our favorites movies and where we'd like to live eventually. We talked about politics and Frankfurt, about the sex shop in the airport, about the bars in the Kstrasse, about New York and Washington State. We talked about everything. Well, nearly everything. The huge pink elephant of our desire for each other was about the only thing not discussed, but we both knew that it was there, and even that knowledge was a kind of progress. The restaurant all around us disappeared as we flew off once again in our own private bubble. Before I knew it, I looked at my watch and it was a few minutes past midnight.

"Dude, I gotta hop. PT is a four-mile run," I said.

"You can drive okay?"

"Oh, yeah," I said. "I'll be fine."

But I wasn't sure about that. I'd had a few more than Paul, and I was feeling no pain, as they say.

"You know, I don't mind driving you back to your place," Paul said.

"No really, Paul, I'm fine. I'm fine," I said. But I knew I probably shouldn't drive, and when I thought about it, I liked the idea of Paul coming back to my place. I imagined his coming upstairs and the two of us jumping each other's bones.

"What about PT in the morning?" I said. "I'll need my car to get to work."

"I can pick you up. It's actually on the way for me. And then we can have lunch here together and get your car."

"And you're okay to drive?" I asked.

"Yeah, I'm fine. I'm cool, don't worry."

He had it all figured out, I thought. In my mind we'd moved from just inside the apartment door to the bedroom, and he would be in my arms, and then he would be in my bed. "Sounds like a plan, dude," I said. "Let's blow this pop stand."

He drove me home in silence, the two of us comfortable enough, now, simply to be in each other's presence without feeling the need to talk. I'd noticed his scent before, but had never had a chance really to stop and take it in for any extended period of time. Now here it was, enveloping me inside his car. It was extraordinary—a clean, fresh, healthy musk—and I found myself breathing it in deliberately, through my nose, my mouth, and thinking (there was no mistaking I'd had a few) about how scents are composed of particles, really, tiny particles, that odor is matter in the end, and that by inhaling the scent of Paul's body I was, in fact, taking pieces of him inside my own body.

As he pulled the car in front of my complex, he said, "I haven't seen your apartment yet. You want to show it to me?" There was an innocence to his voice that confused me. I was trying desperately to think clearly though the mild haze of alcohol. Why would he want to see my apartment at one in the morning? Why would he want to see my apartment at all? The possibility of something happening between us was so overwhelming to me that I couldn't even bear to think about it straight on.

"Why don't you come on up for a minute," I heard myself saying in a voice I barely recognized, something from an old Hollywood movie. Had it sounded seductive? I worried. He said nothing, just followed behind me. We walked up the two flights of stairs to my apartment.

"So here it is, nothing special, really," I said as I pushed the door open and we entered the apartment. And then I yawned. I was very tired.

"Cool. Nice," he said, looking around the place a little, trying to be polite.

"Thanks for the ride, Paul. I usually go in around six. Is that good for you?"

He stopped and turned around in the middle of the room and just stood there with his arms at his side, looking at me, the lighter strands of his dirty-blond hair brightening from the overhead bulb in the kitchen. He looked perfect standing there. I couldn't believe he was here in my apartment, so close to me, his scent actually filling the rooms I lived in. What could he possibly see in me? I asked myself. I mean, I knew I wasn't bad-looking, but Paul was truly in a whole different league. And tonight, now, he looked even better than usual, all that sex in his body. I always thought his body looked like it was built for sex, to be desired and to desire in return. What was he, I was never quite sure, half Italian, half Norwegian, I want to say, something like that, which, when you think about it, is about as perfect a combination as you can get.

We stood there staring at each other, listening to the silence of the night—a passing car, the running shower of a neighbor down below, my little fridge kicking on—the moment almost certainly a prelude to a kiss, I thought. The truth was in between us now, in the air we shared together, and I thought I saw it in his eyes; there was no way out but through each other.

But then suddenly the shower downstairs stopped and Paul shifted and looked away, and the truth got sucked right out the window and pulled off by that passing car, so lonely on the highway in the middle of the night.

"Six is fine, Jeff," he said, starting toward the door. "Guess I'll just see you then." And he opened the door and went out.

"Good night, Paul," I said.

But instead of going straight down the stairs he turned around and faced me again.

"Jeff?"

"Yeah?" I moved toward the open door.

"Do you think I could stay?"

Before I could respond, he was moving to come back in the door. Our eyes locked again, and this time it was as if we were screaming at each other. He was coming right at me and before we knew it we collided, our mouths slammed together, and his tongue was inside my mouth. I was startled. I stumbled back a little bit, with my mouth still locked onto his, and banged my head into the wall.

The kiss was rough; the need was tremendous. Hands through the hair, on the neck, pulling the other's face closer, closer, and then down, the hands fumbling down over the torso, the butt, until our crotches met and our bodies urged us forward, uniting hips and thighs and shoulders and chests. The creaking of jeans aching to pull away from the body, from hands undoing snaps and zippers and buttons, so eager to get to the skin of the other.

I realized then that the door was still open, revealing two male officers of the U.S. Army locked in what must have looked like a hysterical embrace, so I shuffled the two of us toward the door and slammed it shut with my foot, not once pulling my mouth away from his. This felt so good, so right, so beyond the need for explanations or words of any kind. Desire trumps everything.

The jeans came down around the ankles and then off came the sneakers in order to get the scrunched-up jeans past our feet and off us entirely. It never occurred to me to take him into the bedroom. The floor was closer, and the floor was fine. And soon we were both naked and kissing and wrapped up in a tight ball on the hardwood floor. And soon after that we were coming, convulsions, really, almost simultaneously, until our chests were covered and we lay sweaty and spent on the floor, out of breath, and laughing in each other's arms.

"My God," Paul said.

"You said it." I sighed.

"I've been wanting to do that since that first night at Kyalami's," he said.

"Me, too."

We took turns showering and then got into bed. I thought it might be a little awkward, but it wasn't at all. He went to sleep almost as soon as his head hit the pillow, leaving me alone with my thoughts. I was exhausted and wanted to sleep, but I couldn't shut my mind down.

I felt enormously relieved. And happy. And a little pissed, too, thinking about all the time we'd wasted dancing around each other. What if one of us had died in the war? Of course, we'd have never known, so . . . but still, in a way that's tragedy, that would have been a real, bona fide tragedy. No point in dwelling on it, though, I thought, as Paul stirred a little and rolled over next to me.

What now, though? I had no experience with this, and I was pretty sure Paul didn't either. Would we see each other again? Of course we would, I thought, at least if I had anything to say about it. But how would that work? Suddenly, a thousand questions were racing through my head. The logistics just seemed overwhelming. How were we going to do this?

I didn't have the slightest idea, but looking at his face resting on the pillow next to me, that beautiful face I'd been dreaming about for so long, was enough to convince me that somehow we'd figure out a way. It was something we just had to do. He was snoring gently now, and the sheet was only a little more than halfway across his body, revealing a tan shoulder, the curve of his perfect back, one firm ass cheek, and the fine blond hair on his golden legs. I stared at him for a few minutes and then pulled the sheet up over him. For now, I was happy. I was filled with a kind of warm, brown feeling, a feeling of deep satisfaction and safety. I just wanted the moment to last forever.

I woke only a few hours later, at about five-thirty, to find Paul staring at me.

"Hey," he said, softly, "how you feeling?"

"Great," I said, smiling at him, "tired as hell, a little hungover, I think, but great. How about you?"

"Happy," he said, smiling as well.

We both lay there for a few minutes, on our backs, staring up at the ceiling, in silence, but for the occasional car passing outside and the twittering of morning birds. The sun was rising and the bright light of daybreak began to flood through the bedroom window.

"So how come this didn't happen sooner?" I said, breaking through the silence without turning my head.

He took his time to consider before answering. I worried that he might be annoyed by my asking the question. Anxious to see if I could find an answer on his face, I turned my head and looked at him just as he began to speak.

"You know, Jeff," he said, pulling himself up a little and resting his head on the back of his hand, and then looking at me, "I wasn't lying last night when I said that the first time I saw you, that night in Kyalami's, I wanted it to happen. After that I thought about you all the time. I couldn't get you out of my head. But I didn't know what to do. I guess . . . I think I was too afraid of what might happen if I was wrong. I was always, like, you know, 80 percent sure, and then sometimes almost positive, but then something would happen and I'd worry about my career and everything and I thought I was probably imagining the way you seemed to be flirting with me. So all I could do was to hint as strongly as I could, but you didn't seem to be getting it. There were times when I thought I was being so obvious, but then you'd react and I'd be so confused. This is a really tough situation. It's not like I could just come out and say it, you know, ask you out on a date or something. And it's not like you could've asked me—I mean, you could have, it turns out, but you had no way of knowing that. Damn, it's fucked, isn't it?"

"Is that why you didn't bother to keep in touch after you were re-located?"

"Yeah, Jeff, you have to understand how much I wanted us to get together. I mean, it was bad." He laughed at himself a little. "And when it seemed like it was never going to happen, I just couldn't deal with it."

"Believe me, Paul, I understand. I totally understand. It was bad for me, too. Think about how much you wanted to get together with me and multiply it by ten. That's what I was going through." Now, we laughed together, amazed.

"Jeez," I said, "what a waste. My God, five years! You know, if we hadn't met by chance again, it would never have happened, probably."

"I know," he said. "Five years, amazing. And tonight, I'm not sure what convinced me tonight. I guess it was just a leap of faith. I felt it so keenly between us. And then the way you looked standing inside the door. Damn."

"It was really very . . . courageous. I'm so glad you did it."

"Well, I figured even if I was wrong that you were a good enough guy not to rat me out."

I just smiled and rolled over and kissed him good morning.

* *

In the car about an hour later, as we were stopped at a red light, he turned to me and said, "So do you want to see me again?"

"Of course, are you crazy? I want to see you a lot."

We both smiled, and I reached for his free hand and held it for a moment. I was nervous about doing this so openly, worried that someone we knew was going to drive up alongside us. But no one did, of course, and I made it to work on time. I even managed to sneak a quick and very chaste peck on the cheek in the parking lot where he dropped me off.

Within a couple weeks we'd already established a nice routine, seeing each other two or three times a week. I would go to his place or he would come to mine and we'd cook something or eat takeout and then spend the night together. We didn't go out very often because we were both paranoid about being seen together. We didn't feel capable of acting as if we were just two straight buddies because we had trouble keeping our hands off each other. We were convinced, too, that when we were together, even if we did manage to keep our hands off each other for an extended period of time, we still looked too much like exactly what we were: a couple. Going out was too stressful as a result. Occasionally, if we were really aching to get out and do something, we'd make the hour-and-a-half drive to Raleigh, where no one knew us.

It was, while it lasted, the happiest and most fulfilling time in my life. It was the first real relationship I'd had, and I moved through my

days always a little drunk with the newness and thrill of being involved with someone I loved and cared so much about. The relationship had opened up a whole new world to me. This was the closest I'd
come to living what I thought of as a complete life. I'd fulfilled my
boyhood dream of being a soldier, *and* I had someone to share it with.
Having someone in my life, someone to unwind with at the end of the
day, with whom I could be unreservedly myself, put my professional
life as a soldier in a brand-new light, a brighter one, one that gave
everything more meaning and value. I found myself much more mo-
tivated to get up in the morning and go out and do my job knowing
that I had someone to come home to who would replenish me. Not
only did I have the power of a dream fulfilled, but I also now had the
power of two, which is, I've come to believe, the greatest power of all.

Paul and I seemed tailor-made for each other. We shared roughly
the same politics, the same interest in history, and even a similar sense
of humor. We never seemed to run out of things to say. And he was
the smartest guy I knew. No matter what the subject, he had a take on
it; he had something to say about it. His face would light up, signaling
that he had something profound to point out, and he'd say, "Well, you
know . . ." He exuded great confidence and a kind of mastery of the
world around him that I'd never seen in anyone before. There was an
ease with which he moved through the world that I found so attractive. Everything seemed possible when I was with him, and he
brought out the very best in me.

About a month into the relationship we drove to Raleigh to have
dinner. Toward the end of the meal Paul said, "So, listen, I have some
friends coming in next weekend and they want to hang out, so is it
okay if we don't see each other then?"

"No problem, I understand," I said. And I did. "Where you thinking of taking them?"

"Probably here, actually, for dinner, and then, you know, out for
some drinking. I'm not sure I can take the whole night with them,
though. I mean, they're good guys and all, but I've got my limits. So I

was thinking I might break away after and stop by at Legends or Flex for a nightcap. I wanted to make sure you didn't mind."

"You're too much, Paul. Of course I don't mind," I said, smiling. Legends and Flex were two of the big gay bars on Hargett Street in Raleigh.

A week later he called me at the office.

"I really need to see you," he said. "Can you meet me for lunch? Something happened at work today."

"Sure, what's up, Paul? Are you okay?"

"Yeah, I'm fine, but . . . I'll tell you at lunch. How about the Korean place in an hour, say?"

"See you then," I said.

He was already there when I arrived at the restaurant. He'd apparently had a haircut in the last day or so, and it was the shortest I'd ever seen it. It looked really good on him. It always amazed me when I discovered he could do something to make himself even better-looking than before, and I caught my breath a little when I saw him sitting at the table.

Before I could even compliment his haircut, he was telling me what had happened.

"Hey," he said, as I sat down across from him, "somebody from my unit saw me coming out of Legends."

"What, who? What happened?"

"You know those buddies I went out with last weekend?"

I nodded my head. "Yeah," I said.

"Well, it turns out I did break away from them," he said, talking very fast, "you know, like I said I might have to, and I went to Legends for a nightcap and I had a couple beers, and then somebody from the unit must've seen me leaving and it got back to my boss somehow and he called me in. I don't know what to do, Jeff; what am I going to do?" He had an anguished look on his face. His eyes, normally that friendly, open, warm blue, looked haunted and distant now.

"Well, first of all, what did he say?"

"He called me in to talk about a slide presentation that I've been working on. We got through the slides and then he asked me where I'd been last weekend. I told him I was out with the guys. He got a weird look on his face and asked me if I was with them the whole night. I said yes. He said to me, 'That's funny, someone from the shop says they saw you coming out of one of those gay bars up there.' I said that must have been a mistake because I turned in pretty early and what would I be doing in a gay bar anyway. I tried to make a joke, but I was so nervous and he didn't seem to buy it. He looked at me and didn't say anything."

"Okay, so you told him that you weren't there, so don't worry about it. What's he going to do? Listen, it's not like he saw you having sex with someone, for God's sake, so what can he do? Just lie low for a while. Work a little harder and keep your head down, and it'll blow over."

"I don't know about that, Jeff. I mean he even asked me what color shirt I was wearing. I don't know—*fuck*! Why did this have to happen? I should have just gone back to Fayetteville."

"Come on, Paul, don't blame yourself, it's not as big a deal as you think, believe me. He knows how good an officer you are. He'll get over it. Just try to be seen with Jessica at an event or something." Jessica was Paul's beard, a close friend who didn't know about us, but whom Paul took to events as a sort of girlfriend. He sighed heavily and looked away.

"Yeah, maybe. Maybe you're right," he said, but he didn't seem at all convinced.

We kept seeing each other regularly over the course of the next month. Paul updated me periodically on the situation at work. His relationship with his boss went from being friendly and open to formal and distant. Graffiti appeared in the bathroom—"Paul is a fag," that kind of thing. I tried to comfort him as best I could and to help him keep things in perspective. I was willing to do almost anything to accommodate his growing paranoia. We kept up our basic routine in terms of seeing each other, but we started spending most of our time at my place since there were other guys from his unit in the complex where he lived.

But nothing was ever quite the same after that. Something had been poisoned. I kept thinking things would blow over, but his anxiety only grew worse, and it got to the point where it seemed as if he'd never be relaxed or happy again. All that ease I'd admired so much, that confidence, that youthful optimism, had been drained out of him by the constant feeling of being hunted, of being watched and judged and made to feel as if one false move, one wrong word, would put an immediate end to the career he'd spent a good part of his young life working for.

It broke my heart to watch him struggle under this pressure, to see his spirit so diminished. And for the first time in my life I was outraged at what was happening. The injustice of it had suddenly become so clear. It was unfair. It was mean-spirited. I was viewing it from the other side now, the side I should have been viewing it from all along. It was happening to someone I cared about, so in a sense it was happening to me.

About two months later we were having dinner at Chili's. It was a Friday night, and he'd called me at the office earlier and said he needed talk to me.

"You know," he said, after we'd gotten drinks and had ordered our food. "The last couple months have been really shitty."

"Yeah, I know," I said. "But you know I'm here for you, right? And it's getting better, isn't it?"

He smiled warmly at me. "Well, as a matter of fact it's been getting worse. But you've been amazing, Jeff, thanks. That's why it's so hard for me to say what I'm about to say."

My stomach dropped. I felt my forehead getting hot.

"Jeff, I don't want to lose my career. I can't lose it. It's all I have. I really think my boss has moved into high gear and is looking to fuck me over real good. I don't want go to work every day feeling like I've got a target on my back. I don't want to read about myself on the walls of the men's room. I've come so far, and I don't want to do anything else now except be a soldier. So . . . I've decided . . . to get married."

I was thunderstruck. I felt nothing, or maybe everything all at once. For a moment I wasn't sure I'd heard him right. I hoped I'd heard him wrong. I just stared at him with my mouth slightly open.

"Jeff, are you all right? Did you hear what I said?"

"I heard you." Words were coming out of my mouth. Three words strung together—subject, verb, pronoun—a rational sentence. And then another sentence came out, "Who do you want to marry?"

"I've been talking to Margaret—my old girlfriend from back home? We were serious for a long time, and I know it could work with her."

I was stunned, and now silent. I stared at him, the hurt turning to anger, then back to confusion, then hurt again. I was shocked, pissed, deeply wounded, and finally all these words just came rushing out of me.

"I don't know what to say. I'm really confused, Paul. How could I have misread this so completely? How could you do this to me? I mean, you're attracted to men, right? I mean, you don't like women, right? You said you haven't slept with a woman since college. I just can't believe this is happening. And just how's it going to work? Explain it to me, Paul. Explain it to me! You were lying to me, weren't you? You were lying the whole time. Is it me and you just don't want to hurt my feelings? I mean, I'm an adult, I can handle that you might want to move on. I can handle that probably better than this fake marriage shit."

"No, no, no. Please, Jeff, I wasn't lying, believe me. And no, it isn't because I want to break up with you. I *don't* want to break up with you. I *have* to break up with you. I don't have a choice. I want to be able to finish my career, and this asshole is hunting me. I have do this in order to survive. I am gonna do this with her; I'm going to marry Margaret because she's my best friend and, uh . . . as for the sex . . . we've had sex before. It's not like I can't . . . you know, do it."

"That's just ridiculous. Let me get this right, your unit thinks you're gay, and marrying someone is going to solve it? What about Margaret and her feelings? Isn't marriage supposed to be until death do you part? One OER [officer evaluation report] is not going to destroy your career. I think you're a fucking hypocrite, Paul, that's what I think. There has to be something you're not telling me. Did you get caught in the act?" I heard echoes of Greg in my voice here, felt that hard, spring rain on Lexington Avenue, saw Greg on the steps of the Citicorp Plaza, the fountain splashing hard in the downpour, his arms up in the air; it was me now, that was me now. He'd been right, after all. *I wouldn't stay dry* forever, and now I was drenched straight through, I was soaking-wet angry and hurt and lost, losing the most important person in my life. But I wouldn't appreciate the tremendous irony of the situation until later on when it occurred to me how decently Paul had treated me compared to the way I'd treated Greg a decade before.

"Jeff, I mean . . . listen, I know you're hurt, but come on. And no, I didn't get caught. I wouldn't do that to you. You know I wouldn't do that to you. Besides, they would've booted me instantly. Please, Jeff, I'm trying to make you understand. It's about my career. I have a good shot at going to CGSC first look. I'm not gonna lose that."

I couldn't look at him now.

"Listen, Jeff, would you look at me. Jeff, look at me. It's not like we can get married or anything, you know. Can't you see it in the long term? Can't you see what I'm doing? I'm going to be leaving soon and what then? Who knows if we would ever get an assignment together again. It was going to have to end sometime. You knew that; didn't you know that?"

I forced myself to look at him now. "I kind of thought it would end when we stopped caring about each other," I said, my voice cracking a little, but I pulled myself together. "But I guess that's not what you had in mind. Now," I said, "let us summarize, shall we? This is your plan: you're going to discard a good relationship, the best relationship you ever had, you once told me, so that you can use and deceive a long-time friend in order to get to CGSC [Command and General Staff College]? That's pretty fuckin' ruthless. And for what? To run out the clock and get a shitty government pension? I can't believe you think this is right. I don't believe you think it's right. I felt like I knew you up until this moment. Now it feels like I don't know you at all."

"Jeff, I know you're hurt."

"Just be quiet for a minute, you. I am hurt, you're right. I am. I had hoped that things could . . . continue between us. I mean I really . . . care for you." Now I felt tears beginning to well up, but I shut them down out of sheer resentment.

"You're missing the real point here, though, Paul," I said. "I'll get over this, eventually. But you go through with this decision, and you'll never get over it. You'll have to live with it for the rest of your life. Are you prepared to do that? It's you I'm worried about, not me. I'm worried about you making a really bad decision. Think about it. What are you going to do? Imagine your daily life. How are you going to arrange it? Just have affairs to satisfy yourself? I know you know that's fucked up. But shit, listen, I need to go. I have to get out of here." I stood up abruptly and started walking away.

"How are you going to get home? I drove, remember?" he shouted.

"Don't worry about it," I yelled back, spinning quickly through the revolving doors and out to the parking lot.

I walked the five miles home that night, on the shoulder of the highway, never once breaking my stride, walking as if I could walk away from the pain. I cried most of the way. When I wasn't crying, I was thinking how absurd the situation was, and how unfair. All of this heartbreak just because my boyfriend was seen coming out of a gay bar? Was that really the whole story? Amazing. And so royally fucked up. I couldn't get over it. Paul had committed no crime. He'd hurt no one, hadn't damaged any property; he'd done nothing, in fact, but be seen coming out of a bar. And because of that I was losing him.

When I got home there was a message from Paul.

"Jeff, I'm worried about you. Please call me when you get in."

"Fuck you," I yelled, smacking the delete button hard.

I ignored his messages over the next couple of days. On the third day, he came by the office, but I was out. That night my doorbell rang, and I knew it was him. I decided that avoiding him was not going to solve anything. plus I'd begun to miss him already.

"Jeez, Jeff," he said, as I opened the door and he walked into the apartment. "Where have you been? Didn't you get my messages? Or were you just not returning my calls?"

"I got 'em."

"Sooo . . . what's going on?"

"Well. it's obvious, isn't it? I'm hurt, and I need to be alone. I mean the whole situation is fucked. I keep asking myself why I'm in the army, if this is what I have to deal with. I have to tell you, Paul, what you're doing is just stupid. And I really think I'd feel the same way even if I wasn't so personally invested in the whole thing. I've been thinking real hard about this, and I know I can't change who I am, but this? What you're doing is not the answer."

"Jeff, all I want to do is survive. I mean, it's hard to find a job when you're more senior. You're less marketable. I want my pension, shitty as it might be. I love what I do . . . and really, come on, who's kidding who here? You see how they live in the civilian world; you're not like them, neither am I. We're not really gay. I mean I'm not into Donna Summer and the club scene. All they're into is decorating, drugs, and sex. Trivial shit, and I'm not trivial, and neither are you. We'll never fit in."

"Listen, I have one question for you," I said, ignoring his goofy analysis of contemporary gay culture and our place, or lack thereof, in it. Later I'd realize that up until just about the moment the words

how lies beget lies beget lies? I think you're lying to yourself right now. You've already told yourself the first lie—that you can actually pull this off and be happy."

There was a long silence as we stared at each other, standing on the exact spot where we'd made love so frantically that first night several months before.

"My decision is made." He said it simply, although there was a slight hint of regret in his tone, one quiet note that seemed to be asking for my permission and maybe forgiveness.

"Okay, then," I said, giving it to him, apparently.

With that he got up and walked out. And as I watched him go I felt, for the first time in my life, as if I had more in common with the dancing, shirtless, gay-prider than with the closeted gay U.S. Army captain who'd just walked out of my life for good.

CHAPTER TWENTY-ONE

Bob in a Black Velvet Dress

The weeks following the scene with Paul at Chili's were demoralizing, to say the least. I'm not one prone to depression, or even bad moods, really. And I'm not one who generally gets bogged down in any kind of existential speculation, but now I was feeling as if all the meaning had been drained from my life. I simply went about my business, doing everything on autopilot, feeling the whole time as if I had lead weights attached to my legs. As it turned out, Paul hadn't walked out of my life entirely on that day in my apartment. He called several times over the next few weeks, to try to convince me that what he was doing made sense, and to let me know how much he missed me. It was difficult, hearing that, since I missed him terribly, too, so much so that there were times when I almost convinced myself that we could make it work, but then I'd come to my senses and do my best to get off the phone as quickly as possible. Eventually, he stopped calling. The last I heard from him was the wedding invitation I received a few months later. I didn't attend the wedding.

During this time I was sitting in one of the interminable battalion meetings we had to attend all too frequently. My portion of the briefings wasn't until the end, so I would often let my mind wander, thinking ahead to a practical joke we were planning for one of our colleagues who would soon be leaving to assume command. It was something stupid and fun that helped me keep my mind off Paul.

The captain leaving was a great guy and a talented officer. At one point, when he was younger, he'd been heavily into bodybuilding. For some reason there were a lot of photos of him from those days floating around the post. One of his office mates got hold of one of them—a very unflattering shot of him posing in a really tight Speedo. We'd decided to make a bunch of T-shirts with the photo on them and all show up at his send-off party wearing one. I was chuckling to myself in the meeting, imagining the look on the guy's face when he saw the T-shirts, when a soldier poked his head into the room and motioned for me to come out. I quietly excused myself and went to see what he wanted.

"Sir . . . you have a call," he said, looking a little nervous.

"Couldn't you take a message? I'm in the middle of a meeting here," I said peevishly.

He looked at me squarely. "Sir, you need to take this call."

That was convincing enough. The guy had spooked me. I hurried to the phone.

"Hello, Captain McGowan, how may I help you?"

"Jeffrey? Jeffrey, is that you?" a voice, thick with a Scottish brogue, came at me through the receiver. It was Mrs. Gaffney, the wife of the superintendent of my grandmother's building in Jackson Heights.

"Mrs. Gaffney, hello, how are you?" I said, cheering up at the sound of the familiar voice, but then checking myself, realizing how strange it was for her to be calling me.

"Jeffrey, you need to come home immediately. Your grandmother passed away last night. I am so sorry I had to tell you that."

My mind went blank. I was stunned, speechless. I froze up.

"Sir, are you all right?" the soldier said. "Can I get you anything?"

"No, no. Can you give me a minute?"

He walked out quietly, and I closed the door behind him.

Suddenly Mrs. Gaffney's voice came back into focus.

"Jeffrey, are you there? Jeff? Hello?"

"I'm here Mrs. G. What happened?"

"She died in her sleep."

"I'll be home as soon as I can. Thanks, Mrs. Gaffney," and I gently placed the phone back onto its cradle.

I just stood there for a few minutes, frozen in place, listening to the room breathe, as it were. I knew that once I allowed myself to feel this wholly, I'd be a mess, and I still had my presentation to do, so I pulled myself together and returned to the meeting. Though I thought I had it under control, it must've been written all over my face, judging from the way everyone locked at me when I walked back into the room. Taking my seat again I tried to ignore the looks and to lighten, or at least neutralize, the expression on my own face. I sat and stared straight ahead, until it was time to do my presentation, which I did mechanically, with a forced smile plastered across my face the whole time. At the end I made a lame attempt at a joke, and the men laughed politely. I couldn't bear it another moment.

"Excuse me," I said, and I fled the room, going straight to my battalion commander's office around the corner.

"Sir, may I see you?"

"Sure S-Four, what can I do you for?" he said affably.

"My grandmother just died, sir. She raised me like her own son. I need to go home as soon as possible."

His face changed immediately, and he came out from behind his desk and put his arm around me and walked me to the door.

"I'm so sorry to hear that. Take whatever time you need. Don't worry about the paperwork; we'll straighten it out later."

Walking out of headquarters, I began crying to myself. For years I had dreaded this moment. But it had always remained purely theoretical in my head; it never seemed like a real possibility. It would happen eventually, maybe next year, or the next century, but not today, not right now. Talk about kicking someone when they're down! I'd lost my great love and my grandmother, all in the course of a few months.

It sure would have been nice to be able to count on Paul's support at a time like this, but the good old army had seen fit to make sure that couldn't happen. I'd never felt more alone in my entire life.

During the long drive up to New York I thought a lot about my grandmother and how special she was, how she'd managed up until the very end to retain that unique spark she had—staying so active, always going to the senior center at St. Joan of Arc, remaining vitally interested in the people in the building and in the neighborhood, hanging out with her "gray panther" girlfriends, ladies with names like Tessy and Marge and Gertrude and Fran. We talked often on the telephone, and she never failed to mention her friends. And she was always so completely supportive of me, no matter what was going on in my life. Of course, I never came out to her. I'd barely come out to myself by the time she died. And I was convinced she was generationally challenged, so to speak, though looking back on it now, she might have surprised me, who knows?

She was strong and feisty and full of spirit. If I called her and she sensed that I was angry at something, she would tell me to "kick 'em in the knees." She bore a strong resemblance to the Queen Mother, and though she was only five feet three inches or so, she could be quite fearsome when she got going. I loved when she told me about going to rummage sales and finding some god-awful piece of bric-a-brac and haggling the price down by half, from fifty cents to a quarter. Nobody—but nobody—took advantage of Maxine Reid. She spoke with her sister, Maude, every day and had a fight with her every other day—usually over something that had happened more than fifty years before—the most contentious of which was affectionately called the "Maude the mule" fight.

Maxine and Maude, two sisters. One day when she was about twelve years old, Maude was coming home from school, angry and hurt at having been teased by a boy who often razzed her about a popular comic strip character, Maude the mule. As it happened the boy's house was on her way home. When she reached the house, she'd become so enraged at him that she picked up a big clump of mud and hurled it at the front door and then hid behind the neighbor's lilac bush. Apparently no one was home, so she went ahead and plastered the whole front of the house. Well, she got into a lot of trouble for this. It was the main reason why she changed her name to Mary. My grandmother spent fifty years trying to get Maude (now Mary) to admit that she'd been wrong, that her behavior had been far short of ladylike. But until the day she died Maude refused to admit she'd done anything wrong. I think they both just liked the story and liked fighting, and they knew if they ever fully resolved it a lot of the steam would go out of it.

One of the main reasons I think I may have underestimated my grandmother's willingness to deal with my sexuality has to do with a phone conversation I had with her about a year before she died. It went something like this:

"Jeffrey? Hello. Oh, I'm so glad you called. I need your advice about something that's going on in the building."

"Really? What?"

"Well, you remember the Catours on the fifth floor? You know, Father Catour's parents?"

"Yeah."

"Well, they decided to sell the apartment. They want to move to a nicer place. I don't know what could be a nicer place at their age, but they want to go. Did you say hello to them the last time you came home? I hope so. Everybody always asks about you and the army."

I rolled my eyes and bit my tongue. She asked this question almost every time we spoke on the phone. In her view it was worse than a mortal sin for me to come home and fail to say hello to every single person I'd ever known in the building and the neighborhood. And I always made sure to do it since if I missed anybody she'd be sure to find out about it and I'd never hear the end of it.

"Yes, Grandma, I said hello to the Catours the last time. So what happened?"

"Well, they sold the apartment and a, a . . . person bought it."

"A person? Who . . . what's their name?"

"Well, now, Jeffrey, that's what I am calling about, and honestly I just don't know what to do. This person . . . is a . . . man . . . for now, but soon may not be."

I had to think for a second to figure out exactly what she was trying to tell me. "Ya lost me," I said.

"Well he . . . wants to become a woman," she said, with a sharp intake of breath followed by a slow, anxious sigh.

"You mean to tell me that a transsexual moved into the building?"

"Oh Jeffrey! Don't use that kind of language!"

It took every ounce of control I had to keep myself from bursting out laughing. I knew she was totally sincere, that she was really having trouble getting her mind around the situation, and I didn't want to hurt her feelings.

"Well, Grandma, if you're a man and you want to be a woman, that's what it's called. A transsexual. Same if you're a woman who wants to be a man."

"Well, I've never heard that word before. It doesn't sound nice at all."

"That's the proper word. So what is it exactly that you need advising on?"

"Jeffrey, please don't be a pill. This is serious, what do I say?"

"Whaddya mean what do you say?"

"Well, what do I call him? How do I greet him? Does he hold the door for me or do I do it for him?"

"Okay, slow down, Gram, let's take it one step at a time. What's his name?"

"Bob, his name is Bob."

"Okay, then, that's what you call him. Just call him Bob and say hello like you would to anyone else."

"Well, I guess." She didn't seem convinced.

About a week later, I called her to see how things had gone.

"Hello, Gramma, it's me."

"Jeffrey? Oh, I'm so happy you called. How've you been?"

"Good, good, so what happened with Bob?"

"Bob? You mean Barbara."

"Barbara?"

"Yes, yes, the woman who bought the Catours' apartment."

"I thought it was a guy named Bob who bought the apartment."

"Well, the other day I met her on the stoop and I said hello just like you said I should, and ended up talking to her for over an hour. She's really a nice person!"

"So, now you know what do when you see him?"

"Honestly, Jeffrey—her—her name is Barbara, get with it!"

"Sorry, her, Barbara."

"Times, they are a-changing, sonny. You should try to be a little more modern like your old gramma here."

"Well when you put it that way . . ."

I knew that people tend to have different standards for their children as opposed to the children of their friends or strangers. So chances are she would not have been as thrilled about my sexuality as she was about her newfound tolerance of transsexual Barbara living in Father Catour's parents' old apartment. But still, I sometimes liked to believe that she would have come around eventually.

Now, of course, I'd never know. She was dead. The woman who had picked up the slack when her own daughter couldn't meet her responsibility and took me in and raised me like a son was now dead. As I cleaned out her apartment and planned the funeral over the next few days, I was often struck by the finality of it, of death, and how brutal that finality was. The apartment was so quiet now, and I felt so alone in it. There were moments when I was filled with the same horrible feeling I had back in seventh grade when my grandfather died—that nothing would ever be right again, that nothing would ever be the same again. And, of course, nothing ever would be the same again.

I knew that my grandmother had lived a full life and that it was a blessing that she went quickly in her sleep. I could understand all of that, the big picture, so to speak. But the reality of it on the ground was different, harder to grasp. What about those little things I took for granted? Who was I going to call for advice? Who would keep me updated on the weekly *National Enquirer* headlines? Or the gossip in the building? My link to Jackson Heights and New York, to the world from which I had sprung, had been abruptly severed, and I felt unmoored now, homeless, in a sense—I was alone now in the world.

I'm not usually given to emotional outbursts, but, sorting through her things in the apartment, I often found myself crying for no apparent reason. I tried to keep it all together by organizing and prioritizing with military precision all that needed to be done to take care of her affairs and lay her to rest. As the days passed I was touched by how many people dropped by the apartment or simply stopped me on the street to offer their condolences and tell me what a wonderful person my grandmother had been. I didn't know half of them, but they all acted as if they'd known me for years, my grandmother having been so proud of me, apparently, that she'd kept everyone she knew up-to-date on her grandson's life.

On the morning of the funeral, I decided to honor her by wearing my dress blue uniform with full-sized medals. This uniform is considered more formal and can be worn to black-tie and formal day events. I wanted to look impressive so that all these people who seemed to know so much about my life wouldn't be disappointed. I wanted everyone to see what a great job my grandmother had done in raising me, that I had been a good grandson, somebody of whom to be proud. And I wanted everyone to know that everything I'd achieved was due to her loving support over the years.

I tend toward the very formal when it comes to the turning points in life—weddings and funerals and such. I believe that the rituals associated with these events make them easier to cope with. Formality and structure have a way of subsuming all emotion and transforming it into something more, something accessible and edifying.

The funeral took place at the Methodist church up the block from our building. It was a fine old church that lifted your soul. Light flooded through big, gorgeous panes of stained glass on all sides. I waited to receive her on the stone steps alone in my uniform.

A lot of people turned out to bid her farewell. I had a moment of déjà vu, looking at the group of twenty or so little old ladies sitting in a clump toward the front. It was the same group, pretty much, that had come to my grandfather's funeral almost twenty years before. My entire seventh-grade class had come as well, having asked Sister Eileen if they could attend in order to be there for me. It was comforting to be reminded that my grandmother had so many friends, that her life had been so rich with people. Even Barbara (formerly Bob) came to the funeral, dressed smartly in a classic black velvet dress.

CHAPTER TWENTY-TWO

Fort Bragg: Command

Standing on the parade field, the entire battery at attention before me, I watched the well-dressed guests take their seats beneath the camouflage netting. It was a stunning North Carolina morning—cool, a startlingly clear blue sky overhead, a gentle breeze ruffling the netting just slightly. I was about to assume command, having been selected to take over headquarters and service battery.

This ceremony has changed little over the past fifty years. Every commander is given a guidon—a small flag that represents the unit. Originally one of the ways to keep the troops oriented on the battlefield, the guidon today is an anachronism, though the tradition of receiving it still makes for great pomp and circumstance. The ceremony itself is relatively short. The outgoing commander gives the guidon to the battalion commander, who in turn gives it to the new, incoming commander. The torch is passed. The battalion commander then makes a brief speech thanking the outgoing commander and exhorting the new commander to do well. Then the outgoing and incoming commanders make brief speeches, and that's that.

It's a nice, precise ceremony, beautiful in its economy, and I felt tremendously honored receiving the guidon and standing before everyone in that pristine Carolina sunlight. When the battalion commander placed the guidon in my hand, all the grief and pain of the last several months slipped away, and I was filled with a deep sense of satisfaction, realizing that I'd achieved a goal I'd set for myself at the very beginning of my military career. It had been a long time coming, but it had finally happened, and I was thrilled to be leading troops again, as I had in Desert Storm. I believed in the army again. My faith in the institution was renewed as I embraced the serious responsibility the new position conferred. And it had come at just the right time, when I was desperate for reasons to continue in the army, to remain committed to the one thing that had given so much meaning to my life. Knowing that I would have to publicly represent the battery made it easier for me to throw myself into it wholeheartedly as I rediscovered within myself the idealism that had inspired me to join the military in the first place.

I would spend the next two years doing many of the same things I had done before, except now I would be called upon to offer guidance rather than merely seeking it. When it came to the unit, the buck would now stop with me.

And so I was a commander at last. And I was at Fort Bragg. Fort Bragg, North Carolina. If you are a soldier and aspire to greatness, Fort Bragg is the place to be. It's the post with the highest profile. All the hardcore assignments are based out of Bragg. And the sexy ones—Special Forces (Green Berets), the 82nd Airborne, the Delta Force—as well as the JFK School of Special Warfare, where doctrine is formed and foreign armies are trained in tactical warfare.

Bragg is a massive, insulated institution surrounded by more than a quarter of a million acres of woodlands and mountains. The terrain is rough, like the assignments based there. In a word, it's not a place for the faint of heart or mind. To be assigned to Bragg is a great honor, and I am extremely proud to have served there.

Ardennes Street runs straight through the middle of the base. Lined on both sides of the street, with high-rise barracks built in the

1950s, educational facilities, museums, a memorial chapel, and the occasional PX, it often feels more like a small town than the center of an army base that trains some of the world's finest warriors.

I always took my morning run on Ardennes Street, which was closed every day between six and seven-thirty A.M. to all vehicular traffic for just that purpose, so that army personnel like me had a place to run. Having an entire stretch of road closed off for your morning run was just one of the many perks that came with serving in what some called, with little irony, gladiator land. I was never a particularly graceful or fast runner, so I was always grateful that Ardennes Street was flat. In a word, I'm no gazelle, and that's an understatement. I'm closer to, say, a moose on ice skates, actually. But I knew that the surest way to develop endurance for the field was by simply placing foot to ground four miles a day, every day. It wasn't a pretty sight, but it got the job done.

And so it was that I made my daily run one gorgeous spring morning in 1997. North Carolina mornings are truly spectacular, and this one was no exception. I knew I was about halfway done when I looped around the giant bronze statue of the Green Beret standing sentry in front of the JFK School of War. I was always hit with a sudden, strong wave of pride when I passed this statue. To wear a beret was special. It meant that you were highly sought after when the shit hit the fan. I wasn't a Beret, but I was Airborne, which has its own special cachet, so it was a great feeling knowing that you and the men you commanded were thought of as somewhat indispensable. The bronze figure usually gave me the second wind I'd need to get back to the office.

My office was pretty comfortable by army standards. I had a rather large oak desk, a nice couch, and my own bathroom, complete with shower, an amenity that distinguished me from the other officers in my building who had to share showers with the troops. It was just one of the perks that came with command.

After finishing my run, I showered and changed and settled down at my desk to try to get some paperwork done. I had an open-door policy with my troops. I enjoyed being at the center of my battery's daily activity. My men were hardworking, and I felt it was important that they know I was there for them if they wanted to talk. On this day, though, I really didn't want to be disturbed since I had so much paperwork to get through. As I began reviewing soldier promotions and organizing inventories of battery equipment, my phone rang.

"Captain McGowan," I said automatically, expecting one of the usual problems or requests from subordinates that come with being "the boss with the open-door policy." But when I heard the voice on the line, I knew right away that this call was different. The man seemed annoyed, and he was speaking loudly. Turns out this was the call no boss in the army ever wants to receive.

"Yes, hello, sir," the voice said, blunt, uptight, professional, "My name is Sergeant First Class Johnson. Are you the battery commander, sir?"

"I am. How can I help you?"

"Sir, I'm with CID," he said, his voice thickening with a measured authority that filled me with a dreadful, sinking feeling. My stomach dropped. "We need to see one of your NCOs."

It's never a good thing to have the acronyms CID and NCO in the same sentence. You might think of the CID as the FBI of the military world. They wear plain clothes and work undercover, and there's a terrible aura of secrecy about them. They're extremely no-nonsense in demeanor, dealing largely with the nastier, more serious crimes, unlike the standard MPs, who deal mainly with misdemeanor crimes, generally involving too much liquor.

"Well, of course you can see one of my men, Sergeant," I said, "that is, after you tell me what it is you'd like to see him for." I was nervous, but I didn't want the sergeant to hear it in my voice. The stronger I seemed, the more likely it was that I'd get some information out of this guy. The truth was, he didn't have to tell me anything. CID doesn't have to reveal anything about an open investigation. And their jurisdiction runs all the way up to the Capitol Building, and I don't mean the capitol in North Carolina. Anything I could get out of the sergeant would be helpful in keeping the chain of command informed and would invariably simplify the whole process. If it was serious, and when CID called it almost always was, my bosses would be upset if I couldn't explain to them what was happening, so that they could explain the matter to their bosses, and so on and so on.

"Captain, I'm not at liberty to give that information." His peevishness sounded tempered by the awareness that I outranked him.

"All right, Sergeant Johnson," I said, "let's start over, shall we? Who is the man in question?"

"Sergeant Lopez, sir."

I was somewhat relieved when I heard Lopez's name. He was an exemplary soldier and one of the hardest workers in the unit.

"And?" I asked.

"And, sir?"

"C'mon, Sergeant, tell me what this interview is all about?"

"Sir, with all due respect, I can't divulge any information in regards to an ongoing case. You as a captain should know that."

The word *captain* had a little snide lilt to it. This guy is an asshole, I thought. And Lopez was a good man, I knew that, and one of my soldiers, so I wasn't going to give up so easily.

"Well, Sergeant," I said, a little malice in my voice now, "tell you what. If you can't tell me what all this is about, well, then I'm afraid I'll just have to inform the chain of command before I send him to you."

"Sir, that really won't be necessary. I—"

"I'll be the judge of that," I cut in. "You'll hear from me by late this afternoon." And I hung up the phone, cutting off the defensive response about military justice and the law.

I sat for a moment at my desk and took a deep breath. I dreaded the phone calls I now had to make. First, I called Colonel Fazio, my battalion commander at headquarters, and that call went over like a sack of bricks. The second call was to my company first sergeant to get him to tell Lopez to report to my office. I figured maybe Lopez would know what this was about. Then I made a few more calls to higher command at HQ, and everyone agreed that we would cooperate and not interfere. We'd find out sooner or later what they were up to. Just as I hung up the phone, there was knock at my door. It was Lopez.

Lopez was about twenty-seven, with thinning blond hair, a clipped mustache, and a solid build. He was one of the last soldiers in the unit I would've expected to get into trouble. I liked him a lot. He worked hard, did his job well, often went beyond the call of duty, and obeyed the rule of my command to the letter.

"Good morning, sir, you wanted to see me?"

"Yes, come on in and close the door." I smiled at him as he walked in, raised up slightly, closed the door behind him, and stood at parade rest. I shook my head.

"No, Sergeant Lopez, no need for that, sit on the couch."

He walked to the couch. I noticed nothing that would indicate he knew why he'd been called into my office, which only confirmed my suspicion that something else was going on. There was no point wasting any more time.

"All right, Sergeant, let me get right to the point. CID called earlier, and they want me to take you to their command post for an interview ASAP."

Lopez's face turned pale, which concerned me. He was normally an easygoing, cheerful guy—straightforward, I'd always thought, forthright. If he knew what it was they had on him, he'd tell me. That's what I thought, at least. Now it appeared he knew what was going on and was terrified. And apparently he didn't plan on letting me in on it, which was totally out of character for him.

"So is there something you want to tell me, Sergeant?"

"Sir, I haven't done anything wrong . . . that I know of." His voice quivered just slightly, and I suddenly began feeling a little sorry for the guy, though I had no idea why.

"That you know of?" My tone was impatient and annoyed, though I was truly baffled now. "Listen to me, Sergeant. I am going to find out eventually what it is they're looking for. So whether it's you or them, I'm going to get to the bottom of it. At this point I might be the only person who can still help you. But the only way I can do that is if you tell me what's going on. These guys don't play games, Lopez."

He studied me for a moment, carefully, as if he were searching for something, and I thought he was about to open up when suddenly he simply dropped his head into his hands and said nothing.

"Okay, Sergeant. I hope for your sake it's all a mistake. I gave you an opportunity to confide in me and you passed on that chance. Fine. You will report to CID tomorrow at thirteen thirty hours. Have a good day."

He saluted me and walked out, turning his head as he passed through the door and looking back at me with a strange sad look on his face.

Lopez bore heavily on my mind all the next day. That look on his face as he walked out of my office haunted me. It had felt like a wordless accusation. I decided to become proactive in the investigation. He was a good man, after all, and he'd worked hard for me under my command, earning, at the very least, I thought, the benefit of my doubt. So I went to CID.

I had never been in the CID building. It was quite an impressive place. As I entered the sleek, modern lobby, I was reminded of one of the obscene truths of military life—that the farther away from the front lines you get, the more luxurious things become. There were fancy glass partitions and doors and high-tech security cameras all over the place. If it hadn't been for the twelve-foot holding cell, the place could've been mistaken for any big-city office. I was relieved to see that they weren't holding Sergeant Lopez in the cell. It was empty, shining in the soft glare of the indirect lighting.

I slid my ID card into the lock. I was sure that the card had been scanned and that my every move was now being digitally captured by one or all of the cameras. The door clicked open, and I was greeted silently by an attractive woman about my age, a civilian, I was convinced, judging from the expensive clothes she wore. She led me down a pristine white corridor to a sparsely appointed waiting room. A TV attached to the wall in the upper-right-hand corner of the room was tuned into CNN and muted. As I sat down and looked up at the set, I noticed yet another camera situated above the TV, aimed directly at me. A red light at the base of the camera glowed brightly.

The room spooked me. Poor Lopez must be terrified, I thought. I tried not to look at the camera but found myself increasingly self-conscious about it, imagining myself centered on some screen amid a bank of black-and-white monitors, being watched by a group of strangers. Then a man of medium height with closely cropped hair entered and extended his hand to me. He wore a button-down Izod shirt and khaki pants. I felt as if I'd tumbled down the rabbit hole and found myself in some alternate army universe.

"Captain McGowan, pleasure, sir, I'm Sergeant First Class Johnson. Thank you for coming to pick up Sergeant Lopez." Here was my officious CID sergeant in the flesh.

Of course I hadn't come by simply to pick up Lopez. He didn't even know I was here. But it was clear that that's what Izod Johnson thought. It was clear he intended simply to fetch Lopez for me without any sort of explanation. It was clear he felt I had no right to one. His whole demeanor seemed condescending to me, to me personally and to my rank as well, and I almost snapped and dressed him down right there. But I held myself back, though not entirely.

"Sergeant Johnson, before you leave, I must tell you how concerned I am and have been; you know protocol does not warrant a *senior* officer," I pointed to myself and smiled, "to relieve himself from post to drive an NCO back to base, needless to say, and I'm sorry for repeating myself, but I have the utmost concern for the matter at hand."

I'd drawn up very close to the man. I wanted to make it clear to him that no matter how deep his jurisdiction ran, he wasn't leaving the room without briefing me on the situation. He thought for a moment, then curtly nodded his head.

"Very well, Captain, have a seat."

We sat. He folded his legs and clasped his hands on top of them.

"Sir, there has been an ongoing investigation into a prostitution ring on post."

I let out a sigh of relief. The most he'd be looking at behind that charge would be an Article 15, a reduction in rank, perhaps, and the whole thing would stay in-house. There would be no court-martial. But Johnson wasn't finished.

"We have uncovered and broken up the ring, which has been doing business out of Moon Hall. The prostitutes were doing an organized business out of the bar in the lobby, sir. During the course of the investigation we discovered that the ring was not only female—" He stopped talking abruptly. It took me a moment to register what he'd just said. Finally, I said, "So, what is it that you're saying, Sergeant, that Lopez is what—a prostitute?"

"Prostitute, sir? No sir, not exactly. We set up a sting to try to lure in some of the male prostitutes. We, in fact, accomplished our mission and arrested several soldiers. We questioned them and acquired evidence that they were involved in procuring pornography."

The more he tried to explain it to me, the more confused I became. I forged on.

"So Lopez is a pornographer?"

"Not exactly, sir."

I'd had all I could take. I took a deep breath and looked Johnson straight in the eye.

"Give me the charge that you intend to levy against my sergeant; that's all I want from you, Sergeant Johnson."

Johnson looked a little startled. He hesitated before speaking. Then, giving in, reluctantly, he said, "Sir, we questioned the subjects who were arrested, and they gave us the names of everyone who was involved. Through this process we were able to ascertain those soldiers who are known to be . . . homosexual."

Now I thought I might explode. "What is the charge, Johnson?" I said, raising my voice, still looking directly into his eyes. "For the last time, what are you charging Lopez with?" Then, slowly, and more intensely, "What is the charge, Sergeant?"

"There is no charge as of yet. He's part of the inquiry is all, sir, however . . . there is the homosexual issue, sir, and that is where it gets a little complicated."

I stood up. I now had what I needed. There was no charge against my sergeant.

"We believe all of the homos should be chaptered, as I'm sure you do, sir."

I looked away from him. This last bit seemed unnecessary, as if he'd thrown it in in order to prove that his own sexuality was beyond reproof, that he was on the winning team. Replace "homo" with "Commies," and that sentence could have been torn straight from the pages of recent history, the 1950s, say, when unmitigated hatred of communism and Communists was seen as a badge of one's patriotism.

Who knows what Johnson really felt? I think I might even have been able to respect him a little had I thought his antigay rhetoric was based in real conviction. But he was just spouting the party line, there was no doubt about that, and it infuriated me.

How easy it would be for him to end Lopez's career! Hardworking, loyal, honest Sergeant Lopez—who'd probably spent his entire life thinking he had to compensate for his sexuality by overachieving, by always being the best little boy in whatever world he happened to find himself—was now going to be repaid by having his professional life destroyed by some mediocre, goose-stepping, Izod-wearing bureaucrat.

"The prostitutes and pornographers will certainly be chaptered; now we are going to need some sort of administrative help to chapter the rest of the . . . faggots, sir."

I tried to appear indifferent and wholly detached.

"Are we done here, Sergeant? I'm very busy."

"Yes, sir, Lopez is two doors to the right," he said, sneering a little now, and then, as if he'd just thought of a funny joke, he added, "You can take the queer with you, or he can walk back." Hearing this tone and seeing the flash of hatred in Johnson's beady little eyes made me think I might have been mistaken. Perhaps it was real conviction. The way he tried to lure me in with this last remark, to collaborate in a perceived shared hatred of gay men, disgusted me. I was used to hearing this kind of talk, but I'd rarely heard it at this level, rarely heard the tone of voice Johnson had used, drenched in so much hard-boiled contempt.

He stuck out his hand to shake mine. I looked down at it but kept my own hands at my sides. After simply staring at it for a few seconds, I lifted my head up and looked Johnson in the face. The look on my face must have been scary because Johnson took a step back, as if he felt threatened. Apparently it finally occurred to him that he was in the presence of a superior officer who didn't like him very much, so he briskly stepped back, wished me a good day, and hurried from the room.

★ ★

For the most part we rode back to the base in silence, Lopez and I. When he first got in he said to me, quietly, "I know I haven't done anything wrong, sir . . . nothing," and I turned my head toward him briefly and nodded to let him know I believed him. Of course, it wasn't what he'd done, it's what he *was* that they were having a problem with. If that isn't un-American, well, I don't know what is.

I felt bad for the guy. And the fact that I couldn't say anything about myself, the irony of that, was just incredibly depressing. Here I was, a gay man who was probably going to be asked to initiate the persecution of another gay man. Could things get any worse? How could I believe in *this* army? I tried to imagine what he must be going through. And the realization that it could just as easily be me, that it one day *might* be me, was sobering, to say the least. I feared for Sergeant Lopez and for what I might be asked to do. Was it possible to remain in the army as a gay man and still maintain one's integrity? I was beginning to see how impossible that was. I was beginning to see just how compromised I might up end up becoming.

The very next morning there was a message for me to meet Colonel Fazio at HQ. I had my normal horrific four-mile torture session and made my way back to the comfort of my office, where I showered and changed, and when I emerged from the bathroom Colonel Fazio was sitting on the couch in my office, sipping coffee from a plastic foam cup. I was supposed to have met him at his office at nine, but my office was on his way, so he figured he'd just drop by. I smiled as he lifted up a brown paper bag with another cup of coffee in it for me.

"Thank you, sir. This is a surprise, sir. I was just on my way to see you."

Fazio smiled. He was in amazing shape. He could outrun any twenty-year-old on the base. He was tall, about six foot two inches, with gray hair cut very short. He reminded me of the actor Sam Elliot. He was a great guy, easy to talk to, with an excellent sense of humor, and I thought of him as my mentor.

"So, Jeff, you had quite the day yesterday," he said, blowing on his steaming coffee, then chuckling a little before taking a sip from the cup. Before I had the chance to answer he said, "Tell me, Jeff, what kind of soldier is your motor sergeant?"

"A good one, sir. He works hard. Never had a problem with him." I waited for his response. I figured if anyone knew the right way to handle this, Colonel Fazio would.

"Really?"

I looked up from my cup and noticed that the colonel was busying himself with clipping the end of a black Maduro cigar. He then lit it and casually blew out a thick column of smoke. I wasn't sure how to answer the question, so I said nothing.

"So how's his section doing?"

His eyes followed a particularly graceful ring of smoke up to the ceiling, then they slowly trailed down and landed squarely on me. I smiled somewhat guardedly, and just as I was about to speak he broke in again, "So, Jeff, what's up with this bust, anyway? What's going on? What'd they say they're looking for?" Like the rest of us, he didn't like or trust any of the CID people.

"They made multiple arrests, sir. Apparently there was pornography involved." I shrugged my shoulders.

"Seems that this mess has made its way up the chain of command to the corps commander; apparently one of these"—he considered his choice of words carefully—"little queers got an outside advocacy group involved, you know this Don't-Ask-Don't-Tell horse shit and all. There is the potential for some serious blowback behind it all." He laughed again and winked at me, adding, "No pun intended . . . so the process has been slowed down considerably."

"The process, sir?"

He raised his eyebrow at me, then blew another ring of smoke in my direction.

"The process of safeguarding the army. You don't think we'd allow them to stay in, do you?"

"Absolutely not, sir," I answered much too quickly. In all my life, I'd never felt more ashamed of myself than I did at that very moment.

"So tell me about his performance, Jeff."

"He's an excellent worker, sir, never had a problem with him, and the rest of the troops like him."

"Late?"

"No, sir."

"There is talk that the subjects who were outed—you know, the ones who weren't coconspirators—are not going to get sectioned out.

We're not supposed to ask, and this guy certainly didn't tell. Needless to say we're going to have to . . . deal with the situation."

Suddenly the whole thing became clear to me. The colonel expected me to develop a pattern of offenses against Sergeant Lopez, to find fault wherever I could and create a paper trail. This trumped-up paper trail, created by me, would eventually carry enough weight to bring him down. It was a crushing blow to hear this coming from the man whom I'd admired for so long and who'd come to represent for me all that I thought was good in the army.

I thought maybe I could appeal to his reason. "I don't want to sound like I'm not a team player, sir," I said, "but I'm just not getting it."

Colonel Fazio didn't like repeating anything twice, particularly to a handpicked subordinate. He turned deadly serious and leaned into me. "They do not serve in the U.S. Army, McGowan. We find them, we get rid of them. No questions asked. It's been happening since the beginning of time."

"I know the old policy, sir, but I'm aware of the new policy as well, and he never really came forward and said he was . . . gay. So we can't really do anything. It's not fair." I knew I was asking for it big-time.

He lurched forward on the edge of the couch and poked the cigar at me.

"Fair? We are not working in a democracy, Captain. There *is* no fair here. I do not even want to consider the possibility that you don't understand your responsibilities here. Now . . . in *fairness,* I am going to ask you this one last time, is there anything I need to know?"

I dropped my head. I needed to think this out clearly. It was now not only Sergeant Lopez's career on the line but my own as well. Finally, I looked at him and said, firmly, "Sir, I understand your view. But with all due respect, I have to say I am extremely uncomfortable with what it is you're asking me to do."

An eerie calm came over him. He sat back into the couch and relit his cigar. I knew this wasn't a good sign. It was worse than yelling, this silence, because I knew he'd moved to the next level. The colonel was a brilliant tactician. He didn't get to wear those oak leaves for nothing. If he wanted, he could have me demoted to base cesspool cleaner for the duration of my career.

There was no getting around it now. Lopez was fucked, and I was fucked for trying to save him.

"Jeff, where do you see yourself going from here?" he said, refusing to look at me, looking down the ash of the cigar instead. "Increased responsibility requires a broad understanding of army values and an ability to protect the institution." He stood up slowly.

I started to rise, but he pushed the palm of his hand at me. "Remain seated," he said, and walked briskly out of my office.

I just stood there, staring at the closed door, feeling numb at first, then frightened, then very, very angry, and then finally just terribly sad. Most of all I was disappointed in Colonel Fazio. We had talked at great length about his pride in the army's diversity. We had talked about his children at barbecues. He was a terrific husband and father, and not only did I enjoy his company, I liked his family as well.

The truth was I was taking this very personally. It felt as if all the things he'd said about Lopez were aimed at me, too, and that hurt like hell.

Now, I had been on the wrong end of his anger before. And I'd learned that if it turned out he was wrong he'd usually come around and try to make good. This time, though, I didn't care whether or not he came around.

Don't get me wrong. I was as much a careerist in the army as he was. And I knew he could squeeze me out as easily as he intended to squeeze out Sergeant Lopez. What bothered me the most wasn't his hatred (or fear, or both, depending on your point of view) of homosexuals. He was a product of his environment, after all. He'd been in the army his entire adult life, and the army provides little incentive (you could probably argue it provides disincentives) to develop your own thoughts on the issue of gays in the military. Why distinguish yourself from everyone else? What would he have to gain? I can't pretend that I was shocked by his intolerance.

No, what bothered me more than anything was just how personally he'd taken the whole thing, as if Lopez's mere existence (and mine, by extension) in his unit was a personal affront to his character and command. In fact, it had nothing at all to do with him personally. But, of course, he couldn't see that, at least not right away. I spent the next few days expecting a phone call informing me that I was being relieved of my command, but the call never came. When the weekend finally arrived, I tried to relax and put the whole thing out of my mind. On Friday night there was a "hail and farewell," a function we had regularly to welcome new officers to the base and say good-bye to those who were leaving. I sat gloomily at the bar, convinced that any "greeting" on my part would be a waste of time since my days were numbered. Just when I thought I'd head home, I was approached by one of the most beautiful women I've ever known. It was Maggie Fazio, the colonel's wife. She was from Mississippi, a real southern belle. Her father was a retired lieutenant general who'd served stateside for most of his career. Maggie was one of those women who are so stunning and self-possessed that a room changes when they enter it. She had class, and a tremendous sense of self-worth and character. And also a wicked sense of humor. She was a tall woman, with long blond hair, a long, perfect nose, and full lips. We got on together like a house on fire. She was clever and funny and beautiful, and she had impeccable timing. She smiled as she sat next to me at the bar.

"You on the lam from the New York authorities, old boy?"

I smiled. "Apparently I'm wanted in all fifty, I'm told."

"Don't be so hard on yourself, Jeff. . . . Things have a way of coming round." Her presence was always like a gift. I breathed easy for the first time in days. Maybe the death blow was not so close after all. "Has he told you anything, Maggie?"

"Oh, hells bells, Jeff, you know how he is. When someone is twisting them on him, all he does is talk about them but not really about the issue at hand. You, of course, have been the topic of conversation for a number of dinners and breakfasts. I have never seen the man quite so angry; now why not tell me your side of the story?"

I told Maggie Fazio the whole story. She was an intense listener, periodically nodding her head, putting me at ease with an occasional "uh-huh" or "ah" or "I see." It felt good to get it all out and to have such a sympathetic ear. I ended up with this:

"To go after this man was no different than going after someone because they're black or a woman. I believe in fairness. Soldiers have to know that if they follow the rules they will be treated fairly. Lopez did nothing wrong. It was a witch hunt at best, and as much as I like your husband—you know how much I like the colonel, right? [Maggie Fazio nodded her head]—I just couldn't let myself be a part of it. Whether he was gay or not never really entered into the grand scope of things. If he was, the policy states that we shouldn't ask, so technically he deserved a reprieve. But they still want him out—by any means available. It just isn't right."

I finished off my third whiskey and was about to say good-bye to her when she tilted her head at me and smiled.

"He is a handful, Jeff, isn't he?" she asked, rolling her eyes and laughing softly. "You can't blame him for doing something he thought was right by the old guard, yes?"

I nodded. And I couldn't blame him, really.

"But, Jeff, I get it. I get it," she repeated, patting my hand, "and I know for a fact that eventually he'll get it, too."

With that she stood up, gently kissed my cheek, and disappeared into the crowd, leaving behind a trail of Opium perfume. I didn't know what to feel now. Maybe she was right. Maybe the colonel would come around. But even if he did, it wouldn't be soon enough to save me. I was doomed. I hunkered down and ordered another whiskey.

That Monday I went into the office earlier than usual. I'd planned actually to start going through my desk, so convinced I was that

Colonel Fazio was going to give me the ax. When I walked into the room, the first thing I noticed was an envelope lying on the floor, a few feet from the door, as if someone had slipped it underneath. I opened it. Inside was a card with a picture of a gorilla on it. The card read, "It takes a big man to know he was wrong." Below that, in the undeniably strong handwriting I'd come to recognize instantly, was the signature, Colonel Joseph Fazio.

Sergeant Lopez survived without any adverse action taken against him, but when it came time to reenlist he refused to consider the possibility. He could read the writing on the wall: there was no future for him in the military.

It was really the final nail in the coffin for me, I knew that I was no different from Lopez, and I was smart enough to know that I might not have a godfather to save me in a similar situation. I knew that when my command ended, I would leave the army. It was a bittersweet decision, but I had achieved many of the goals that I had dreamed of as a boy, and I felt that I wanted to live a complete life without the artificial restraints of this hermetically sealed culture.

CHAPTER TWENTY-THREE

Driving North, Home

I t w a s a dull, gray morning in March 1998 when I set out to make the long drive from Fort Bragg in North Carolina to New York. The trip is roughly fourteen hours and I-95 gets dull quick, so I stopped in Raleigh first to get some books on tape—the newest Clancy and a Michael Crichton and a Grisham. I wanted to keep my mind occupied, to escape into stories of the lives of others in order to forget about my own for a while.

I left Fort Bragg knowing that I was going to leave the army. But even though my mind was made up, every time one of the tapes would run out and I'd find myself alone in the silence, searching for the next tape, I had trouble believing it was really happening. I'd spent my entire adult life serving my country, and now, just when I'd gotten word that I'd been promoted to major, I was walking away.

I was afraid, unsure about the future, unsure about almost everything. The only thing I was certain of was that I couldn't serve in the U.S. Army anymore. The actors' voices on the books on tape gave me solace. Nothing had to be decided today. I was taking a thirty-day leave, so I would have plenty of time to think things through. I'd held on to the apartment in Jackson Heights after my grandmother's death, and now I was going back there to find my footing for a new life. I would base there as I looked for a place to live in Kingston, New

York, where I'd been assigned as an adviser to the National Guard, and where I would finally submit my resignation.

I had no idea what the future held or even where to begin. I was now confronting a possibility that had never before occurred to me: civilian life. I did know, however, that I wanted to confront this new life on my home turf, New York. The army had sent me all over the world, but when the choice was finally up to me, there was no doubt in my mind that New York was the place I wanted to be. I was coming home.

It was dark by the time I approached the Holland Tunnel on the Jersey Turnpike and the Manhattan skyline came into view. The mere sight of it was invigorating. All my worries and fears slipped away as the energy from the great sparkling city reinvigorated me. All at once I knew everything was going to work out fine. I would find a job. I would create a new life for myself. My old self-confidence returned anew. So much possibility now. So much hope. Everything was up!

I would be living with almost nothing for the next thirty days since I couldn't have my things shipped up until I'd found a permanent place to live in Kingston. At the end of my leave, I would figure out what to do. The assignment I had was pretty laid-back. I would have plenty of time to make decisions and get a plan together.

Living without my stuff was somewhat liberating, and I was able to relax and enjoy my time off. I reacquainted myself with the city, caught up with all my neighborhood friends, went out a lot at night. I also got to spend time with my great-aunt Mary, aka Maude, my grandmother's sister. I'd made a special effort to keep in touch with her after my grandmother's death since she was confined to her apartment nearby in Elmhurst and her only company was often just the home health aid who came regularly to care for her. Having a relative close by again in Jackson Heights was a blessing. She was eighty-nine years old and seemed to cherish the opportunity to share memories with a beloved grandnephew. I spent hours listening to her tell stories about my grandparents and my mother and father, helping me fit together pieces of a puzzle that had for so long remained stubbornly resistant to understanding and leading me toward a newfound appreciation of my family. Hearing her stories, I was amazed at the accumulated wisdom that can be found in a single life.

One day when I was sitting in her kitchen drinking a cup of coffee, she looked at me and said, "You know, Maxine was right."

"What?" I said.

"She was right," she said, shaking her head and looking off into the distance, a faint smile rising into her face.

"Right about what?" I asked.

"I shouldn't have plastered Scotty Gallagher's house with mud. It was very unladylike. . . . I should have thrown a rock instead. Maude the mule, indeed!"

That night my great-aunt Mary passed away quietly in her sleep.

And so I set about arranging her affairs and preparing for the funeral. Since all of my possessions were in storage, I had to buy something to wear for the funeral Mass at the Church of St. Agnes near Grand Central Terminal. I decided to go to Brooks Brothers and Barneys.

As I walked up Madison Avenue, I was a little bit awestruck by the displays in the shop windows and by how stylish everyone was dressed. And they all seemed to be in such a hurry, fueled by the sheer energy of life in the great metropolis. I'd grown so accustomed to the dreary conformity of military life that I'd forgotten how exciting civilian life could be. This was definitely not the PX!

As I passed the Calvin Klein window on Sixtieth Street, I noticed a tall man with wild curly hair walking toward me down the avenue, a little black pug at his heels. He had on a trench coat, with a blue blazer and a pair of khaki pants underneath. The words "Park Avenue" popped into my head. He was strikingly good-looking, with a wide, sensual mouth, a fine, prominent nose, and a deep tan that set off his blue eyes nicely. With an athletic build and a firm stride, there was something about him that just seemed to exude fine, healthy living. The little black pug was very well behaved and seemed as smart and interesting as his owner.

We made eye contact as we passed, and he smiled. I was intrigued. When I reached the first Barneys window, I stopped and looked back to find that he'd stopped and was standing in front of the Calvin Klein window. I stared at the handsome mannequins, trying to appear nonchalant. Every time I'd look over, he'd turn his head back to the window, the pug sitting obediently at his feet. We went back and forth like this for a few minutes until finally he came over and introduced himself.

"Hi . . . my name is Billiam. I am very bad at this." he said, laughing a little at himself, though clearly sizing me up. Later on he'd tell me he was trying to figure out if I was gay or straight, single or married, by "reading" the way I was dressed and the shopping bags I was carrying. Eventually we'd come to affectionately label this process "doing a Willa," in honor of his niece Wilhemina, who has the uncanny ability to make deadly accurate character assessments based solely on a person's shoes and how well he or she accessorizes. It seems to be a genetic gift of the van Roestenberg family that kicks in at a very young age.

Apparently he liked what he read. "Would you," he said, "um . . . like to go for a beer . . . or a cappuccino?"

"Both." I said, smiling now.

From that moment on we were virtually inseparable. We spent the next several hours getting to know each other at Nello's, an upscale trattoria on Madison Avenue in the sixties. Time flew by so quickly. Amazingly, there were no gaps in the conversation, no uncomfortable stretches of silence; the whole thing felt as if it was meant to be. After a few hours we exchanged numbers and split up, agreeing to see each other not the following day but on the day after that.

I could've just gotten the E or R train not far south of Nello's but I was so excited at having met Billy and at being back in the city again that I decided to walk awhile. The renovation of Grand Central was nearly finished, and I'd not yet seen it, so I figured I'd walk the roughly twenty blocks south to Forty-second Street, check out the terminal, and catch the 7 train back home to Eighty-second Street in Jackson Heights. Making my way down Madison Avenue I reviewed the afternoon with Billiam, hearing his words over and over again, seeing his face, hoping I hadn't said anything too stupid. Thinking about it filled me with a kind of hope, a sense of possibility, that I'd never experienced before. There was no way of knowing, of course, how things would turn out with Billy, yet I sensed right away that something very, very special was happening, and I felt determined to get it right. I was a walking cliché now, heading south on Madison Avenue, a young man in the city whose step had suddenly been lightened by the prospect of love.

I cut over to Park Avenue and rushed through the Helmsely walkway and then entered the Pan Am Building (it's the Met Life Building now, and it was that day, too, but for some of us it will always be the Pan Am Building) and made my way through the lobby and to the escalators that would take me down into the great vaulted concourse of the newly renovated Grand Central Terminal. As the sleek escalator dropped me slowly down into the main room, I was stunned by the transformation. The big Kodak sign was gone, allowing a full view of the giant windows up on the east side. The old ticket windows were gleaming with freshly cleaned brass, and none of them housed Off Track Betting. The air was smoke-free, and that fact seemed to make the ceiling all the more impressive. The great mural of constellations covering the ceiling had been deeply obscured when I'd last been here in the 1980s. Now it sparkled as clear as a night sky in upstate New York. Later on I couldn't help seeing this as a kind of sign of my own newfound clarity regarding my sexuality and my whole life. That all the smoke and grime that had rendered the great muraled ceiling nearly invisible in the eighties was just like all the ambivalence, all the indecisiveness, all the pain of denial I'd put myself through during that time. And now all the smoke and grime was gone. I could finally see, and having met Billy, the clarity seemed to become even more profound, the ceiling seemed to reveal a universe that had been, a mere decade before, inconceivable to me, unimaginable, unreachable. Now here it was, looming so grandly over the freshly scrubbed train station, and seeming so close I felt, as the escalator gently deposited me onto the soft marble floor, almost as if I could reach out and grab a handful of stars and rearrange the Milky Way.

I stood for a moment in the center of the room, by the great brass clock set atop the information desk, and took the whole thing in, feeling immensely relieved and happy. And just as I was about to head off east toward the subway, I thought I saw two boys sitting on one of the counters across the way. Cigarette smoke fluttered over the head of the smaller one, while the bigger one seemed to be chewing on a large piece of gum. Their hands were locked together beneath the bigger boy's left thigh. I thought I could smell smoke there, and the strong smell of, what—a strawberry Starburst, maybe?—but then the image disappeared, and I knew I was seeing things. I knew it was Greg and me, the memory unspooling. The image came and went so quickly that I tried to conjure it up again, but no matter how hard I tried, I couldn't coax it back. It wouldn't return, those two boys were gone forever, I knew now, and so I got on the escalator to go down to the subway. Just as I reached the bottom, just as I passed the heavyset nun in full nun regalia, who was always stationed there at the bottom of the escalator on a stool with her cup, all my newfound clarity and joy was suddenly tempered and enriched with sadness, the sadness of regret over all the time I'd wasted, over all the youth I'd misspent.

But then I was on the train, and before I knew it we were bolting out of the earth at Hunter's Point and I was feeling reinvigorated. There's nothing like it, the way the train just emerges from beneath the ground on the Queens side, having just crossed beneath the river, and then rises up and up and makes the great sweeping curve north until the skyline of Manhattan appears to your left just behind the bridge. We pulled abruptly into the Queensboro Plaza station, the old

Redbird rattling on the elevated, just as an N train pulled in on the other side, so that it felt like two roller coasters competing at Coney Island. The doors opened, then closed, and the train lurched forward again. And as the N veered off dramatically to our left, heading north into Astoria, and we started the climb up to Forty-third Street, I began to feel doubtful.

How could I be sure that this wouldn't be a replay of Paul? Wasn't this too good to be true? Suddenly all the pain I'd experienced from Paul came rushing back to me, and I found myself wanting to run and hide. But I'm being ridiculous, I thought to myself, as we rushed past the apartment windows at Fifty-second Street nestled right up next to the train tracks, revealing brief snippets of private lives—a man standing in front of a television set, a woman crossing a room. Billiam is out (of the closet, that is), I told myself, and I'll soon be out of the army, and this isn't going to be anything like Paul. By the time the train rolled into Woodside I'd decided that life was about taking risks, that just because I'd been hurt once didn't mean I'd be hurt again, that I'd be a fool to pass up an opportunity to make something with Billiam. Not only was I attracted to him, I was really impressed with his intelligence as well, and his sophistication. And you know what, I thought to myself, after all the trauma with Paul, I think I deserve a shot at a relationship in this new, healthier context. So when the doors finally opened at Eighty-second Street, my mind was entirely made up: I would pursue a relationship with Billiam. That's what I would do.

And so for the third time the light switch was flipped on, and this time nothing stood in the way of letting that light shine as brightly and freely as possible. My new life had begun to take shape, and all my anxiety about changing careers and fitting into civilian life were now made bearable by the presence of this special man who seemed to have arrived at just the right moment, as if on cue.

Before I knew it I was meeting the family, something I'd never done before. Billy's sisters, Yvonne and Andrea, share his striking good looks. At that time Yvonne lived on Eighty-sixth Street on the East Side, not far from Central Park. When he took me to meet her, we walked in and were met by a tall, elegant woman, who bore a strong resemblance to Julia Roberts, with thick brown hair, and, despite being pregnant with her daughter Helena, a near perfect figure. She wore one of those smiles that manage to put everyone at ease instantly, and I knew right away that I was going to like her a lot. Next to her stood her husband, Chris, a tall, blond, sturdy fellow, with handsome features, who, it turned out, is a kind of Renaissance man—an accomplished corporate finance banker and oil painter. Seeing the two of them together I couldn't help thinking that I'd somehow managed to stumble into an F. Scott Fitzgerald novel.

I was nervous at that first meeting, but it quickly became clear that they accepted me for who I was and were prepared to open their home to me with the same generosity and kindness they offered to everyone.

Soon thereafter, Billy took me to meet his sister Andrea, and her husband and daughter, at their home in Westchester. Like her two siblings, Andrea is stunningly beautiful. The moment I met her I was struck by her fierce intelligence and warmth. She's so open and easy to talk to that she quickly took me into her confidence. To this day she is one of the people I turn to for advice. Her husband, Bill, a successful trader, comes from a large and wonderful family, and whenever we spend the holidays with them it's always a raucous good time. The aforementioned Wilhelmina was only ten months old when I first met them, and she was already showing signs of being very precocious. I would be remiss if I did not mention the three children who followed, Helena, Claudia, and Harrison—all of whom are destined for greatness.

That first month of our relationship was truly magical. Since I was on leave and had nothing better to do, we were able to spend a lot of time together, whenever Billiam's busy work schedule permitted. It was just so easy and right, I could not believe it. It seemed as if time stopped whenever we were together, as we laughed and talked about everything under the sun. He was funny, smart, good-looking, and kind; in short, a dream come true. I knew even then that I was in love and that I would spend the rest of my life with him. It was the kind of conviction that starts in your gut and then expresses itself in the mind.

The neatest thing, which was also a little intimidating at first, was the fact that he was so comfortable in his skin. The old adage that opposites attract could not have been truer in our case. For so long I'd had to censor myself and try to fit in; Billiam just *was*, and it was great. I was champing at the bit to be drawn out of my comfort zone and create a new life for myself, and Billiam was the perfect man to help me do it.

★ ★

So here I was, this kid from Queens, suddenly thrust into the town-and-country set, and they took me in like one of their own. I was part of a family that accepted me hands-down and provided me with all the love and support I needed to transition from the army to civilian life. I was a lucky man, indeed.

And I was quickly learning just how wrong I'd been. So much that I had thought was entirely out of my reach—love, family, and the deep satisfaction that comes with them—was, in fact, quite possible. All it took was honesty. I had to find the courage to be honest with myself, and after that, everything fell into place. That did not mean that it came easy. I had to work for everything, and for the first year or so it was very hard.

Transitioning from military to civilian life was in some ways like immigrating to a new country—that's how different I found things. So many of the rules in the civilian world were completely different. A lot of it was better—the freedom to be with Billy openly for one, and that's a big one; some of it not so much—figuring out how to dress appropriately for work took some real time and effort; and some of it was actually a little scary—job security, for instance. One of the most glaring differences was the absence of the structure and predictability I'd grown accustomed to in the military. People no longer stood up when I walked into a room. I no longer had a driver. And since I'd reached the rank of major and had a pretty substantial tenure with the army, I had to take a hefty pay cut. So, a lot of the fears that Paul had expressed to me were in part valid, but nothing that time and hard work could not overcome.

I chose to go into pharmaceutical sales because I figured it would give me the opportunity to help people in some small way after having spent most of my adult life focusing on how to kill them. I quickly learned what it means to be an entrepreneur and to have to hustle. The upside to all this was that I had someone in my life who loved and supported me. There was no law that barred my relationship with Billiam or forced us into the kind of weird secrecy that destroyed my relationship with Paul. And there was, of course, no longer my fear of being found out, which had ruined my relationship with Greg. The light was lit. The genie was out of the bottle for good. We could be and do whatever we wanted.

I would be lying if I said that I found this easy to deal with initially. I was so used to being closeted and in denial that I had to unlearn (and am still unlearning and probably will be for the rest of my life) all the ingrained habits and ways of thinking that characterize the kind of unintegrated life I was living. Time, though, is the great healer, and I have managed to shed much of the paranoia that was part of surviving in the army.

Over the years my relationship with Billiam has undergone many changes as we've struggled with my adjusting and all the normal ups and downs of life. And through this we've both grown individually and we've grown together as a couple. When I talk to our straight friends, I'm often, still, struck by how much we have in common, that we are, in the end, just like them, good people working, and sometimes struggling, to stay together and pay the bills.

About a year into our relationship we decided to buy a house in the New Paltz area. We chose the Hudson Valley because of its great beauty and proximity to New York City. We were a little leery of what our reception would be, since it is definitely small-town America. What we found was a wonderfully open-minded community that welcomed us from the very beginning. After introducing ourselves to our neighbors, we met the town supervisor at the time, Judy Mayle, who graciously extended an invitation to both of us to sit on the zoning and planning boards. We accepted immediately, because we both believe in public service and want to help out in any way we can. I serve on the planning board and Billiam is on the zoning board. One year, I even ran for a seat on the town council.

In the early days of our relationship I'd not given much thought to the idea of getting married. But all that changed in 2003 when Billiam attended a debate among the local candidates running for the legislative seats in Ulster Country. That night he came home bursting with excitement about one of the candidates, whose name was Jason West. His exact words to me were, "He is destined to do great things." One of the main reasons Billiam said this was because Jason was the only candidate for any office he'd ever known who publicly supported same-sex marriage. After that night, he followed his campaign intensely and became an avid supporter.

After Jason was elected mayor of the village of New Paltz, Billiam got to know him better and asked him if he really meant what he said about supporting same-sex marriage. The answer was still yes. Over the next several months Billiam kept in contact with him and helped him formulate how to best go about doing it. Truthfully, I did not think that it would happen because I thought it was against the law, but every time we talked, Billiam assured me that there was a legal basis for it.

A couple months later, we met a gay couple—Charles Clement and Maurice Zinken—who had moved to the area from Holland to open a bed-and-breakfast. Charles is American. He is an extremely talented artist and has the wisdom of several lifetimes. From the first time we met, I knew that he would be a close friend of mine till the end. Maurice is Dutch, and easily one of the smartest people I've ever met, speaking four languages fluently. They'd been married in Holland where same-sex couples can do so legally. From the start I was impressed by their great generosity. They opened their home to Billy and me and treated us with kindness and hospitality on an epic scale. What they teach me every time I am around them is that any limitation in my life is generally self-imposed, and I can change it if I want to. They're two truly amazing human beings who, in a very real way, have become my heroes. Their relationship should be the subject of a book of its own.

One night they invited us over and toward the end of the evening casually popped their wedding video into the VCR. I think to a certain degree their marriage wasn't entirely real to me until I saw the video. Almost from the moment it began playing, I was awestruck by the beauty of this happiest of rituals. And suddenly seeing two men there instead of a man and a woman made so much sense; it looked so natural, so right. It was a wedding just like any of the weddings I'd attended over the years for my straight friends. But seeing the evidence of their freedom to marry so clearly in front of me shook me to the core and inspired me deeply. The very next day, I asked Billiam to marry me.

We thought we'd simply have a commitment ceremony, until Billiam told Jason about it and convinced him that the time had come to act on his convictions. San Francisco had begun to conduct weddings, and the momentum was building. And the rest, as they say, is history! Billiam and I were the first same-sex couple in New York State to get married, thrusting New Paltz onto the national stage.

For me it was a natural next step. I love Billiam, so why shouldn't I have the freedom to marry him and to commit myself to the responsibility of that marriage? As for the fact that we are the video clip you see every time the issue appears on television, well, that was just really frightening to go through. The pressure to be dignified and not put your foot in your mouth on your wedding day was nerve-racking. I shudder to think what it must feel like when the scrutiny is negative. Thankfully, once again everything turned out okay.

As a result of this very public act, I have been blessed in countless ways. The first wedding gift we received came, amazingly, from Greg, with whom I'd completely lost touch. I've heard from old army buddies and college friends. Every week it seems that people I knew long ago contact me to tell me they support me and that they want me back in their life again. All in all, not bad for a kid from Queens.

If you had told me fifteen years ago that in the late winter of 2004 I would announce I was gay and get married to another man on national television, I would have said you must be smoking crack and would have recommended therapy. Then again, I guess I am living proof that you can teach an old (though not *so* old, really) dog new tricks.

Epilogue

MAY 2004

It was a brutally hot Sunday, the temperature reaching up past ninety, and Billy and I were walking across the Brooklyn Bridge in linen and seersucker. We were marching along with a few thousand others from Brooklyn to Battery Park in support of same-sex marriage. We would be speaking at the rally in the park later on. The walk over the famous bridge was a first for me, and I savored every minute of it, watching the magnificent skyline sparkle in the bright spring sunlight. Occasionally my vision would be drawn to the lower end of the island, and I'd feel a twinge of pain, that odd absence, looking for the two graceful towers that should have been there but were not, just blue sky opening out to New Jersey, a clean wound now, perhaps, though a wound nonetheless.

What was most striking to me about the march was how young everyone seemed to be. Everywhere I looked, I saw a sea of young faces, smiling and laughing, eager to show the world that their relationships have value and that they're entitled to the freedom to marry and are prepared for the responsibility it entails.

Later on, after finishing my speech in the park, I was accosted by two kids from Scarsdale, Cindy and John. Both were dressed comfortably in T-shirts and shorts. They told me they were both straight and part of the gay-straight alliance at their high school. I'd heard of such organizations but wasn't quite sure what they did, so I took the opportunity to pepper both of them with questions. They seemed a little surprised that I was so clueless about the gay-straight alliance phenomenon. I explained to them that I didn't get the chance to meet many high school kids these days but was grateful that they'd filled me in. Toward the end of the conversation, John said to me, "Mr. Mc-Gowan, you're a hero. We just wanted to thank you for all that you're doing."

If they only knew! My life was an example of everything you *shouldn't* do, at least when it comes to being true to yourself. In fact, I had spent the last fifteen years doing everything in my power to deny and evade the truth about myself, hardly the stuff heroes are made of. Yet, by an odd twist of fate, I'd been blessed (cursed?) with my own fifteen minutes of minor fame—enough, at least, to have made an impact on these two serious teenagers from Scarsdale.

During the media circus that surrounded our marriage ceremony, reporters frequently asked me if I was now going to become an activist. To me that word conjures up images of ponytailed people in tie-dyed shirts, bearing strident manifestos, an image that is about as far away from the person I am as can be imagined. And so when John said the word *hero*, and I saw the expression on his face and on Cindy's face, two earnest children looking up at me in my linen and seersucker, I cringed, feeling entirely unworthy. The truth is, as this book shows, I haven't spent years of selfless sacrifice in support of the movement, and I have no right to pose as someone who has.

If I have done anything to advance the just cause of equality for gay people, it was by accident, a result of simply finally making the decision to act. Powerful change often comes from the least likely of places. All it takes is one ordinary person doing one extraordinary thing. The civil rights movement is replete with examples of this. Whether it was Rosa Parks refusing to sit in the back of the bus or Sergeant Leonard Malevitch coming out to his air force commander in 1975, these were simple people who had the guts and the integrity to stand up for what they believed was right. What I've done doesn't even begin to come close to what these people did. I'm not in their league. The point is, we all have a role to play, and we can all make a difference to one degree or another if we only make the decision to act.

Why have I written this book? How have I arrived at this point? These questions can be answered with a few more very simple questions. Why not me? Why not now? What do I have to gain by remaining cautious, hidden? Immersed in the antigay culture of the military for so long, I mistook being reasonable with conformity, with doing my soldier's best to squeeze myself into a box made for others. I believed being reasonable meant sacrificing personal fulfillment for the sake of my profession, and as a result I spent the best part of my young adulthood as only half a man. Those days are now over.

What it is, finally, is a question of integrity. I came to believe that not only do I have a responsibility to myself to be honest and open about who I am, I have a responsibility to the people around me as well. That is integrity, and without it, I'm nothing. Ironically, I learned that lesson from the army, the very institution that would have excluded me had I been open about my sexuality from the start.

Writing this book has given me the opportunity to come clean about who I am and to provide a glimpse of what it is like to serve our great nation. I am the man I am today because of the military. Everything I've achieved, everything I have, I owe to the United States Army.

I hope that this book will spark a conversation about changing the rules that govern the debate surrounding gay people and the services. Today, we serve honorably at all levels of the military, as we have since the dawn of history. We should be able to do so openly. So what should be done? The first step would be to remove the prohibition against homosexuality in the Uniform Code of Military Justice and allow gay men and women to serve openly, as the Canadians, the British, the Australians, the Israelis, and others have already done. I understand that changing the law is much easier than changing the culture. Still, we have seen the successful integration of African Americans and women into the armed services, so there's little doubt that over time the same kind of integration would work with gay service members. The training used today to educate soldiers about women and minorities would require little change to ensure that gays were included.

The broader culture has embraced gay men and women in unprecedented ways over the last decade or so. We've gone prime-time, in fact, with shows like *Will and Grace* and *Queer Eye for the Straight Guy* regularly winning the battle for network ratings. The mainstreaming of gay Americans makes it all the more imperative that the military catch up with the culture at large and put an end to a discriminatory policy that seeks to continue to define gay people as second-class citizens and unfit for service. Morale and unit cohesion depend largely on strong leadership and integrity, not on whether the man next to you happens to be gay.

We are diminished as a nation when our institutions fail to live up to the ideals of democracy. And the military is diminished when it fails to allow all Americans who are qualified to serve openly and proudly on behalf of their country. When the awesome and terrible decision to go to war is made, all Americans must take ownership of what follows, and all Americans—rich, poor, white, black, gay, and straight—must close ranks and do their duty.

Let us marry. Let us serve. For we, too, are Americans.